Published by Gadfly Press (d.b.a.)
  Owner, Robert E. Lynott, for self-publishing only
  8925 SW Homewood St, Portland, OR 97225

Library of Congress Catalog Card Number 93-81357

ISBN 0-9618077-1-7

For sale by mail only, no discount, no return

Price $ 19.00 plus $ 3.00 for Priority mailing

This book was written on an IBM clone PC, monochrome screen,
386/25, 30 meg hard disk, HP Deskjet 500 printer. Layout,
homemade diagrams, paste-up, and printing of camera-ready
pages by author. Software, Word Perfect 5.1 for DOS. Details
for aid to other self-publishers. Photocopies self-service at
neighborhood Kinko's copy store.

Cover photo by Gertrude E. Myers, deceased. See page 93.

Printing arranged through a broker, Dean R. Burn, "Catalogs
and Books are Our Specialty," P.O.Box 226, Ryderwood WA 98581,
Telephone and Fax 206-295-3505. He arranged printing of my
first book in 1987. His experience, skill, advice, and encouragement are gratefully acknowledged.

The 1987 book, The Weather Tomorrow, Why can't They Get It Right,
is still in print. It has been re-recorded with Library of Congress,
removing copyright, placing it in public domain, dated Feb. 16, 1993,
reference: volume 2798, page 334. Price $ 10.00 plus $ 2.00 for book
rate mailing. Paper, 5 1/2 x 8 1/2, 183 pages, not illustrated. It is
about the restrictive politics of weather forecasting, which apparently
had never been openly published before. Three thousand copies have been
distributed. It predicted a "Coming Shakeup," but directed primary
blame on one of the activists, the NWS, instead of the propaganda mill
and de facto Board of Directors, the American Meteorological Society.

Corrections after press time, 10-25-94, or not handwritten

p 75 col 2, 17 lines from bottom, spelling "Doppler,"
        and elsewhere
p 82 col 1, 11 lines from bottom, DFW is Dallas-Ft. Worth
p 93 col 1, last line. World Almanac explains Daylight
        Savings time did not begin until 1967.
p 134, date of SLE raob plot should be 8-18-94

CONTENTS

PREFACE

In *The Weather Tomorrow, Why Can't They Get It Right?*, self-published in 1987, I tried to explain the political and bureaucratic reasons why weather forecasting was dying. As an indoctrinated member of the American Meteorological Society since 1940, my faith in its scientific integrity was absolute. That faith also included academia, at least those parts devoted to science, especially physical science, and of course, meteorology.

As a forecaster, my perspective mistakenly assumed the problems in public weather forecasting were caused by an invasion of federal bureaucrats, who placed self-interest above noble scientific advances and public service.

Now I'm more experienced in coping with the power structure. The forecasting business was not invaded by federal bureaucrats. That part of academia which is concerned with the science and technology of meteorology, specific universities, created the American Meteorological Society in 1919. Its avowed objective is the development and dissemination of such knowledge, and the advancement of professional applications.

The first half of the objective led me to believe the AMS was primarily a scientific society, and that professional activities would naturally follow high standards of ethics. I was naive.

The advancement of the professional elite in the weather business has been extremely successful. With an enormous budget for propaganda it deluges the public with self-promotion. Behind the scenes the corporate, academic, military, and federal bureaucratic leadership in the field of meteorology places priority on increasing power and control.

Why is this second book published? Because local weather forecasting ought to be the prime product of the weather business. It's almost non-existent because the arrogance of the weather bureaucracy maintains a monopoly on local weather forecasting for one abominable purpose, to retain excessive rewards for the selfish leaders.

I resigned from the American Meteorological Society in 1990 after 50 years as a member. My purpose is freedom to criticize the unauthorized and unfair monopoly in local weather forecasting supported by its members.

Gadfly Press is merely a d.b.a. for my self-publishing efforts. No conventional book publisher can afford to challenge the authority and prestige of the multi-billion-dollars per year weather business. The word gadfly was a self-definition of Socrates, a Greek philosopher executed by draft of poison in 399 B.C. for impiety and corruption of youth. A modernized definition of a gadfly is that of a constructive critic. Critics are rarely popular, often dismissed as complainers, soreheads, rejected job seekers, or at least a curmudgeonly old crank.

What can earnest fair-minded citizens do about this scandal? Not much in the near future. We can try to inform others. We can try to make democracy work. Unfortunately, such effort is often overwhelmed by the better-paid efforts of opponents.

Meanwhile here is a plain inexpensive book to promote a better understanding of the mechanics of a branch of physical science called meteorology, or simply weather.

Bob Lynott   September 28, 1993

INTRODUCTION

I was a local weather forecaster in Portland, Oregon for 25 years. It took more time to learn the job than it should have.

If you read this book, I promise you will understand how weather works. You will learn how to predict the weather for tomorrow better than anyone you know unless that one has also read this book.

I'll explain how you can make your own forecasts, more accurate than those of the National Weather Service, providing you have access to the necessary information. Such will be easily available when the federal monopoly is broken. Then we can discontinue the cost of imitation forecast offices of the federal government.

However, recent plans tout doubling the number of these offices and doubling the staff at each. As these projected changes occur, you will learn the elitist definition of "professional applications." More tax dollars will disappear, and federal forecasting will continue to be little more than reporting the latest observations.

You won't earn a PhD by studying this book. But you will understand most of the fundamentals of weather forecasting as I understand them. My knowledge, like that of everyone, is incomplete and probably inaccurate in places. Any suggestion for revision is welcome.

Discussion is the lifeblood of a genuine scientific environment. If someone has an incorrect idea, let it twist in the wind. Later, carefully consider any which survive the ventilation.

The book strives to follow common sense which really means uncommon sense, because of its lack in the world. Sense means logic, which is my guidance, even my religion.

In true scientific method, not the warped one often supported, the search is simply for truth. Like a navigator making a correction in course, when new information or comprehension reveals past error, a quick correction is made. Such revision should be admired.

I'll strive to avoid ambiguity which sometimes creates tedium, presumably a lesser evil. The sequence of topics may appear disconnected at times. Knowledge doesn't bloom along a garden path to be picked for a bouquet.

Knowledge is three-dimensional. It overlaps and intertwines with other knowledge. Learning requires much backtracking and adjustment of concepts. Explanations may be abbreviated at first, to be filled in later. None are ever complete.

A knowledge of mathematics is not required. That's an admirable subject but its importance is often exaggerated in elementary texts about weather.

I'm not a scientist in the presently cheapened sense of the word. I'm a technician. Some might call this a book on popular science. Actually, it's a book on unpopular science, meaning a lack of modern hype, glamour, razz-ma-tazz, and awe.

I assume the reader is familiar with customary programs by weathercasters on TV. Such presentations vary with local personalities, but most conform to the style and content of national cable weather shows on CNN and The Weather Channel.

This writer was also on TV, for 14 years (1954-68), freelance employment, with no station equipment except a gray "black-board" and a felt-tipped pen. I made my own forecasts. The upper air pattern was suggested by a single line, which nowadays is wider, colored, often pulsating, and described as the jet stream.

I was granted the AMS Seal of Approval #39 for Television Weathercasters in 1962, only after I complained to the AMS Council about an absurd restrictive rule. The hindering was because I was a "trouble maker" for the local Weather

Bureau, sometimes contradicting its forecasts.

In those primitive days (at least in Oregon) I was inspired by the opportunity to bring the art of weather forecasting to the public as never before, encouraged by the adage, a picture is worth a thousand words. Probably influenced by the war-time speedup of personal education, my naiveté exuded confidence that progress in technology could now attain accurate prediction of the "weather tomorrow." Television would relay the predictions quickly.

Somehow, the dream has faded.

* * *

Weather is a result of the physics of the atmosphere. Soon you will know a lot about it and enjoy its wonder.

Brief Resumé of Author

Born July 1914, Cedar Rapids, Iowa
Aug 1933-Mar 1940 Multigraph printer,
    Rock Island, Illinois
    (my home was in Davenport, Iowa)
Mar 1940-Dec 1941 Junior Weather Observer,
    Des Moines, Iowa
Dec 1941-Jun 1942 Weather Bureau, Wash. D.C.
    (banished to Daily River Stages,
    department of Hydrology, but told
    transfer was related to war effort)
Jun 1942-Jan 1946 Air Corps, U.S. Army
    (Draftee to Master/Sergeant)
Jan 1946-Sep 1946 Radiosonde Observer,
    Great Falls, Montana (grade SP-6)
Sep 1946-Jun 1947 Student, College of Education,
    Great Falls, Montana (courtesy GI Bill)
Jun 1947-Jun 1949 Student, University of Chicago
    (courtesy GI Bill, awarded B.S. degree)
Jul 1949-Nov 1953 Local Forecaster,
    Weather Bureau, Portland, Oregon
Nov 1953-Apr 1968 "Mr. Weatherman," KOIN-TV,
    (Part-time contract employee) Portland
May 1960-Apr 1974 Fire Weather Forecaster,
    Forest Service, Portland, Oregon
    (Seasonal to May 1968, then full-time)
Jul 1983-Present, Gadfly role against Forecasting
    by Government.

Chapter 1. The Jet Stream -- So Called

This chapter is an introduction to the horizontal circulation of the earth's atmosphere. Unless otherwise stated, all discussion applies to the northern hemisphere. Only slight amendments are needed to apply concepts to the southern hemisphere.

It's about the "upper air," not circulation of wind near sea level or even within one vertical mile above sea level. It will focus on the 500 millibar level (500 mb) which varies in elevation, but averages near 18,000 ft MSL (above mean sea level).

The average atmospheric pressure at sea level is 1013 mbs, as measured by a barometer. That means the 500 mb level is about the midpoint of the mass of the atmosphere, a rather obvious place to observe the general pattern of winds aloft.

Atmospheric pressure was first measured precisely by a mercurial barometer, which measured the length of a column (liquid) of mercury, the weight of which balanced the weight of a corresponding column of air extending to the top of the atmosphere. That made standard (average) sea level pressure at 29.92 inches of Hg. Pressure is better defined as force per unit area. For those who want detail, a millibar is a force of 1000 dynes per square centimeter.

The top of the atmosphere is difficult to define, because with increasing elevation the molecules of gas are farther apart. Even at the orbit altitude of space shuttles, there probably are a few lonely molecules.

Physicists have defined a Standard Atmosphere, assumed to be near average conditions over the U.S. at 40 deg latitude. It estimates the top of 99% of the atmosphere to be near an elevation of 100,000 ft, where pressure is about 10 mb. That seems far overhead, but it is sobering to realize such "top" is only 19 miles from our ocean beaches, and only 18 miles above Denver. An impressive demonstration of scale is to draw a circle, with a diameter equal to the width of this column (3.0 inches) to represent the sphere of the earth. Even with a sharp pencil the thickness of the line will exaggerate the 19 mile thickness of the atmosphere. The diameter of the earth is about 7900 miles which is 500,544,000 inches. Nineteen miles is 1,203,840 inches. Drawn to same scale, the pencil line should be 1/139 of an inch wide (1/416 of the diameter of circle).

Although seemingly thin, such layer of atmosphere is the frame of reference for events we describe as weather. The origin of that word is related to wind, which ordinarily is defined as horizontal air movement. However, most weather processes are associated with vertical air movement. Most vertical movement occurs near the surface of the earth, within an elevation of about 10 miles near the equator and about 5 miles near the poles, making the frame of reference even thinner.

The patterns of horizontal wind are displayed on weather "maps," called synoptic charts. That means they present a synopsis or summary for a specific time and specific altitude. The measurements or "observations" are made simultaneously. Because clock time varies with longitude and maps include more than one time zone, the time is listed as GMT, Greenwich Meridian Time, as per zero longitude. Recently the designation for time has been revised to UTC, Universal Time Coordinated.

However, this book is for elementary instruction for the general public in the USA. One goal is to make learning as convenient as possible. Citizens here are accustomed to temperature in degrees Fahrenheit, and to most measurements in English units. Everyone in the world in any technology knows GMT refers to universal time. Also, GMT already had changed once to Greenwich Civil Time,

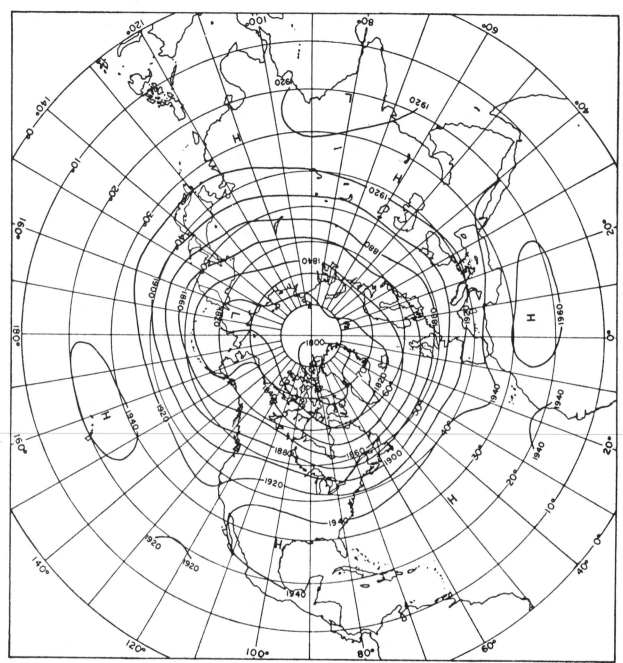

U.S. Weather Bureau

FIG. 1.032*b*.—500-mb height (10's of feet) in July

which was about as needless as UTC.

When the USA changes to the metric system we all can learn the new units quickly. Such knowledge is about as important as your brand of soda pop.

Traditional textbooks in synoptic meteorology begin with an explanation of wind patterns at the surface of the earth. Because more than half of the earth is covered by the oceans, and sailors were unusually vulnerable to storms, the first weather maps were for sea level.

My slow and awkward education began with such maps, learning to plot data from coded teletype messages, many relayed from radio. In 1940 the "upper air" was in the early stages of discovery, first explored by mountaineers, then balloonists, by instruments attached to kites and later to airplanes, and eventually the ingenious electronic radiosonde lifted by a small free balloon.

Discussion will now soar approximately to 18,000 ft, to the 500 mb level

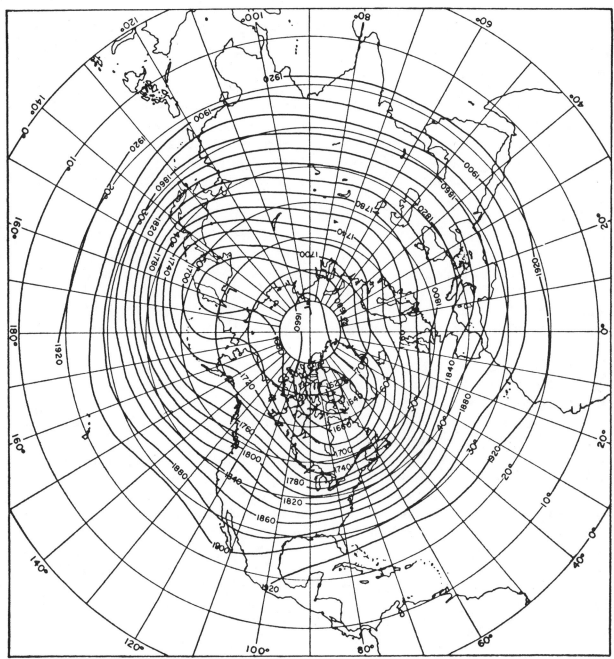

U.S. Weather Bureau

FIG. 1.032a.—500-mb height (10's of feet) in January

which is not really "level," but nearly so. The wind pattern there usually provides a better framework for beginning the three-dimensional analysis necessary for making a forecast.

On the preceding page and this page are charts for the 500 mb level, charts you will never see in a forecast office, because they show a climatological average of wind flow for the entire northern hemisphere, for midwinter and

midsummer, derived from many daily maps at those times. The ever present troughs and ridges are not shown because over time they cancel each other out.

The maps are "polar projections" in geographic terms. All meridians of longitude converge to the North Pole and parallels of latitude are curved. The reader is urged to refer to a common spherical globe during any discussion of a very large area.

These maps attempt to show an entire hemisphere, but areas are shrunken near the north pole and enlarged at low latitudes.

Superimposed on the base map of polar coordinates and outlines of land areas are contour lines for the 500 mb surface, similar to the familiar contour lines for elevation on a topographic map. Such lines are labeled in feet, with final zero omitted. The interval is only 200 feet, a trivial distance vertically, considering the vast distances horizontally.

The actual wind blows along these lines when all forces are in equilibrium. The direction is from west to east, which on this map of a hemisphere, appears circular with a counter-clockwise curvature.

Spherical geometry is a strange subject for nearly everyone. For example, if you stand at the north pole, a view in any horizontal direction is toward the south.

In our narrow everyday world we use rectangular coordinates, as on road maps, or the usual walls of a room. In the world of weather forecasting the earth has polar coordinates, which rotate counter-clockwise on a map of the northern hemisphere. In the southern hemisphere upper winds also blow from west to east, but in a clockwise direction around the south pole as our view is reversed.

Such pattern is caused by the Coriolis Force, after the name of an early explainer. Any substance moving in any horizontal direction has inertia to keep moving in that direction. However the lines of direction are turning to the left, of which we are unaware by any physical sense.

Because our frame of reference for direction (in rectangular coordinates) is rotating, and the inertia of a moving mass of air is straight ahead with respect to a point in space, and if no deflective force exists, such as higher pressure in the same horizontal plane, the path of that mass on a geographic map curves to the right.

Sometimes it is claimed that the CF is not really a force but a sort of convenient conversion to a new framework, something like converting miles to kilometers. However, inertia is a force. If one ties a small stone to a string and swings it in a cirle, the string is a deflecting force to the path of the stone. If the string breaks, inertia will propel the stone straight into a tangential path. The CF is an inertial force.

The rate of potential turning by the CF at the north pole is one revolution per 24 hours, or 15 degrees per hour. That may seem slow, but with no deflective force such as higher pressure, within six hours the direction can curve 90 degrees to the right. *Then why do all these contour lines, which are streamlines of air flow, all curve to the left?*

Answer: because there is a deflective force, higher pressure (in the same horizontal plane) to the right of each contour, and lower pressure to the left, facing downstream. However, pressure is everywhere the same on the 500 mb chart (although altitude varies slightly as shown by the contours). The chart slopes upward to the right of each contour. The first adjacent contour is 200 feet higher.

If the actual pressure of point #1 on an 18,000 ft contour is 500 mb, and point #2 is at the same elevation of 18,000 feet under the adjacent 18,200 ft contour, the pressure at point #2 must be more than 500 mb, because point #2 is 200 feet lower than the elevation where pressure is 500 mb.

Atmospheric pressure increases downward, absolutely always. Pressure always decreases upward. Never forget that. The rate of increase or decrease in pressure with altitude is rapid. Near sea level it is about one millibar per 30 feet. Therefore comparisons of pressure from one geographic location to another must be at the same altitude.

This may sound unduly complicated. In practice it merely means higher contours are equivalent to higher pressure at any given location and elevation.

Early weather maps described pressure at sea level, and such continues today. Sea level means a horizontal surface worldwide, which changes as the direction of gravity changes with latitude, ignoring the tiny departures by waves and tides.

The first upper air charts also were for a constant elevation, such as the 10,000 ft chart, forerunner of the present day 700 mb chart. The aneroid barometers in radiosonde instruments measure pressure, not altitude (but altitude can be computed quite precisely).

On the two 500 mb charts of mean contour patterns, what makes the contours higher to the right? There are two physical causes, and usually both are operating. One involves the contraction or expansion of air masses with cooling or warming, and the other is the result of the CF on air in motion. The interplay between the two causes is the focus of much attention by a forecaster.

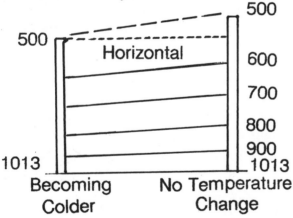

Consider the first cause. Refer to diagram, a cross section view of the atmosphere from sea level to the elevation of a pressure of 500 mb. The vertical scale is expanded for clarity. If both the left and right columns had the same pressure at the bottom, and the same change in temperature with elevation, the elevation of each column would be the same at 500 mb (not shown). Assume the left column becomes colder. Molecular motion in the gases would slow and the length of the column would decrease.

Assume a slower rate of cooling in each imaginary column toward the right, with no cooling at the right. The "pressure surface" of the 500 mb chart (dashed line) would tilt, sloping downward to left. All pressure surfaces below 500 mb would also slope toward the cooler column, but become more horizontal approaching sea level, assuming no change in pressure there. If columns in the right half of cross section warmed as the left half cooled the tilt in pressure surface would increase (revealed on the 500 mb chart by closer spacing of contour lines). Such explains the effect of changes in temperature only (no horizontal air movement). However, such tilt would initiate horizontal movement. (An example of difficulty in explaining dual processes one at a time.)

Next consider the effect of wind flow only, without change in surface pressure or change in temperatures in a vertical column of air. Because of the spherical shape of the surface of the earth, and because the earth is revolving, the CF is a deflective force produced by the inertia of moving mass.

(Mass is defined as anything that has weight, that is affected by gravity. Gravity is an extremely strong force, downward and vertical, as per the familiar plumb line.)

Because the inertia of a moving body is proportional to the velocity of that body, the CF increases if the windspeed increases. The CF is extremely weak compared to gravity. Its only discernible influence in the atmosphere is to change the compass direction of moving air. The concept of compass direction applies only to the local horizontal plane. The CF itself does not increase or decrease horizontal windspeed, but its deflection (to the right) of moving air molecules can have pronounced results. This is an intriguing example of composite forces.

If all parts of the atmosphere had

the same temperature and pressure at each elevation, equilibrium would prevail. The atmosphere would be stagnant. Bound to the earth by gravitation, it would revolve with the earth as a seemingly stationary gaseous shell.

As partial proof of this idea, note that the two 500 mb charts fail to reveal contours within 20 degrees of the equator. Horizontal winds in tropical regions, although temporarily strong in local areas because of local imbalances, display very little persistence in any direction. There are no significant areas of enduring temperature contrast. And the CF is almost non-existent at low latitudes because of spherical geometry.

In most of the early texts which I studied, "the CF decreases to zero at the equator." Why? The earth at the equator rotates at same rate as at the north pole.

The CF is very weak, at best, at north pole and gradually decreases because the horizontal plane of a compass card tilts from the plane of rotation at the pole. (The variation of CF with latitude is a sine function, with a value of 1.00 at 90 deg, 0.71 at 45 deg, 0.65 at 40 deg, and 0.17 at 10 deg.)

The earth is a sphere rotating on an axis, a straight line from north pole to south pole. In discussion of rotation such axis is the basis for reference. Viewed from above, as on a polar projection map, the axis is a point. A point is a position in space, without width.

The concept of rotation of the pole itself is meaningless, but the rotation of a polar projection map is obvious. One may envision rotation in a "plane of rotation," perpendicular to the axis of rotation. At the equator the plane of a compass card (horizontal as always) is perpendicular to the plane of rotation of the earth (which is vertical at the equator)

For demonstration, pierce a business card with a sharp pencil as shown. Hold pencil vertically, and rotate card counter-clockwise in horizontal plane as at

north pole. Walk across room, while rotating pencil and gradually tilt pencil to horizontal, top of pencil tilting toward you, representing the changing conditions as

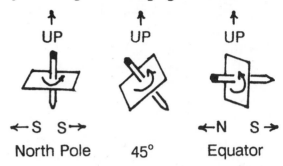

you travel to the equator, and the plane of rotation becomes vertical.

From my file of "almost useless information," at the equator the CF continues as an inertial force only for west winds, upward, and east winds, downward, and for north or south winds no effect when exactly on equator, where both latitude "north" and latitude "south" decrease to zero, as does the CF in the horizontal plane. For practical purposes, compared to the massive force of gravity, the CF does disappear.

There exists an entire book about the coriolis force, but this is all you need to know to understand weather maps. You may be surprised at what this weak force does to wind patterns.

In the popular science of weather, the physics of rotation is a neglected subject which this book will strive to explain. Here are a few facts which may

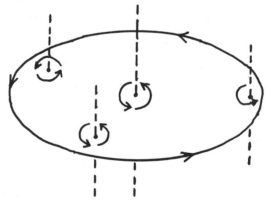

not be apparent initially. (1) Although rotation on a flat disk is obvious in a collective sense, all parts are rigidly connected and rotate as a solid body. (2) Each unit of mass in the solid disk, each molecule, also is rotating at the same rate. Also each unit of mass is moving around the circumference of a circle with a diameter twice the distance of the unit from the axis of rotation. Such motion doesn't appear to have its own axis because we observe the composite motion of rotation plus the linear motion along the circumference. The linear motion obscures the rotational motion. (3) Each unit of mass in the disk has its own invisible axis of rotation, parallel to the axis of the disk.

Look back at the two 500 mb charts, for the climatological average of wind patterns for summer and winter. The initial cause is the temperature difference between the polar area and those areas toward the south. For any given pressure, the molelcules of air are closer together (occupy a smaller volume) when cold than when warm. In winter, the latitudinal temperature differences are greater. The arctic is much colder, but with little change in the subtropics and even less in the tropics.

The pressure surfaces aloft tilt downward in cold air masses, with the greatest tilt in winter. The force of gravity is proportional to density. Density is mass per unit volume, which is same as weight per unit volume at any given location for non-moving masses. Density also is a neglected subject.

Volume is a three dimensional concept. Mass is composed of particles of material substance, the small particles of which are invisible to the eye, such as molecules. Even these vary greatly in weight, the usual measure of mass. The greater the number of particles in a given space (volume) and the greater the weight of each, the greater the density of such volume.

Molecules of gas are in rapid motion, with velocity proportional to temperature, darting in all directions.

Uncountable collisions occur between darting molecules and against any other obstacle such as an aneroid barometer, or the inside of a confining container (e.g. a pneumatic tire). The collective bombardment of gas molecules is measured as pressure.

Molecules of air exerting superior pressure will push back molecules exerting less pressure. Hence, in a horizontal plane, air moves from a location of higher pressure to one of lower pressure, in the direction of the "pressure gradient." By convention and logic the pressure gradient force is always directed toward lower pressure (horizontal plane only).

(Brief detour needed here) Air is a gas, actually a mixture of several substances, where pressure is exerted in all directions. The atmosphere is unconfined in the sense of a closed container, but is definitely confined by the strong force of gravity. Air at the surface of earth is compressed by the weight of all layers of air above, which creates the standard pressure (meaning average) of 1013 mb at MSL. Any position moving upward will measure decreasing pressure, and vice versa downward. Hence all discussion of pressure gradients refers to a horizontal plane.

Air is thin stuff. Horizontal movement is easily achieved by a comparatively weak pressure gradient (and easily deflected to the right by the weak coriolis force).

The day to day changes are one of the greatest shows on earth, and if you learn how they work you can predict the weather for tomorrow!

The reason upper winds blow along the contour lines on the 500 mb chart (with higher contours to the right), and the average direction is west to east, and the greater the local slope of the 500 mb pressure surface the greater the speed of the wind, is because: (1) the atmosphere usually is colder toward the north, (2) horizontal pressure gradients push air

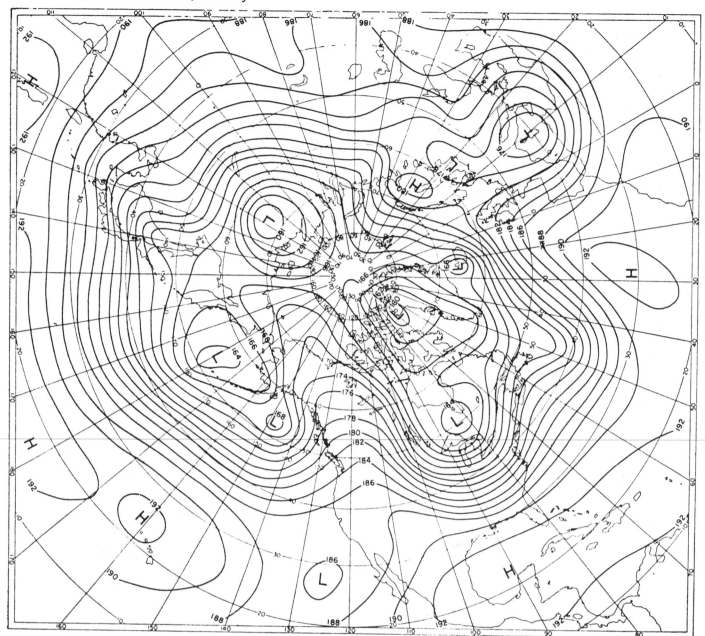

FIG. 7.02b.—500-mb analysis (based on *Daily Series, Synoptic Weather Maps, Northern Hemisphere Sea Level and 500-Millibar Charts*) for 1500 GCT, 1 March 1950. (Contours are labeled in hundreds of geopotential feet.)

toward any area with lower pressure at the same elevation, (3) the CF deflects wind to the right which soon increases the higher pressure already there, until (4) the increase in pressure gradient balances the CF, ending additional deflection (unless the windspeed increases, and CF therefore increases, and a new balance is soon reached.)

The small diagram in next column is a plan view (from above) showing initial air flow from high to low pressure (wide arrow), with immediate deflection by CF (small arrow). Finally, the CF

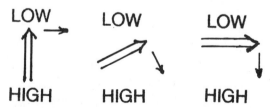

balances the pressure gradient, and wind blows along the contour line.

The large chart at top of this page is a 500 mb analysis for a given hour derived from observations made simultaneously. The chart is a "snapshot", a still picture of a moving pattern, and not a display of climatological averages.

There is considerable similarity to the previous polar projection maps, with a general counter-clockwise airflow around the north pole. In the jargon of meteorology such direction of rotation is called "cyclonic," and a clockwise circulation is called anticyclonic. The broad band of circumpolar contours displays kinks pointing approximately southward, which are "troughs," (called valleys on a topographic map). The less conspicuous bulges of contours northward are ridges. If the northern part of a trough has one or more localized circular contours, it is called a "closed" Cold Low.

The physics creating the localized Lows (which means a center either of low elevation, or a center of low pressure if measured on a horizontal plane) are the same as that which creates the huge polar Low on the climatological maps. Each localized Low or trough is a pocket of cold air pressing southward from the everlasting supply over the pole.

A beginner in synoptic meteorology should remember that weather maps are displayed on flat sheets, and atmospheric motions are on the surface of a sphere. The polar projection maps shown here are for textbook purpose. Usually a forecaster is looking at a map which has rectangular coordinates, or nearly so, rather than a map with polar coordinates. For forecasting in a specific region, e.g. the Pacific NW, weather maps are limited to much smaller areas than shown here.

The reader should not assume from the climatological charts first displayed that the circular contour lines are merely "harmony" with the circular geographic parallels (depicting latitude on the globe). Their shape, viewed from a position above the north pole, results from the prevailing center of cold air over the pole, which in turn results from the physics of astronomy.

If by some absurd magic a large mass of the coldest air on the northern hemisphere was centered permanently over the "lower 48 states," the pattern on the climatological maps would shift accordingly. The center of the Cold Low would be about over Kansas City.

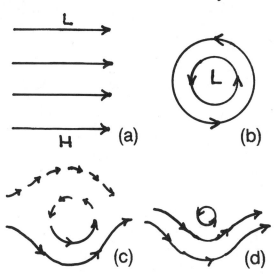

In plan views immediately above, whether the contours appear as straight west to east windflow (or some other direction) as in (a), or whether they are circular as in (b), is probably in the difference in scale of the two areas. In both circulations lower pressure and colder air prevail to the left, facing downstream. If for any reason the two patterns are superimposed, such that the air in the center of (a) became the coldest (instead of at north edge), the composite pattern would reveal some of the shape of (b), as suggested in (c).

In the northern half of (c) the gradients of both temperature and pressure are now reversed. During the transformation the initial winds in that area would tend to cancel each other, as suggested by the broken streamlines.

The result is the formation of a trough as in (d). If the pocket of cold air has only a small effect, the trough is shallow, meaning a minor deflection. If the cold air is very cold, the trough is deeper with major deflection and probably will produce two or more closed contour lines (see examples on map of March 1st).

In short, a trough is a composite pattern of circular flow around a Cold Low and straight line flow. Recognition of composite activity is extremely important.

The reader probably realizes already that the ridges between the troughs, ridges which bulge northward and display clockwise turning of windflow are areas of relatively warm air. Pressure surfaces always bulge upward in warm air, and sink downward in cold air, as a vertical column of air expands or contracts with changes in temperature.

Sometimes, especially in areas in middle latitudes, the southward intrusions of cold air masses, and the accompanying northward advance of warm air masses, create remarkable bends or kinks in the band of west winds around the coldest regions.

Cold Lows or cut-off Warm Highs, meaning they are localized circulations temporarily independent from the broad band of "westerlies" displayed on the climatological charts.

Ordinary troughs and ridges move slowly toward the east, embedded in the general flow of air, with faster progression in the "flat" troughs and ridges, and slower progression in the pronounced deflections. When cut-off circulations appear, the general west to east circulation is disrupted, and progression usually stops. Sometimes the cut-off centers even retrograde toward the west. Cut-off circulations present big problems for forecasters.

These explanations may seem complicated, but with frequent access to upper air maps (available every 12 hours) the maps become familiar and fascinating. The shape, slope, location, and changes with time for both troughs and ridges are closely related to local weather. There are numerous other indicators for forecasting, to be described in following pages.

In this preliminary chapter about upper air wind patterns, the phrase "jet stream" was mentioned only in the title. Television weathercasters often refer mystically to the big arrow on their map graphics. The treatments often are distorted, and seldom educational in explaining the connection with impending weather events. If you are a long-time watcher of TV weather shows, the explanations in this short chapter must surely differ from your experience.

The term jet stream appeared soon after World War II, reportedly because U.S. bomber planes encountered westerly winds while approaching Japan that nearly equalled their airspeed. The jet aircraft engine was under development, but not yet on the bombers. The "jet stream" was an ideal headline to promote governmental research grants for the fledgling technology of meteorology (which technology captured my ambitions, especially for public weather forecasting).

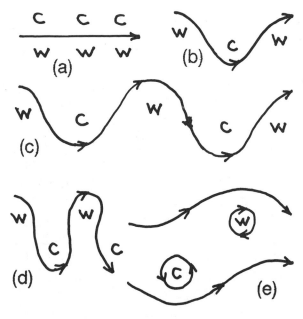

In the plan views above, (a) shows a long stretch of west winds with cold air to the north and warm air to the south. Cold air may bulge southward and warm air bulge northward, as shown in (b) and (c). In some cases the deflections are sufficient to create closed circulations of "cut-off" pockets of cold or warm air, as in (d) and (e). Often these are called cut-off

In my copy of the Glossary of Meteorology (1959) published by the AMS, the jet stream is defined as:

> Relatively strong winds concentrated within a narrow stream in the atmosphere... a jet stream of maximum winds embedded in the mid-latitude westerlies, and concentrated in the high troposphere. The question of the maintenance of the jet stream is a cardinal problem of theoretical meteorology...it is discontinuous and varies greatly from day-to-day....a jet stream is indicated wherever it is reliably determined that the wind speed equals or exceeds 50 knots. [57.5 mph]

I suggest the outworn term be respectfully laid to rest in our weather museum.

However, always pay attention to areas where the contour lines are relatively close together, meaning the winds are stronger. That is where horizontal temperature differences are the greatest. Look closely for signs of "bad weather" (to be discussed in the next chapter).

The polar projection maps in this chapter are photocopies from the remarkable book, "Principles of Meteorological Analysis" by Walter J. Saucier, published by The University of Chicago Press in 1955.

In his preface dated 10-1-53, he wrote: "Without the contribution, assistance and encouragement of a large number of associates this book never would have materialized. Most of the credit goes to the students whose scientific curiosity was the force and whose patience gave life to experiment."

I bought my book from Professor Saucier, in which he inscribed: "With best wishes to a former student--Bob Lynott--one who helped make this a reality."

My help(?) was minimal. However, in 1947-1949 I was a student at U of Chicago, financed by the "G.I. Bill." Saucier taught a lab course, Weather Analysis and Forecasting, with 10 hour credits per quarter. Attendance was from 1 to 5 pm five days a week. There were about 50 students in the class. At end of course (3 quarters) in June 1948 I was at top of the class, tied with John Hope, who also had served as an Enlisted Forecaster in the Army Air Corps in World War II.

Dr. Hope completed a brilliant career with the National Weather Service, and he appears on the Weather Channel as an expert on hurricanes.

In the fall quarter of 1948 I was in a 300 level course in Advanced Analysis taught by George Cressman, PhD candidate. I won a competition for a part-time job as "relief" synoptic analyst for Dr. Cressman (8 hours a day, Saturday, Sunday, and holidays only, $110 month).

Although I had been warned by the admissions office that the Department of Meteorology no longer offered bachelor degrees, and I must work toward at least a masters degree (their programs led to research only), I was grateful to obtain admission. My real goal was public forecasting.

After 8 consecutive quarters I was granted a Bachelor of Science degree, as an exception, presumably for high grades in courses related to forecasting. The University credited me with an earned 60 quarter hours in meteorology alone, plus advanced credit of 25 quarter hours in meteorology for academic training in the Army Air Corps.

Note to reader: On the next two "book" pages, actually four counting both sides, are two "extra" weather maps. One is a 500 mb map already shown on page 8. The other is a northern hemisphere Sea Level map for the same date, March 1, 1950, which will appear again on page 15. 20

The extra maps can be removed from the book. With no printing on back, they can be superimposed on a light table, or pressed against a back-lighted window.

My Desktop Light Box of 9x12 inches cost $53 in 1987 at an art supply store. Such investment is useful for do-it-yourself forecasting to reveal the changes between successive charts. You can make your own. I recommend its use.

Maybe this little exercise will help stimulate your interest in real weather maps, and how to properly use them to make genuine forecasts.

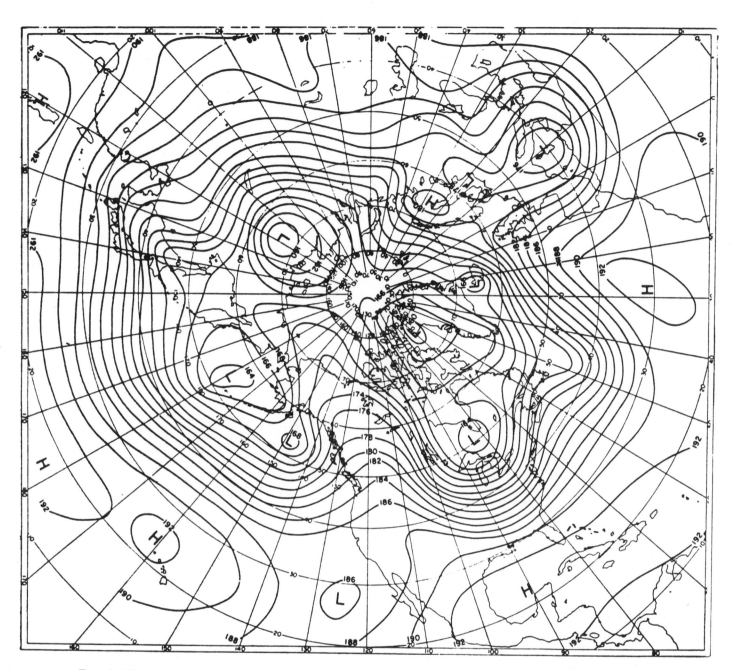

FIG. 7.02b.—500-mb analysis (based on *Daily Series, Synoptic Weather Maps, Northern Hemisphere Sea Level and 500-Millibar Charts*) for 1500 GCT, 1 March 1950. (Contours are labeled in hundreds of geopotential feet.)

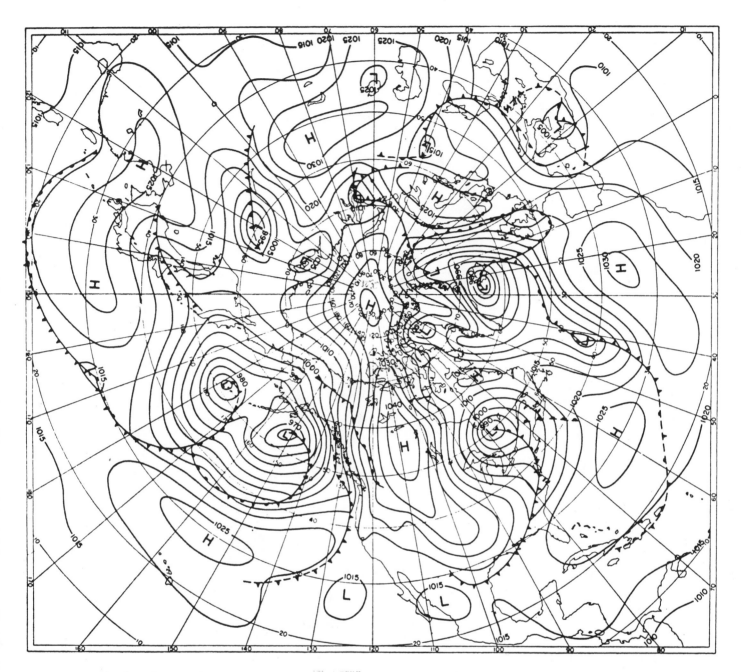

FIG. 7.02a.—Sea-level pressure and frontal analysis (based on *Daily Series, Synoptic Weather Maps, Northern Hemisphere Sea Level and 500-Millibar Charts*) for 1230 GCT, 1 March 1950. (Units of pressure are millibars; fronts are entered in standard symbolic form.)

Chapter 2. The Sea-Level Map -- Also Called the Surface Map

Everything should be made as simple as possible, but not simpler.
--Albert Einstein

Keep in mind the historical development of the technology of meteorology, which uses many parts of older established fields of knowledge, such as physics, chemistry, geography, and mathematics. Academic authorities, stretched to comprehend the entire encyclopedia of physical knowledge, sometimes require too much mastery of the related subjects, and not enough integrated comprehension of the many portions needed for this applied technology.

Although an understanding of the "upper air," at least the mapping of flow patterns, was mostly developed during the last sixty years, the first chapter began on that topic. The patterns are simpler, and easier to understand.

The surface map is prepared from measurements on the surface of the earth, which is not all at an elevation of sea level. Considerable complexity results from the character of the terrain. The very term "local weather" introduces a topic difficult to summarize adequately on a map. However, real surface maps, not the show-biz maps on TV, are remarkable examples of ingenuity.

By use of symbols, abbreviations, and a few coded numbers, a surprising amount of information is displayed. For those of us old-timers, it's delightful to see all that stuff without the labor of plotting the "station model" from codes, and drawing all those isobars. I'm sure I drew at least 50 miles of isobars early in my career, and I mean about 3,168,000 inches on a map table. At least it seemed that much. Nowadays we have time to think about what we are looking at.

After the invention of the barometer it was discovered that air pressure at each location, even at sea level, varied slightly from day to day, and the variation seemed to suggest impending change in the local weather. Sailors soon learned to watch both the sky and the "glass," meaning a mercurial barometer.

The discovery of meaningful patterns of pressure over non-local areas followed the invention of the telegraph. The local pressure not only varied from day to day, but the geographic patterns of pressure moved, and changed shape, in a systematic way. Such change and movement were soon related to the wind, and to the general weather itself, good or bad.

The early maps were drawn for areas at or near sea level, the usual locations for population centers, which even today are associated with ocean shipping. As population moved inland from coastal areas, to higher elevations, the barometer readings were not in harmony with sea-level measurements. Soon a system of "reducing" surface pressure readings (actually increasing them) was developed to meaningfully compare such pressures with coastal areas.

Hence the pressures plotted for stations above sea level are "computed" so that isobars (lines of equal pressure) can be drawn on surface maps, making that pattern a sort of sea level map. You will soon learn such patterns vary from the patterns on 500 mb maps. However, the patterns are partly dependent on each other, and the differences are excellent indicators for weather forecasting.

Again, we need to recognize the climatological averages for windflow patterns at sea level, as presented in the previous chapter for the upper air, such as the 500 mb "level."

[The 500 mb chart is a depiction of contours on the 500 mb pressure surface, which is not quite level. The shop-talk label is understandable, from the habit of the earlier sea level chart. Isobars (on sea level charts) and contour lines (on upper air charts) should be interpreted similarly, as depictions of patterns of wind flow.]

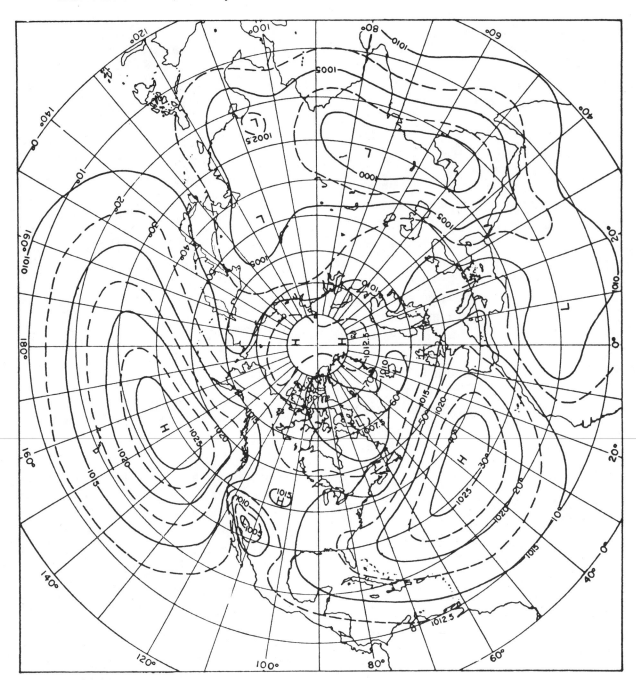

U.S. Weather Bureau

FIG. 1.031*b.*—Sea-level pressure (mb) in July

On this page and the next page are the longtime average patterns of pressure, as depicted by isobars (lines of constant pressure) for sea level in the northern hemisphere. Average patterns for July and January are presented. The pressure actually measured in land areas, at varying elevations, is adjusted to a higher value to extend isobars over those areas. (See later discussion about barometers.) The isobars are labeled in units of millibars, with a 5 mb interval between solid isobars, and intermediate dashed-line isobars.

These mean pressure patterns are not of a synoptic sea level chart for a specific time. They reveal the "semipermanent" features such as the Pacific and Atlantic Highs of summer and winter, the summer heat Lows of California and most of Asia, the pronounced winter Aleutian and Icelandic Lows, and the strong Siberian High in winter.

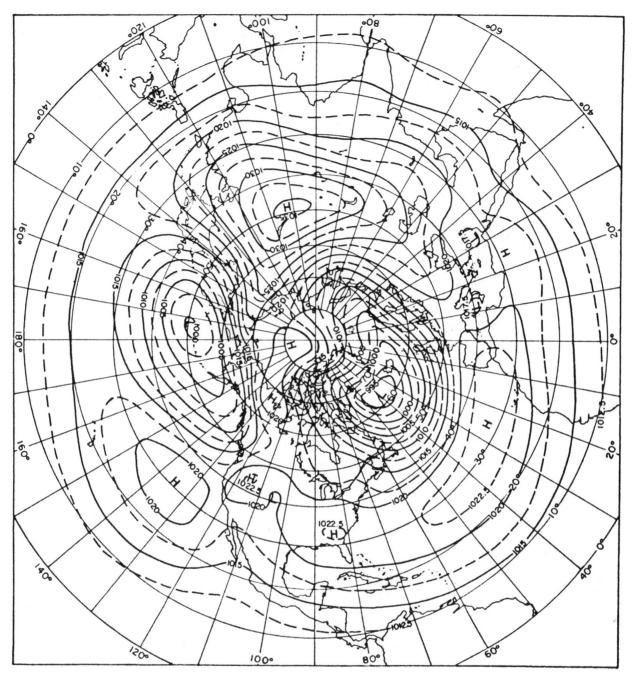

FIG. 1.031a.—Sea-level pressure (mb) in January

U.S. Weather Bureau

These "average" isobaric maps exist only vaguely in the memory of a forecaster striving to interpret the synoptic maps for today and maybe for the last two days (four maps each day). Climatology is useful for reference, but "real time" forecasting must cope with the present departure from normal. Real time means right now. Normal means average, for various periods in the past.

Consider the imaginary problem of a forecaster in Portland, Oregon on January 9, 1880. An observer of the U.S. Army Signal Service measured a sea level pressure of 967 mb, the lowest ever recorded. The map above indicates an average January pressure of about 1018 mb. Portland measured a pressure of 977 mb with the windstorm of October 12, 1962, described later in this book. (Highest gust 116 mph).

Compare the climatological map above with the synoptic map on the next

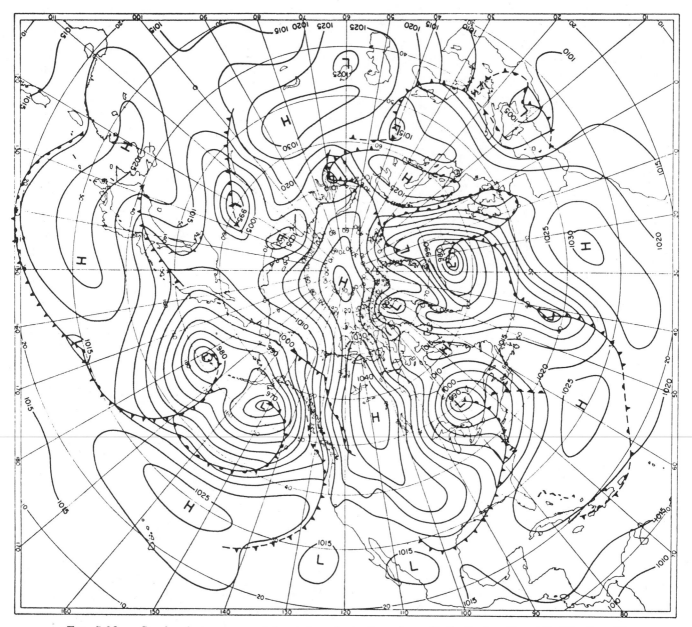

FIG. 7.02a.—Sea-level pressure and frontal analysis (based on *Daily Series, Synoptic Weather Maps, Northern Hemisphere Sea Level and 500-Millibar Charts*) for 1230 GCT, 1 March 1950. (Units of pressure are millibars; fronts are entered in standard symbolic form.)

page, which is the same sea level map as on page 13, slightly reduced in size. Although for a date only slightly after the January climatological map, it looks much different. There are more Highs and Lows, of greater intensity, more isobars closer together, and air mass fronts, sometimes called storm fronts. However, a local forecaster doesn't need to study the synoptic maps for the whole northern hemisphere. But he should be aware of nearby broadscale patterns which helped create, and may still be influencing, the existing local conditions.

Note the following features on the synoptic map above: (1) two low centers in the north Pacific and Gulf of Alaska, related to the Aleutian Low; (2) the band of relatively high pressure across the Pacific from Japan to east of Hawaiian Islands, which reveals the persistence of the Pacific High even in late winter; and (3) a vigorous Low over Iceland with a new Low approaching from southeastern Canada.

Central North America was exper-

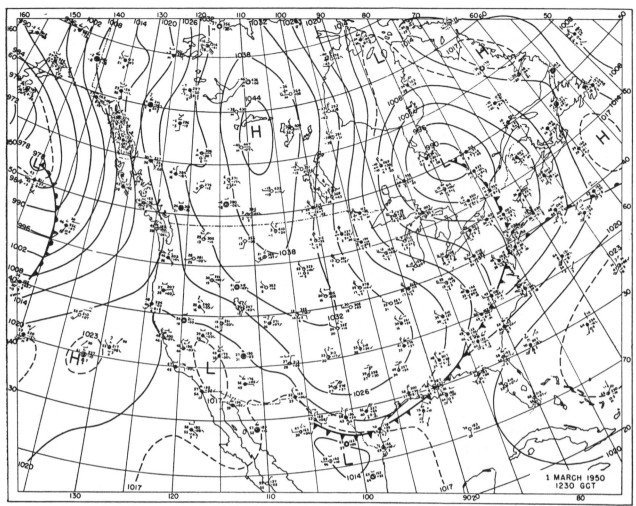

FIG. 9.02a.—Sea-level chart, 1230 GCT, 1 March 1950

iencing a major arctic outbreak. This helped generate an intense storm center just north of the Great Lakes, shown dramatically on both sea level and 500 mb charts. An elongated surface High had pushed a cold front southward to the Gulf of Mexico.

The storm center near the Great Lakes is a good example of a Cold Low, where the upper air Low is almost directly above the surface Low, meaning cold air throughout the layer from the surface to 500 mb. See upper air map page 11. 13

On the other hand, the elongated surface High, at least that portion west of longitude 90°, the meridian near Kansas City, is an example of a Warm High, even though the air is cold near the surface. At 500 mb a warm ridge extends from Yukon Territory to near El Paso, Texas. The warm air aloft moved over western North

America, in advance of storms from the Gulf of Alaska. The strong winds aloft, south of the Gulf storms, under influence of an increased Coriolis Force, deflected some air to the right which increased the pressure gradient toward the Low center. As the upper Low intensified, higher pressure built ahead of the trough. As streamlines curve to the left, warmer air on right side is "advected" northward. Also, as will be explained later, air gradually sinks in a High or a ridge, which warms the air by compression.

The surface map above is also copied from Professor Saucier's book, Principles of Meteorological Analysis. The copyright has expired, but a reprint is available from Dover Publications Inc., code number 65979-8, $12.95 plus $3.00, (catalog available). Address: 31 East 2nd Street, Mineola, New York 11501.

The reader will see little resemblance between the sea level map on previous page and the weather maps on television. Saucier's map is 43 years "old," but its purpose is to inform, not entertain with bold colors, pulsating jet streams, putting satellite pictures in motion, and icons such as yellow disks with spikes.

As a reader you are a serious forecast user, a SFU, or a potential SFU. Let others enjoy the hype of the market place. Occasionally when they want to know the weather for tomorrow, they will come to you. Begin as an amateur, but with self-confidence. Later, when the federal monopoly on local forecasting is broken, you might become a professional forecaster, with benefits comparable to other skilled occupations.

In one way I look back on the early days after World War II as the golden age of forecasting, but it really wasn't. There was rapid progress, but more like the childhood of forecasting, memorable but not as satisfying as the accomplishments of middle age, the age which is now beginning in the art and use of local weather forecasting.

* * *

The remainder of this chapter will discuss airmass "fronts," which always appear on a Sea Level map. In turn, that means a quick review of the airmass concept, which now gains little attention.

During World War II and a few years afterward, the focus was on observation of existing conditions, which was still mostly of surface conditions, but forecasters were striving to include the third dimension. The almost frantic effort led to distortions and exaggerations (such as the concept of the jet stream).

On sea level charts today you will see Lows and Highs portrayed by isobars which remain very important, and airmass fronts, which have obvious value but are not as important as everyone thought in 1945. The emphasis on airmass fronts was because upper air data was very scanty.

Direct measurement of pressure, temperature, and relative humidity along a vertical line in the atmosphere was difficult. Kites were slow and limited to low elevations, airplanes were expensive, and risky for human life, especially in adverse weather. Radiosonde instruments provided the great leap forward in the science of weather. In my opinion, that was a greater step than the overblown and overcostly satellite "imagery." That last word is a classic example of puffery.

Gleanings from my dictionary: Imagery-- mental images; employment of vivid descriptions in writing or speaking; metaphoric representation as in music or art; figurative language, especially when used for ornament. From my vocabulary: cloud pictures of exaggerated value, compared with the numerical measurements of radiosondes.

In the days of surface weather observations only, forecasters had to speculate, and make careful estimates of the temperature and relative humidity at successive elevations in the air above. Every clue was wrung from the surface data, including eye observations of the clouds from below. Many individuals developed a "weather eye."

Weather maps provided vital information for wind patterns beyond the horizon. Man looked upwind, as best he could, to estimate where the local air of today was yesterday, and the day before.

An airmass is defined as a large mass which had acquired a set of standard characteristics (approximately) from its former location--the arctic, tropics, ocean, or continent. From trial and error, and much logic, considerable skill developed in predicting the local weather for tomorrow by determining where that air is today.

As an airmass moved, the leading edge was called a front, such as a cold front, a warm front, or a combination called an occluded front. As might be expected, the classifications and the shorthand graphics on the maps were overly stereotyped and categorized. The value of some indicators were exaggerated, and attempts at precision overdone.

The term "airmass front" needs better explanation than what we see and hear on TV, read in the newspapers, or in many popular science books. One period of early stimulation in meteorology was during World War I. A front was a war zone, a No-Man's Land in which enemies tried to kill each other. To this day, a weather front is often described as a "battle line" along which physical forces are competitive. Which airmass will win?

There is no conflict along a weather front. The activity is merely adjustment of physical differences, according to the "laws" of physics, which in weather are mainly those related to gravity, change of state of ordinary water, and the rotation of the earth.

The adjustments from imbalances to equilibrium often are accompanied by wind, fog, precipitation, or unwanted events. When man doesn't understand the physics, events often appear mysterious or frustrating. With understanding, those events usually can be predicted. Even if one dislikes the ensuing conditions, one prefers to be forewarned.

Air masses were labeled as maritime or continental (lower case m or c), or arctic or tropical (capitalized A or T). A third designation was added for airmasses newly arriving over warmer or colder earth surfaces (lower case w or k). The k meant cold, because c was already in use.

Thus, "mPk" meant maritime Polar cold, meaning it was colder than the new surface over which it was flowing. Also it was being warmed at the bottom, making it more unstable. "mTw" was for maritime Tropical warm, such as air moving northward from Gulf of Mexico in winter.

Nowadays, because observations both surface and aloft are more numerous, forecasters have numbers rather than imprecise adjectives.

Although fronts are drawn as lines, they are zones of demarcation, with main attention on ordinary temperature. The zones vary in width and in difference between temperatures, and may be intensifying or dissipating.

The main problem in the interpretation of fronts is that an air mass is a three-dimensional concept, and the surface map is a two-dimensional display. An airmass is a huge glob of gas, meaning the simple gaseous "state" of matter, and matter is any batch of molecules. [Be patient with help for beginners in physics because that is a neglected subject.]

The airmass concept is concerned with the lower part of the atmosphere (the part which is directly responsive to conditions on surface of the earth) and any boundary of the mass which maintains significant difference from another mass.

The following sketches illustrate the stylized and oversimplified boundary zones between cold and warm airmasses.

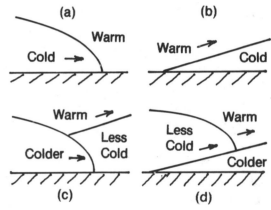

These are cross-section views near land or sea surfaces for (a) cold front, (b) warm front, (c) cold occluded front, and (d) warm occluded front. The separation between cold and warm air is a sloping surface.

Cold air advances as a wedge lifting the warm air ahead, but friction with the surface slows the advance slightly. Warm air, less dense, slides up over warm air. Occluded fronts are "upper" fronts, "bitten off" from the surface. Labels are sometimes quaint.

* * *

The evaluation by a forecaster does not come only from a surface map or an upper air map, but also from radiosonde graphs and hourly airway reports not appearing on the surface map. Yes, even from satellite cloud pictures, which are especially useful over sparse data areas.

Keep in mind that weather maps are just one of the ingenious ways to display what is going on in the thin invisible stuff called the atmosphere. How is it moving horizontally and vertically, what are the present changes in pressure, temperature, and water vapor content? What will the weather be like tomorrow? That last question is the important one, and after you read this book you will know the answer is not as difficult as the NWS says it is.

You will also understand better why corporate interests (which includes the consortium of universities who created the American Meteorological Society) are maintaining a monopoly on local weather forecasting. Of course, Congress is involved too, because it makes you pay double or more for what public weather forecasting ought to cost.

When voters are informed, and awakened to their self-interest, maybe amateur forecasters can obtain the necessary data which are now hidden by crafty rules, policies, and other obstructions to handicap their effort.

The next chapter will discuss some basic physics of any gas, to help in the fourth chapter of "What Makes a Low?" That is a fascinating question.

Chapter 3. Heat, Pressure, Density

Although local weather forecasting is based on the physics of the atmosphere, only an elementary knowledge of such physics is needed. What puzzles this writer is the seeming lack of the elementary knowledge by both citizens and a sizeable proportion of TV weathercasters.

My goal is to explain the "needed" without losing the reader's interest in forecasting. That means short trips to the supply room of nuts and bolts, and quick return to building the reader's forecasting machine which will outclass the crude robot in Washington D.C.

Three important concepts in the physics of air are Temperature, Pressure, and Density. The first two are easy to measure directly, and density can be derived. Usually, one needs only to recognize comparative density without burdening oneself with a number.

Temperature is a subtopic of heat, which in turn is a subtopic of Energy. Energy is anything that can do work. Work, in physics, means movement against an opposing force. Hence energy is anything that can start motion or maintain motion against an opposing force. Heat can do work if harnessed to produce motion.

Heat is a familiar thing, but an explanation can become complicated. It involves both the kinetic energy and potential energy in molecules. Only that energy which can be transferred from a warm body to a cool body is heat.

Heat often is explained as the energy of molecules in motion, which is true if we also include energy which has the potential of adding to the motion of molecules. The total heat in a body at rest is the sum of the energy of that molecular motion, called the kinetic energy of the molecules, and any potential energy that can be converted to kinetic energy while the body remains at rest. That potential energy for heat is related to intermolec-ular forces, usually in liquids, which are electronic in nature.

Horace G. Deming in his book "Fundamental Chemistry," (1947) pointed out that it is incorrect to say that the motion of molecules produces heat. The motion is heat.

Temperature is an easier concept than heat. It's a measure only of the kinetic energy of molecules, not any potential energy, and the measured value is usually used for comparisons. Temperature determines the direction of flow of heat from one body to another body. If both bodies are at the same temperature, no heat is transferred. This does not necessarily mean that each body contains the same quantity of heat.

The ordinary concept of temperature is the degree of hotness or coldness as measured on a specific scale (Fahrenheit in the U.S.) by various types of thermometers. All scales are arbitrary, and convertible, and each has reference points.

The common reference points are the boiling point of water and the melting point of ice (at sea level for both). Physicists also refer to Absolute Zero, meaning the lowest possible temperature on any scale. Theory assumes molecules are without motion (without kinetic energy) at that point, and devoid of any heat. Molecules cannot become colder. On the other hand, there is no upper limit to any temperature scale. There is only the limit of available energy to increase the speed of gaseous molecules, jostling one another, or the rate of vibration or spinning of molecules in liquids and solids, which in comparison to gases, are relatively fixed in space. At sufficiently high temperature all molecules presumably are gaseous.

The reference point on the Fahrenheit scale for the melting point of ice is 32° and the boiling point is 212°. The zero was supposedly determined at the lowest temperature to which water could be cooled by the addition of ice and salt, as in making ice cream at home. If you are young, ask your grandparents about that. The 100° mark was presumed to be normal human body temperature. Absolute zero in terms of Fahrenheit is -460°.

The seldom used Rankine scale

	C	F	K	R
Boiling point	100	212	373	672
Melting point	0	32	273	492
Absolute zero	-273	-460	0	0

Reference points on scales for Celsius, Fahrenheit, Kelvin, and Rankine

begins at absolute zero, and using increments like Fahrenheit, shows 672° at the boiling point.

The Celsius scale is nearly universal (formerly called Centigrade for obvious reason). It begins at the melting point of ice, and with larger units than Fahrenheit, reaches 100° at the boiling point.

For all practical purposes the more common phrase, the freezing point, is the same as the melting point of ice. For science, a change of state during rising temperature (such as the boiling point) is determined more precisely than during falling temperature. Also, very small drops of liquid water, common in the atmosphere, often cool far below 32°F before solidifying to ice.

Liquid water has strong surface tension, especially around tiny droplets. When molecules form bonds in the crystalline structure of ice, they occupy slighly more space. The surface tension of a droplet resists such expansion. (How can anyone claim that physics is dull?)

The Kelvin scale, with same size units as Celsius, begins at absolute zero, and is widely used in science, to avoid the annoyance of minus numbers.

It is incorrect to say that 100°F is twice as warm as 50°F. In absolute units 100°F is about 10% warmer than 50°F.

In meteorology there is another measure of temperature which is dependent on pressure, called the potential temperature. But first, we need an explanation of atmospheric *pressure*.

The age-old subject of weather, which even animals seem to understand fairly well, has a large built-in problem. Air is matter in a gaseous state. The molelcules, like any other kind, are extremely small and hence invisible. Also, the molecules are spaced far apart, compared to those in a liquid or a solid.

However, considering their small size and wide separation (compared to liquids) air molecules reveal considerable energy of motion, or kinetic energy. According to Horace Deming (1947), a molecule of oxygen in the atmosphere at sea level at ordinary temperature travels at a speed of about 900 mph, and moves less than one-millionth of an inch before colliding with any other molecule.

Actually, the so-called collisions may not be contact in the sense of two billiard balls. They suffer no wear or tear. Maybe, as they approach actual contact, electronic forces act to repel each from the other. After all, the molecules are in the gaseous state because they have too much kinetic energy to bond with partners, even the same identical kind. Because of the high speed, the motion is assumed to be straight-line until a collision occurs.

The pressure exerted within a gas is the force of collective impacts, in a random chaotic manner. Air is thin stuff but at sea level it is exerting a force equal to a weight of 14.7 lbs on each square inch. It should not be surprising that slight variations in such pressure can move that thin stuff around quite a bit, movement which we call wind. Take note, pressure variations are important for forecasting.

If the reader wonders why the "hyperactive" molecules don't fly off into space, just remember that immense force called gravity. The earth is a huge mass of liquid and solid, with a core of iron, compared to an infinitely small air molecule. Then why aren't those air molecules compressed into a shallow high density layer very near the surface of the earth?

Well, they are, as explained on page one. When 99% of the atmosphere is compressed into a layer about 100,000 feet thick, that is impressive. However, the force of gravity is balanced by the combined force of all those molecules darting about at 900 mph (at sea level). As elevation increases, the concentration of molecules becomes less, and the bombardment decreases. Hence pressure decreases with elevation, as per selected values in table at bottom of page.

Variations in temperature in the atmosphere create corresponding variations in the pressure-height relationship. Values in the table are from the U. S. Standard Atmosphere, defined for scientific and engineering use, a frequently used "yardstick." For example, air-pressure altimeters for aircraft, the most common kind, are built to that specification. Radio altimeters (radar) are more precise, and more expensive.

The U. S. standard atmosphere assumes a sea level pressure of 1013 mb, a surface temperature of 59°F, and a lapse rate of 3.6°F per 1000 ft from sea level up to 35,332 ft.

At that elevation the temperature is -67°F and the pressure is 235 mb. From there up to 65,000 ft, where the pressure is only 55 mb, the layer is isothermal, meaning the same temperature everywhere in the layer. For our purpose here, local forecasting, the temperature for such altitudes is almost meaningless.

A comprehension of the physics of gaseous pressure is vital in understanding other topics, such as evaporation and condensation, buoyancy, and lapse rates in the atmosphere which depart from the average depicted in the standard atmosphere. The term lapse rate means the rate of change in temperature with elevation, which usually decreases upward. Such rates influence vertical movement of air.

Pressure in a gas is closely related to *density*, the final topic in this chapter. Density is mass per unit volume, and volume means space, such as a cubic foot or a gallon. In meteorology, to keep track of a fixed amount of mass (air molecules), such a mass is labeled as a parcel.

The word parcel is odd, but common synonyms are inaccurate. The intent is to refer to a batch of adjacent molecules and to distinguish them from the surrounding air. A sample is a portion representative of the whole (and a parcel might not be). A bubble is a body of

```
Elevation  Pressure  Pressure
  (feet)     (mbs)   (inches Hg)
 102,336       10      0.30     99% of atmosphere lies below
  53,170      100      2.95     90% of atmosphere lies below
  32,000      274      8.10     Airliner
  29,000      313      9.25     Summit Mt. Everest
  18,280      500     14.76     50% of atmosphere lies below
  11,235      664     19.50     Summit Mt. Hood, Oregon
   9,880      700     20.67     30% of atmosphere lies below
   4,780      850     25.10     Denver is 500 ft higher
Sea level    1013     29.92     Air pressure 14.7 lbs/sq in

1 millibar = 0.02953 inches Hg      1 inch Hg = 33.8622 mbs
    Near sea level, an increase in elevation of 10 ft reduces
    pressure .01 inch Hg, or 1/3 millibar (30 ft = 1 mb)
       At sea level, 1 cubic foot of air weighs 1.22 ounces,
       and 1,000,000 cubic feet of air weighs 76,000 lbs.
       That is a cube of only 100 feet on each side.
```

gas within a liquid or solid, enclosed by a visible liquid film or solid shell (which is not quite correct). We could describe a parcel as a bubble of air inside the atmosphere. A parcel may be any size but tiny compared to an air mass.

Most substances, in the conditions of usual environment, exist in only one of the three "states," gas, liquid, or solid. A solid has all molecules arranged in rigid position, at least apparently. Liquid molecules are partly free. They flow to the bottom of a container and assume the shape of the container. The molecular bonds (some sort of electronic attraction) are still strong except at the boiling point of the particular liquid. Some substances can melt or solidify within natural conditions. Water is common in all three states both on the earth's surface and in the atmosphere.

Gaseous molecules are almost entirely free. They are comparatively far apart but the spacing is obviously related to density, and that spacing can change markedly with changes in temperature and pressure. In the atmosphere, pressure varies much more than temperature.

Gases don't flow to the bottom of a container, they expand to fill all parts of a container. If the container is not closed, collision with other moleclues beyond the container is the only restriction on expansion, except for gravity.

Because the atmosphere is not confined except for gravity, air has a remarkable ability for almost instantaneous adjustment in expansion or compression for changes in temperature and pressure, both of which change density.

The density of a solid or a liquid can be measured by weighing, and dividing by the volume. For a given number of molecules the volume is essentially constant because (for these) the density of the atmosphere is insignificant. For water, a pint is a pound the world around. Comparisons of density are usually easy. A bucket of sand is heavier than a bucket of sawdust.

For weather forecasting we don't need to know the details of all the conditions. Comparative evaluations are often sufficient, and some conditions can be assumed to remain unchanged during the comparisons.

For example, to compare the density inside a parcel of air with the density of the surrounding air, we can assume that for short periods of time the pressure remains the same. Then density will vary only with the temperature, a simple thing to measure. If temperature inside is equal to temperature outside, the densities are the same.

If the parcel has been positioned over a hot spot (such as sunlit paving) and attains a higher temperature than the surrounding air, the parcel is now less dense, and therefore probably buoyant. The pressures at the same elevations in the local area will have equalized as the parcel warmed and expanded.

A smaller number of fast molecules can exert as much pressure as a larger number of slow molecules. Thus, a bucketful of warm air weighs less than a bucketful of cool air (at same pressure).

Why does air expand when warmed? Because a warm molecule moves faster than a cool molecule. Amid the countless collisions, the warmer molecules in a parcel, with greater impact, push and shove the surrounding cool molecules until the pressure inside equals the pressure outside (almost instantaneously). Equilibrium will be maintained only if the warm molecules maintain the higher temperature (thus higher speed).

Conversely, a parcel losing heat, compared to the adjoining parcels, will be compressed, until its greater density of cooler (and slower) molecules equals the pressure outside the parcel.

Although we can't see such action, we can easily measure temperature and pressure, and make eye observations of those processes which become visible.

Chapter 4. What Makes a Low ?

This topic is about the common "extratropical" low pressure centers which always involve air masses of contrasting density (cold air and warm air). In formal scientific papers such a Low is called a cyclone, (and a High is called an anti-cyclone). The prefix "extra" means "not" (tropical). In some parts of the world tropical storms are also called cyclones, and in the U.S. tornadoes are sometimes called cyclones. The words Low and High are more convenient.

Here, the word Low excludes tornadoes and tropical storms because those events have significant special features. The so-called "heat Low" is also excluded, because it doesn't involve a cold air mass.

The common Lows on sea level maps first appear when pressure falls enough at an observation station to require the drawing of an enclosing isobar, which was not on the preceding map. Continued fall in pressure reveals the development of the Low, often called its "deepening."

The recipe for a Low requires two main ingredients, a mass of cold air sliding under an adjacent mass of warm air. The energy for the interaction is from the force of gravity, directed downward, and the Coriolis force, directed horizontally toward the right, deflecting the upper winds which blow horizontally in the zone between cold and warm airmasses, as shown in Chapter 1.

The speed of those winds depends on the contrast in temperature between the airmasses, and the CF is proportional to the windspeed.

Such "disturbance" tends to produce precipitation and strong winds, generally described as bad weather. Lows move in the direction of the upper level winds, as revealed on the 700 and 500 mb charts, because each Low involves upward motion of air from the earth's surface.

The rising air is swept along with the upper level winds, which are blowing in horizontal planes.

The logical way to develop an understanding of an event involving multiple processes is to study one action for its contribution, and then another. Strive to integrate the parts, keeping in mind how each part may affect the others.

Air pressure at the surface results from the pull of gravity on the air above the point of measurement. Envision a column of air (of any small diameter) extending to the top of the atmosphere. Of course, the air on either side of that column is pressing against the column, but that doesn't add to its weight because the force of gravity is always vertical.

If pressure continues to decrease at the bottom of a column in spite of convergence at the bottom, somewhere above air must be diverging out of the column. Furthermore, air must be rising between that lower convergence and upper divergence.

The force of gravity controls both the rising of air (buoyancy) and the sinking of air (anti-buoyancy).

(Note:) In meteorology the upward motion of air is called "convection," horizontal motion is "advection," and downward motion is "subsidence."

In the world of popular science, explanations sometimes are made too simple, and become misleading. Everyone knows that warm air tends to rise. Many don't know why.

To levitate means to rise into the air and float, in apparent defiance of gravity. If the rising and floating are real, not part of a dream, or illusion created by a magician, such action is because of, not defiance of, gravity. When a toy balloon filled with helium escapes from a child's hand, it is being pushed up by the surrounding air which is more dense than the helium.

This is Archimedes Principle describing buoyancy, the reason boats float on water. The idea is more difficult when one can't see the water. The invisibility of air, understandably, continues to mystify a lot of people.

The solving of mysteries is part of the excitement of learning. Ordinary visible examples may provide clues.

Children often play on a teeter-totter, a rigid board pivoting on a fulcrum. If two children of equal weight sit on the ends, and the fulcrum is centered, the loaded board will balance. If a heavier child sits on one end, that child will move down, and the lighter child will move up.

Another example is the need to shake a bottle of salad dressing, to mix the heavier herbs with the lighter oil. The first analogy involves solids, the second involves liquids. Both illustrate comparative buoyancies, in which the bodies or liquids are free to respond to the force of gravity according to their densities.

Parcels of air are extremely free to move, being a gas which weighs only 1.22 ounces per cubic foot even at sea level. This value of density assumes the "standard conditions" of 1013 mb pressure, and 59°F temperature.

If a Low (extratropical) appears on a surface map and pressure falls, an inter-action between a warm air mass and a cold air mass has already begun. Consider the motion generated in a stationary parcel of warmer air of one million cubic feet (not really a very large parcel of air) at a temperature of 79°F, in the path of a cold front. Compare the buoyancy of the warm parcel with that of an advancing cold parcel of equal volume but with a temperature of 59°F. Assume a pressure of 1013 mb in both parcels.

In this arbitrary circumstance (volume and pressure equal in both parcels) density will vary only with absolute temperature, inversely. The two temperatures are 519 and 539 in Fahrenheit units on the absolute scale (Rankine).

Having previously rounded off the weight of one million cubic feet at 519° Rankine at 78,000 lbs (bottom page 25)

the warmer parcel will weigh only 0.96289 (519/539) of 78,000, or 75106 lbs. With a difference of nearly 3000 lbs, the relatively buoyant parcel of warmer air will be lifted as the heavier parcel slides under it. Although 75,106 lbs of mass is now farther from the earth, 78,000 lbs of mass is closer.

So gravity always wins if not temporarily opposed by a stronger force. Be careful when climbing a ladder.

The difference in density between cold air and warm air is an imbalance which gravity adjusts by pulling the colder air downward, and spreading it horizontally, just as rivers flow into the ocean.

Please accept some assertions here, to be explained later, to assist the main development of ideas.

When warm air rises because of buoyancy it also cools because of expansion in the lower pressures above. This introduces another process.

Air is a mixture of gases, one of which is water vapor, which ranges from about 1 to 5 percent of the total mixture. Any condensation of water vapor releases a significant amount of heat. Rising air cools as it expands in the lower pressures aloft.

Such "adiabatic" cooling is partly offset by the "latent heat of condensation" (both to be explained in detail later). The release of latent heat renders the rising air parcels even more buoyant than before, encouraging upward motion.

Thus, air rising in the area of a developing Low will be accelerated upward if clouds form and precipitation occurs, which is nearly inevitable.

Finally, there is the effect of the Coriolis Force. The CF is directly proportional to the speed of the horizontal winds.

The horizontal winds in the atmosphere are created by the horizontal pressure pattern. Conversely, the horizontal pressure patterns are created by the winds. Any temporary imbalance can soon approach equilibrium because air has low density, meaning its inertia (tendency to keep moving at the same speed, which might be zero, and in same direction if it is moving) can be changed much more easily than liquid or solid substances.

This chapter has been difficult to write, partly because I've never been able to answer, adequately, the title question. I posed this question in 1940 soon after entering the weather business at the bottom of the ladder. I've never found an adequate answer in the "literature" which I could understand.

Here are some simple diagrams which might help a reader (or confuse one even more). These are oversimplified. Flat sheets of paper and elementary sketches, even when accompanied by words, can't fully describe three-dimensional motions.

Keep the following mechanism in mind. If a glass tank, with a removable

separator in the middle, is filled with cold water on one side tinted blue, and with warm water on the other side tinted red, and the separator is removed, the blue water will lift the red water even if a little mixing occurs at the boundary.

The next two diagrams suggest the motions generated during the formation of a surface Low. The action is more complicated than in the "density channel" illustrated above. As cold air approaches the area where the surface pressure is falling, the upper trough is also approaching.

The leading edge of an upper trough is the zone of strongest winds aloft (usually in the southeast quadrant of the trough or "closed cold low") because the coldest airmass lies to the NW, and the warmest airmass lies to the SE.

Although the sloping wedge of the cold front is lifting warmer air as it slides underneath (a response to the force of

gravity), the rising warm air is entrained by the horizontal winds aloft, and is swept away, thereby encouraging the rise of air from below. The visible drift of smoke from a chimney or campfire is similar.

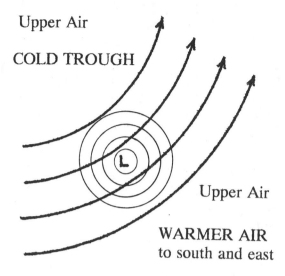

In meteorology the term divergence means the horizontal spreading of air currents. Convergence means horizontal flow toward a point or central area.

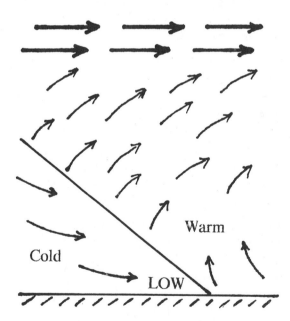

Of course, convergence toward a point, such as the developing Low at the surface, need not be in equal amounts from each direction. And divergence away from a point does not uniformly spread outward like spokes in a wheel.

In this explanation of the formation

of a Low at the surface, the multiple actions are described one at a time, a characteristic of a textbook. In actual forecasting the effort is to quickly peruse the maps, raob charts, and hourly airway reports for (1) a general comprehension of existing conditions as revealed on those sources, (2) the recent trends leading up to the present conditions, and (3) indications of changes underway at the present.

The easy problem is when the scene is quiet, with little or no change occurring. The decision-making process is merely to predict more of the same. But when a new surface Low appears on the map, and the pressure is falling rapidly, and the conditions in the surrounding areas are favorable for intensification of the Low, then the forecaster focuses on specific indicators. The main one is the rate of change in central pressure of the Low. The subject of pressure, both at the surface and aloft, will be the topic for the next chapter.

Chapter 5. Pressure Versus Altitude

Humans live in a physical world that is mostly horizontal, in two dimensions so to speak. Weather exists in a world of three dimensions. A forecaster must learn the basic physics of the invisible atmosphere. The beginner may feel bewildered among the new complexities of that third dimension. New knowledge is unfamiliar. The goal is to get acquainted quickly.

It's easier than anticipated. Although details are explained one at a time, they soon blend in general understanding. You need not remember all details. Look them up later if needed.

The words altitude, elevation, and height are interchangeable. They mean distance above a reference plane which usually is sea level unless otherwise stated. Such measurements are needed in both aviation and meteorology. Accuracy is especially important for aircraft when a pilot is approaching a runway under blind flying conditions.

The concept of the Standard Atmosphere based on presumed average conditions of pressure vs height at latitude 40° in the U.S. was introduced on page 25. Atmospheric pressure can be measured at any attainable elevation, with satisfactory accuracy, by an aneroid barometer which is far more portable than a mercurial barometer. If manufactured specifically to translate pressure values to the corresponding elevations defined by the Standard Atmosphere, it is renamed an aircraft altimeter.

However, as various wind patterns move across the landscape, actual pressure at a given position varies significantly from day to day, and even hour to hour. In this special situation a clever solution was devised long ago, via what is called the *altimeter setting*. But it requires two aneroid barometers, one on the ground and one in the aircraft, frequently tested to make exactly similar measurements.

It works this way. Each aneroid barometer responds to local air pressure, at whatever altitude that might be. Although the Standard Atmosphere always lists a pressure of 29.92 inches of mercury (29.92 Hg) for sea level (zero altitude), both the aircraft communicator on the ground and the pilot in the air, will temporarily adjust to a "computed" *sea level pressure* (to be explained soon). That usually is more or less than 29.92.

The rigid scale of the Standard Atmosphere, is manually adjusted on each instrument by a thumbscrew, to begin the altitude scale (zero) at this temporary pressure value, now called the *altimeter setting*. The known altitude of the airport runway will now appear in a small inset window on the large dial of the communicator's aneroid barometer. Although the instrument is responding to local pressure, the large dial will display the temporary *altimeter setting*.

That setting is included in hourly airway reports, and is relayed to pilots via radio upon request. A pilot needs to know his altitude. His altimeter, properly adjusted (in a small inset window) to the temporary basic pressure, will display altitude according to the yardstick of the Standard Atmosphere.

If he lands on the runway, his altimeter will indicate the elevation on his large dial, identical to what shows in the inset window of the communicator's instrument. If he doesn't land and passes overhead nearby, he knows his flight altitude as acccurately as technology can determine. Even if the indicated altitude is in error by a few feet, any nearby aircraft is enduring the same error. Collisions are extremely unlikely. How clever!

The two partner instruments are merely aneroid barometers, but the large dials are calibrated to different scales.

Altimeters also are needed for navigation between airports to maintain assigned flight levels, to avoid mountain peaks, and reported altitudes of severe turbulence, icing, cloud layers, and unfavorable winds aloft.

Unless rules have been changed recently, pilots navigating below 18,000 ft MSL are required to adjust their altimeters if significant changes are noted in the successive *altimeter settings* reported from weather stations enroute.

Fortunately, the ambient pressure (meaning pressure in local position in atmosphere), also called the *station pressure* in meteorology, rarely varies more than 4% from the listed value in the Standard Atmosphere. However, the ambient pressure is not needed by a pilot, and is NEVER inadvertently communicated as the *altimeter setting*. Such error is impossible under the procedure I have taken pains to explain.

I know of a tragic example of misunderstanding about ambient air pressure. May it never be repeated.

A medical technician was calibrating a radiation machine for treatment of cancer patients. It aimed a beam of electrons very accurately at cancerous tissue. Such tissue is more vulnerable to damage by radiation than is the surround-

NACA STANDARD ATMOSPHERE ALTITUDE-PRESSURE TABLE

Inches of mercury	.00	.10	.20	.30	.40	.50	.60	.70	.80	.90
	feet	feet	feet	feet	feet	feet	feet	feet	feet	feet
0									80 522	78 056
1	75 850	73 854	72 032	70 357	68 805	67 361	66 009	64 740	63 543	62 411
2	61 337	60 315	59 341	58 411	57 519	56 665	55 844	55 053	54 292	53 557
3	52 847	52 161	51 496	50 852	50 228	49 620	49 030	48 456	47 898	47 354
4	46 824	46 307	45 803	45 310	44 829	44 358	43 898	43 448	43 007	42 575
5	42 151	41 737	41 330	40 931	40 540	40 156	39 779	39 408	39 044	38 686
6	38 334	37 989	37 648	37 313	36 983	36 659	36 339	36 024	35 714	35 408
7	35 106	34 809	34 514	34 222	33 934	33 649	33 367	33 088	32 812	32 539
8	32 269	32 001	31 736	31 474	31 214	30 957	30 702	30 449	30 199	29 951
9	29 706	29 462	29 221	28 982	28 745	28 510	28 276	28 046	27 816	27 589
10	27 363	27 140	26 917	26 697	26 479	26 262	26 048	25 834	25 622	25 412
11	25 204	24 996	24 791	24 587	24 384	24 183	23 983	23 785	23 588	23 392
12	23 198	23 005	22 813	22 622	22 433	22 245	22 058	21 872	21 688	21 505
13	21 323	21 142	20 962	20 783	20 605	20 429	20 253	20 079	19 905	19 733
14	19 561	19 391	19 221	19 052	18 885	18 718	18 553	18 388	18 224	18 061
15	17 899	17 737	17 577	17 417	17 259	17 101	16 944	16 787	16 632	16 477
16	16 324	16 171	16 018	15 867	15 716	15 566	15 416	15 268	15 120	14 973
17	14 826	14 681	14 536	14 391	14 247	14 104	13 962	13 820	13 679	13 539
18	13 399	13 260	13 121	12 983	12 846	12 709	12 573	12 437	12 302	12 168
19	12 034	11 901	11 768	11 636	11 505	11 374	11 243	11 113	10 984	10 855
20	10 726	10 599	10 471	10 344	10 218	10 092	9 967	9 842	9 718	9 594
21	9 471	9 348	9 225	9 103	8 982	8 861	8 740	8 620	8 500	8 381
22	8 262	8 144	8 026	7 909	7 791	7 675	7 559	7 443	7 327	7 212
23	7 098	6 984	6 870	6 756	6 643	6 531	6 418	6 307	6 195	6 084
24	5 974	5 863	5 753	5 644	5 534	5 425	5 317	5 209	5 101	4 994
25	4 886	4 780	4 673	4 567	4 462	4 356	4 251	4 146	4 042	3 938
26	3 834	3 731	3 628	3 525	3 422	3 320	3 218	3 117	3 016	2 915
27	2 814	2 714	2 614	2 514	2 415	2 315	2 217	2 118	2 020	1 922
28	1 824	1 727	1 630	1 533	1 436	1 340	1 244	1 148	1 053	957
29	863	768	673	579	485	392	298	205	112	20
30	− 73	−165	−257	−348	−440	−531	−622	−712	−803	−893
31	−983									

SMITHSONIAN METEOROLOGICAL TABLES

6th Revised Edition, page 273, Publication 4014, 1958 (my copy, purchased 1959, cost $4.00)

Fed. Meteorolog. Hndbk No.1, Surface Observations, U.S. Dept. Commerce, NOAA, 1988, presents the Stand. Atmos. from S.L. to 10,731 ft, as per ICAO (Internat. Civil Aviation Org.). Difference varies from 0 ft near sea level to 5 ft at 20.00 inches Hg.

ing healthy tissue.

If the "dose" of radiation is adjusted to within a range of error not more than 4 or 5 percent, it will kill or weaken cancer cells, and not seriously harm nearby healthy cells, which can recover from a limited amount of radiation. The intensity is adjusted by a meter which "counts" the molecules of air which have been "ionized" by a practice shot (no human target).

At sea level, in more dense air, the molecules are closer together. At higher elevations, in less dense air, the air molecules are farther apart. A given dose affects fewer molecules. The dose meter must be adjusted to the ambient atmospheric pressure. For a given dose the count is lower in less dense air than the count at sea level.

The technician called the nearest FAA Flight Service Station, and asked for the "pressure" without identifying himself as a non-pilot, and with no specification of pressure he wanted. When a motorist drives into a gas station and says "fill 'er up," he doesn't mean root beer.

The communicator, having answered as many as 10,000 requests during his career for an *altimeter setting*, gave the caller the number displayed on the large panel dial of an aneroid barometer. It showed "sea level pressure," adjusted slightly for aircraft altimeters as needed.

Such a large number would be obvious to one who knew ambient pressure decreases upward, and that the altitude of the radiation machine was 3600 ft.

In the long established Standard Atmosphere, the ambient pressure for 3600 ft is 26.23 Hg, not 29.92. With incorrect adjustment for an ambient pressure in more dense air at sea level, in the less dense air at 3600 ft the count of ionized molecules in a practice shot appeared too low. Intensity was "cranked" up to attain the ionization count for a proper dose in more dense air, which was an overdose.

This error was repeated for a period of over two years. A total of 592 patients were treated with radiation 14% greater than intended.

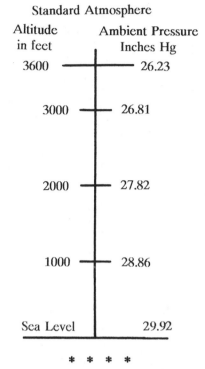

How is the *sea level pressure* computed for a weather station that is not at sea level? Measurement by a barometer is easy on a ship at sea, or on a sea coast. What is done for Denver, Colorado widely known for its altitude of a mile high, or Lakeview, Oregon at 4800 ft?

The ambient pressure can be measured at the station. An additional pressure for the weight of an imaginary column of air down to sea level can be added. Such addition lacks precision because imaginary columns can't be measured exactly.

Discussion now is about approximations, which is a large part of the world of a forecaster. It is claimed that mathematicians seldom are good forecasters. If so it probably is because their training tends to emphasize precision.

Forecasting is more of an art than a calculation. Its a blending of different skills, some of which are intangible. This explanation is about a problem that can't be solved precisely in terms of numbers.

Note regarding page 25

The box at bottom of page listed values, some approximate, from the U. S. Standard Atmosphere.

The text stated that such standard assumes a sea level pressure of 1013 mb, a surface temperature of 59°F, and a lapse rate of 3.6°F per 1000 ft from sea level up to 35,332 ft. Such numbers result from conversion of metric units used by physicists, to the English units familiar to most of expected readers of this book.

It also assumes the air is "dry," (devoid of water vapor), and that air (a mixture of several gases) behaves as a "perfect" gas. Such assumptions are more than adequate for altimeters and forecasting.

	Metric	English
Sea level pressure	760 mm Hg	29.921 in Hg
Sea level temperature	15°C	59°F
Isothermal layer	-55°C	-67°F
Temperature lapse rate	6.5°C/100 m	3.566°F/1000 ft

However, it can be solved approximately, and with sufficient accuracy for most purposes, both in aviation and weather forecasting. Again we use the handy yardstick of the Standard Atmosphere.

For aviation altimetry we use two reference points, the unchanging known altitude of the airport runway, and the temporary measurement of the ambient pressure at that location. On our yardstick (a fixed scale describing ambient pressure versus altitude above MSL) we measure downward on the altitude scale to zero, and identify the "computed" ambient pressure associated with zero altitude on the yardstick. Our variable end-product is the temporary sea level pressure, called the altimeter setting.

Often it is not 29.92 inches Hg. If airport pressure varies upward, the altimeter setting goes up. If airport pressure varies downward, the altimeter setting goes down. The same computation is made for determining the *sea level pressure* for meteorology, except for one refinement for greater accuracy.

The Standard Atmosphere assumes a linear (straight line) decrease in temperature with increase in elevation.

There is no adjustment for cold air or warm air. In cold air, for a given pressure, the molecules are closer together, and in warm air, farther apart. In a term useful in meteorology, the "thickness" of layers of the atmosphere, from one pressure level to another such as from 1000 mbs to 900 mbs, varies directly with temperature.

Special tables, or a special slide rule, are prepared for each weather station to allow for the assumed mean temperature in the imaginary air column from the station elevation down to sea level. The mean temperature is midway between the present observed temperature and such temperature 12 hours ago.

Fortunately, most terrain is within low elevations, compared with the variations of altitude for aircraft. Airliners often fly above 30,000 ft. However, for aircraft, two aneroid barometers are used for a cross check with each other. Each is actually measuring ambient pressure at the same place.

For weather forecasting, to draw sea level isobars for terrain above sea level, there is only one barometer, at the top of an imaginary column of air. A forecaster must remember that "reductions" to

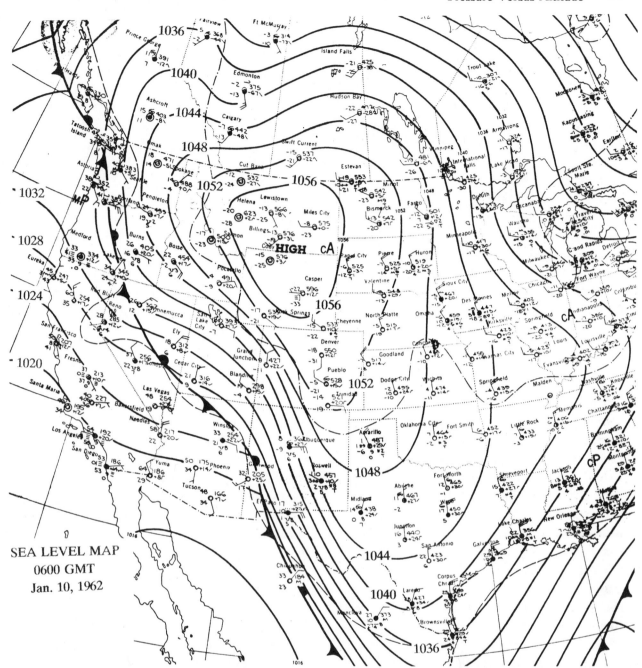

SEA LEVEL MAP
0600 GMT
Jan. 10, 1962

sea level are skewed to higher pressure when station is abnormally cold, and to lower pressure when station is abnormally warm. A cold column of air is heavier than a warm column, even when imaginary.

The Weather Bureau sea level map above is copied from the magazine Weatherwise, page 106, June 1962, published at that time by the AMS, in article by David Ludlum, "Extremes of Atmospheric Pressure in the U.S." Caption: "The Great January 1962 Anticyclone crested over Montana and Wyoming. Pressure at Helena, Montana is shown at 1062.3 mb (31.40")." That was, and possibly still is, the highest pressure ever officially reported in the U.S.   Great Falls reported 31.34".

The altitude of the Helena station was not given. It lies in a narrow valley in the Rocky

Mountains. A 1993 road atlas lists Helena at an altitude of 4157 ft. The map shows a temperature of -20°F, clear sky, and calm wind. At time near midnight, conditions are ideal for radiation cooling and hillside drainage, but resulting in a comparatively shallow layer of very cold air. Hence some exaggeration when applied to a column of 4157 ft. Compare Blanding, Utah and Denver, Colorado. Differences: temperature 37°F, pressure 25 mb. Light surface winds (however, Albuquerque 25 mph). This is a dramatic weather map.

As might be expected, sea level maps for those areas near sea level provide more dependable pressure patterns for analyzing surface windflow.

Note: although the above map is enlarged 40% from source in "Weatherwise," it still needs a hand magnifier for details. Even a 10x is sometimes useful, and not only for weather maps or illustrations in weather books. (It seems to me there is more fine print nowadays.)

* * * *

You probably already assume that the row of asterisks above mean a changing of the subject, maybe small but significantly. You also know this book is informal, something like a one-to-one tutoring, or a lecture to a small group. You know I have limitations. One is that I'm not a mathematician, although I struggled long and hard before realizing only modest skill is necessary for forecasting. One of my very best friends (dating back to 1932) is a mechanical engineer and a mathematician.

The subjects of altimetry and reduction of station pressure to sea level focus on a single geographic location. Local weather forecasting does too, with regard to the end product. But it also intently analyzes atmospheric processes in the surrounding area.

Obviously it's impossible to "measure" conditions in every cubic foot of the atmosphere, even up to 18,000 feet (which altitude usually is sufficient). It is necessary to establish weather stations, most of which are at airports, naturally. These provide the vital hourly airway sequences. At some of these stations, radiosonde observations are made every 12 hours.

In spite of such abundance of data, compared to 1940 when I entered the weather business, the present day clamour for more data, when existing data seems inadequately utilized (at least from what I can gather from television), it seems more a clamour for larger appropriations. We don't need to "slice" the atmosphere into more layers, so unseen storms won't sneak through.

What we really need are more serious forecast users to learn how to make their own forecasts, and get the government out of its imitation effort.

After the above straying from pressure versus altitude, the final topic is to call attention to two slices in the atmosphere other than the sea level chart and the 500 mb chart, which are the 850 mb and the 700 mb chart, analyzed every 12 hours. There are also routine charts for 300 mb and 200 mb, but I never bother and neither need you.

Upper air charts are for specific "pressure levels" simply because raobs (radiosonde observations) measure only pressure, temperature, and relative humidity as the instrument is lifted by a small balloon. Such levels "undulate" in altitude, usually with seemingly modest change, but such changes are significant as indicators of changes in weather.

As shown in box on page 25, the approximate elevations of the 850, 700, and 500 mb charts are 5,000, 10,000, and 18,000 feet. When you gain access to such upper air charts, you will find the contour lines are labeled in meters, and the charts themselves are called 850 hpa, 700 hpa, and 500 hpa. Hectopascals now replace millibars, but they are identical units.

The vertical distance between charts is described as "thickness," which is a direct evaluation of the mean temperature between the two pressure levels.

Variations in temperature and relative humidity along a vertical axis of decreasing pressure are plotted on graphs called adiabatic charts. The next chapter on temperature and the little known public concept of potential temperature will help clarify the mysterious third dimension of the atmosphere.

Chapter 6. Adiabatic Change in Temperature

Because air is a mixture of gases, and often moves upward and downward, involving expansion or compression, a forecaster must be constantly aware of the automatic change in air temperature which accompanies that vertical motion. Such change is called adiabatic, meaning without loss or gain of heat. This explanation is an extension of that on pages 24 and 25 about the kinetic energy of gas molecules.

Those molecules are so small, and knowledge of them (at least mine) is certainly limited. Kinetic energy is measured by speed and mass. It takes energy to get a particle of mass moving, and that energy can be transferred by collision, as when a golf ball is struck by a club.

The following seems to satisfy me. A parcel of air contains a certain number of molecules colliding with each other. The parcel has an imaginary spherical wall around it, which of course is merely the crowd of molecules surrounding it. Assuming no expansion of that wall (or shell) and no loss of heat energy by radiation (which needs explanation elsewhere) the temperature remains constant. The molecules rebound from the wall without loss of motion (kinetic energy).

If the parcel expands, the wall moves away from each approaching molecule which slows its rebound speed. Kinetic energy is lost, and by definition, temperature decreases.

If the parcel is compressed, the wall moves toward each approaching molecule, which transmits kinetic energy to it, and its temperature increases.

However, there is no change in total heat energy during these changes in the volume of the parcel. The kinetic energy is spread out into more space during expansion, and squeezed into less space during compression. The total energy (heat) is diluted or concentrated.

Thus we have another complication because of the third dimension of altitude in the world of the atmosphere. Soon it becomes familiar, and we just recognize it as part of the environment. For convenience, a new term was invented, called the *potential temperature*.

If there is need to monitor the temperature of an air parcel that is moving up or down, but not actually gaining or losing any heat (and its "ordinary" temperature is changing because its volume is changing) we can label it with an unchanging "potential temperature." That is the temperature of a parcel subjected to pressure of 1000 mb, which is near sea level.

To identify this label we use the Kelvin scale (see page 24) which is handy because it has no minus numbers. Its units are the same size as Celsius. We need familiarity with Celsius because of use world wide for coding radiosonde observations.

The Kelvin scale reminds us to not forget that both Celsius and Fahrenheit scales have an arbitrary position for zero, and that zero Kelvin is very much colder, It means an absolute absence of heat.

It should widen our perspective about the exaggerated concerns for climatic warming or cooling. Frozen water begins to melt at zero Celsius. That chilly point is 273^0C above "true" zero. At sea level the Standard Atmosphere is rated at 15^0C and few places, even in the tropics, swelter above 45^0C.

Keep in mind that air pressure varies rapidly upward and downward, and a significant variation in temperature accompanies rising or sinking of air.

The mathematics of the variations were developed long ago by physicists, as were many other processes in weather. For the convenience of forecasters, many of the relationships have been illustrated by graphs and numerical tables.

On the next page is a nomogram called an adiabatic chart. A nomogram represents numerical relationships to

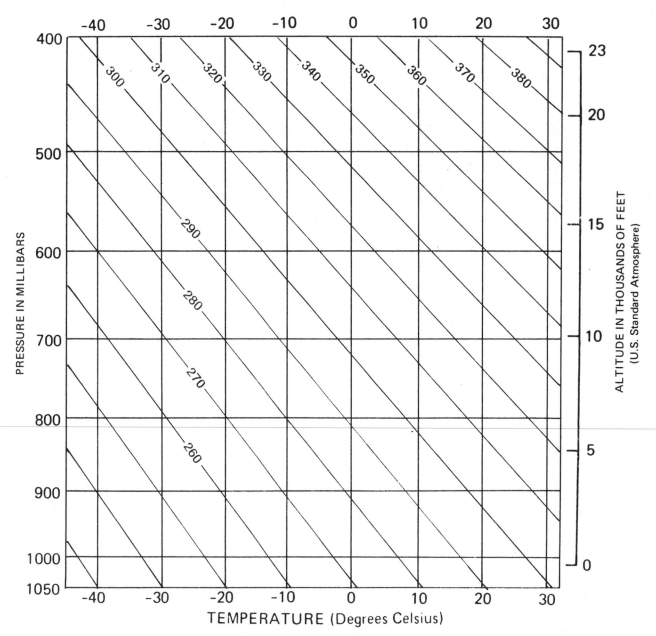

quickly find the answer to a calculation. Method of use often is obvious. Locate a position defining the temperature and pressure of a measured parcel. If the parcel moves adiabatically to another pressure level, follow the sloping lines, or a non-printed parallel line to the new pressure and new temperature in Celsius.

The sloping lines are called dry adiabats, which means there must be no condensation or evaporation within the parcel (which would add or subtract latent heat). Actually, the parcel may contain water vapor, but that mass must remain unchanged for a dry adiabatic process.

Bear in mind the nomogram merely illustrates how temperature within the atmosphere changes if the pressure changes (and those must be the only changes). It is not a map or picture of a vertical slice of air. An air parcel can move straight up or straight down.

The sloping lines, informally called adiabats, are designed as straight lines to simplify the pressure-temperature relationship. It also makes the altitude scale on the right margin almost linear (as per the Standard Atmosphere yardstick). The pressure levels gradually spread farther apart as density decreases with altitude.

A sharp-eyed reader may note the adiabats are not quite parallel. They converge to a point where there is no heat energy, no pressure, and no need for us to even think about it.

The adiabatic changes also apply to large masses of air, not only to small parcels. Here is an example of how lack of attention to broadscale adiabatic change can hinder a forecaster.

The localized upward motion of air, called convection, is often dramatic because of association with thunderstorms, whirlwinds, and hurricanes. Downward motion of air usually is gentle and broadscale, and hence subtle.

A major part of my forecasting career was associated with "fireweather" in the Pacific Northwest. Of course, a constant concern was the onset of especially low humidity (very dry fuels burn faster) which is turn results from high temperature.

In the world of television forecasting cold air sweeps horizontally from the north, and warm air arrives horizontally from the south. In fireweather, danger often arrives from above, where the air always is *warmer* than down here where we live and the trees grow.

By warmer I mean containing more heat energy per unit of mass (as per pound of air). However, because the molecules of air up there are farther apart they move more slowly, and display lower "temperature" on a thermometer. But they have a higher potential temperature, which can't be read directly by a radiosonde.

In the central lengthwise valleys of California there is a semipermanent feature of the sea level map, called a heat low, in the warmer parts of the year. There are reasons. California lies at the southeast corner of the north Pacific High, where air subsides as it curves clockwise and spreads away from the High. The central valleys are encircled by mountains.

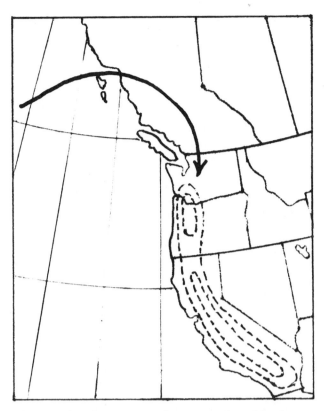

Even the low coastal mountains hinder inflow of cool marine air. In the schematic map above, the heat low is shown by dashed lines.

In western Oregon, where conditions are less favorable, the Willamette Valley will develop a heat low during a summer hot spell. The weathercasters explain the hot weather moved northward from California. But they never mention it the day before.

Actually, Oregon develops its own heat low independently. A fireweather forecaster is always watching for the Pacific High to "nose in" over Vancouver Island and British Columbia. Which happens when the upper air charts show an upper ridge developing there. A good fireweather forecaster knows at least 24 hours earlier the heat low is coming "from above," and from the north before it supposedly arrives from California.

The nomogram on page 40 is for simplified introduction. It's too small for the routine plotting of "raobs," meaning radiosonde observations. The next two book sheets, printed one side only, should

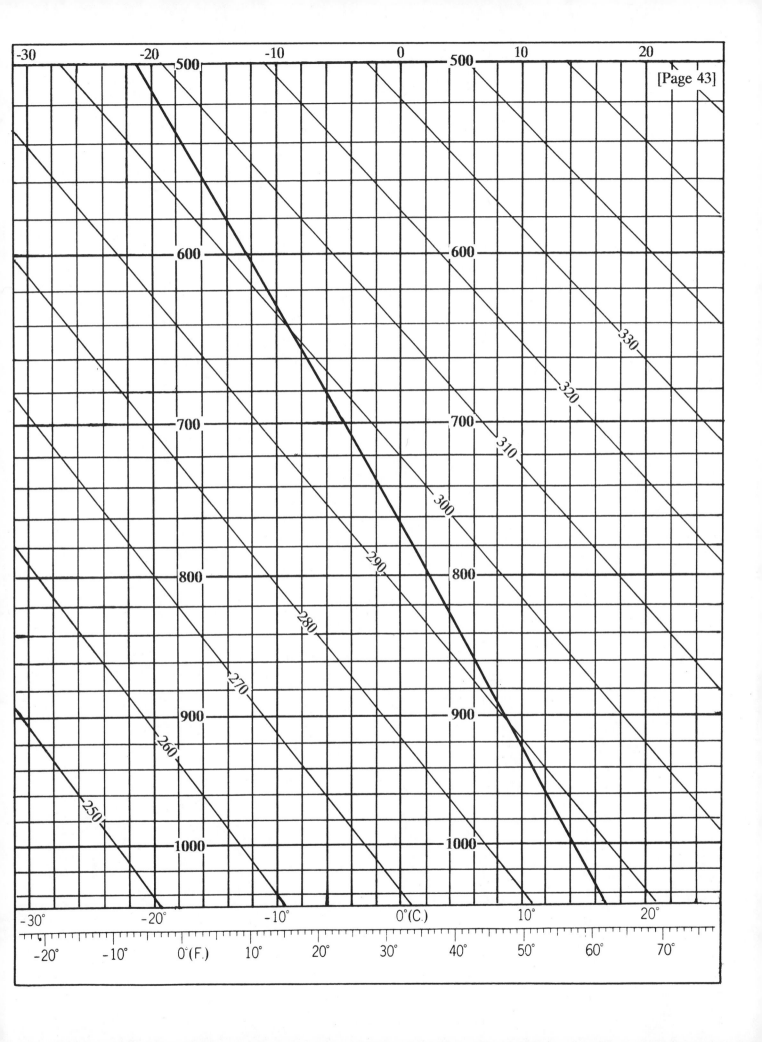

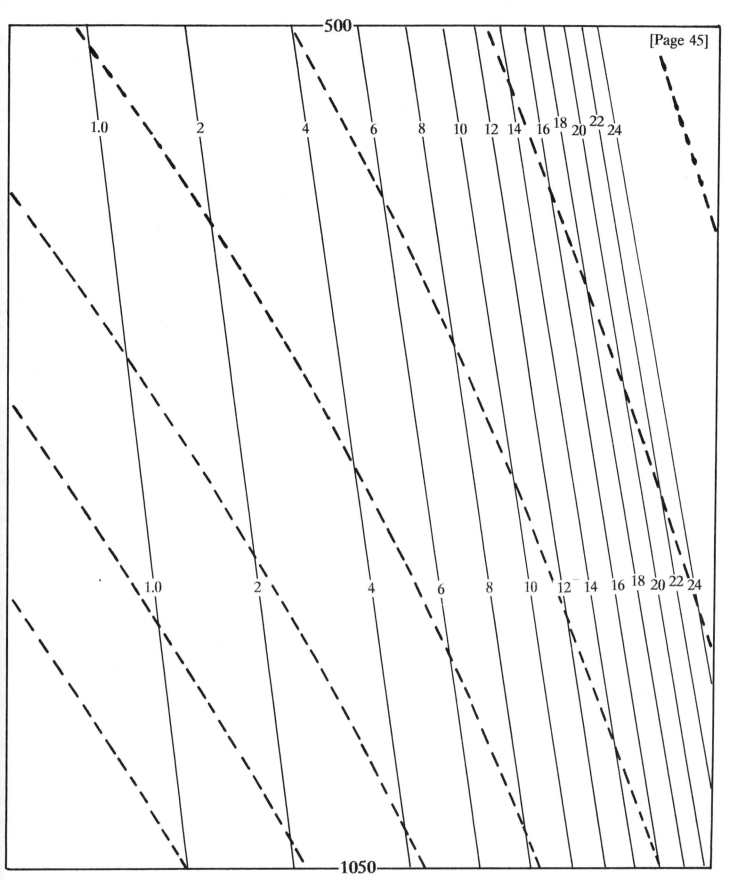

OVERLAY for adiabatic chart:
Dashed lines are "moist adiabats,"
also called pseudo-adiabats.
Solid lines for saturated Mixing Ratio.

be preserved for photocopying. These are homemade adiabatic charts photocopied from the center section of a pseudo-adiabatic chart 16x16 inches used by the Weather Bureau in the 1960-1970s.

The section is full-sized but limited to what can fit on a letter-sized page. The original chart is printed in brown ink with a blue ink overprint for lines pertaining to water vapor in the atmosphere. Such chart (also called a Stuve diagram) is awesome for a beginner. To reduce awe the "moist adiabat" overprint is shown separately on page 45.

A forcaster has only occasional use for moist adiabats and saturated mixing ratio lines. If needed, a light box is handy. Also there is little need for plotting soundings in very cold or very warm air.

The horizontal lines are drawn for intervals of 20 mb instead of 10 mb, and vertical lines for intervals of 2^0C instead of 1^0C. To avoid clutter, the lines on the overlay are pruned.

An explanation of plotting a raob will be postponed. That is quick and easy, and needed only for raob stations in your nearby area, usually for 2 or 3 or 4. Also you need only to go up to 500 mb, which is about the mid-point of the entire atmosphere. As a forecaster for 25 years I can't remember needing higher information.

Judging from what I see on TV, and since the introduction of satellite pictures, I doubt the public even knows about the radiosonde observations every 12 hours. Also I wonder if the so-called forecasters ever study them. However, I do know why public forecasting is deteriorating, and so will you after reading this book.

First, there is need to discuss topics in the next chapter. However, a brief description of the radiosonde instrument is appropriate here. Also, a monument for it should be designed and erected at the University Corporation of Atmospheric Research at Boulder, Colorado, to remind the PhDs working there.

Maybe they could be persuaded to create a new department to research ways to make routine observational data (obtained at taxpayers' expense) available for DIY (do-it-yourself) forecasters at little or no personal expense. Such a department would not cost more than one million dollars per year and save much more money. The imitation local *forecasting* fiasco of the federal government could then be discontinued.

Citizens could either make their own forecasts, or obtain real forecasts from local entrepreneurs who establish individual reputations in the market.

The radiosonde is a very light-weight device carried aloft by a helium filled balloon. It measures pressure via an aneroid cell, temperature via an electronic thermistor, and relative humidity via a chemical film across which the electrical resistance varies. The instrument contains a radio transmitter. A technician on the ground interprets the signals and computes the data needed for upper air charts.

The measurements are made under obviously variable conditions. A free balloon rises to heights well above those of cross country airliners, amid all kinds of weather conditions. The accuracy is not as precise as such measurements on the ground or aboard ship, but they are made at the right place, in the vertical dimension of the atmosphere.

Upper air maps are not dependent on a single observation location. The contour lines and isotherms (or any other iso-line) are drawn for logical continuity from one geographic location to another. Any single measurement significantly different from those adjacent must be evaluated on a scale from acceptable to doubtful to discarded.

Radiosondes were a tremendous advance in meteorology. They will be around for a long time, like barometers. We need to reestablish fixed shipboard sites where there are no handy islands.

Chapter 7. Water Vapor

All "matter," (which is anything affected by the force of gravity) can exist in three states-- solid, liquid, or gas. Clean dry air, other than water vapor, is a mixture of several gases which never exist in a liquid or solid state under natural conditions. These gases, never condensing in the atmosphere, have unchanging proportions of total dry air volume.

Nitrogen is listed at 78.09%, oxygen at 20.95%, argon at 0.93%, and carbon dioxide (in non-polluted areas) at 0.03%. That totals 100%. Air contains traces of seven other gases, not worth mentioning in weather forecasting.

Water vapor must be described separately. Even as a gas, it seldom exceeds 4.00% by volume except in tropical air masses. It is invisible as a gas, and commonly observed in the atmosphere as drops of water, which fall out if heavy enough, or seem to float if tiny and light enough. The same applies to the variety of ice particles.

The substance of water is remarkably influential in how weather works. When water vapor condenses to liquid the change releases a surprising quantity of heat called latent heat. Understandably, the evaporation from liquid to gas absorbs heat at the same rate, the heat seeming to disappear. Such results help illustrate the difference between heat and temperature (page 25).

The nomogram overlay on page 45 covers the same range of temperature and pressure as the adiabatic chart on page 43. The bold dashed lines are called moist adiabats. They could be labeled with "equivalent potential temperature" values, which belong only in your unimportant information file.

However, you will note that the "slope" of those lines in the right half of the nomogram is substantially different than the slope of dry adiabats. They show a slower rate of cooling for ascent of air

which has already become "saturated" with water vapor. We will explore information either unknown or poorly understood by the public, in spite of 45 years of TV weathercasters.

In my opinion this is only one of many weather topics deliberately hidden by the power structure in the weather business, for selfish reasons to be explained in last part of this book. The lame excuse is that the public is not interested in "technical" information, or lacks ability to comprehend.

You soon can judge for yourself. It isn't that complicated. You must understand it before becoming a do-it-yourself forecaster.

People can understand details of processes which are important to them. We learn how to read, how to cook, make home repairs, play musical instruments, take care of our car, and catch fish. In my case, I'm not much of a sports fan because often I can't understand what is happening. My wife tires of explaining things.

Back now to dry or moist adiabats. No air in the world of forecasting is absolutely dry (devoid of water vapor). Until the content of water vapor reaches saturation, meaning 100% relative humidity, the vapor behaves like the other gases, cooling with expansion and warming with compression as shown by the dry adiabats on page 43.

Relative humidity can't exceed 100%. With accumulation of vapor molecules exceeding a certain number within a given space (which varies with temperature and pressure) some will attach to each other, creating liquid water or maybe ice. Any air which rises also cools from expansion (because pressure decreases with altitude). If cooling proceeds below the former dewpoint, condensation occurs, which releases latent heat, which offsets some of the cooling from expansion, and helps to maintain buoyancy for additional upward motion. That is why rain is sometimes a "cloudburst."

In everyday language the word saturated usually means wet, drenched, thoroughly soaked, as with a liquid. In the physics of the atmosphere, saturated means a parcel of air contains as much water vapor as possible. Any excess will condense into liquid or ice.

A forecaster need not know all the intricacies of molecular physics, but there are adequate descriptions, terms, and definitions. First, it may be helpful to remember that although air is a mixture of gases, the atoms or molecules of each gas never combine chemically with the others, and only water vapor ever changes state. When we say that air is composed of different gases, actually it is space that is occupied by an assortment.

Each gas behaves as though it were alone although they bump into each other. The total pressure of the mixture is the sum of the partial pressure exerted by each gas, according to its molecular weight and concentration. If a parcel is not changing its volume, each gas is at the same temperature, which means the same *average* kinetic energy for each molecule. These facts have been helpful to me in learning the physics of weather. In the routine tasks of forecasting there are many habits to acquire, as shortcuts.

Here are some definitions:

MIXING RATIO--the ratio of the mass of water vapor to the collective mass of other gases in a given volume, such as a parcel, usually expressed as grams per kilogram. See the labels on the overlay on page 45, for the straight, almost vertical solid lines. Those values are for parcels of air at 100% relative humidity. The label 8 means 8 grams of water in 1000 grams of other gases. If relative humidity is 50%, then water content is only 4 grams.

Note the decreasing space between the solid lines toward the right margin. I only included saturated mixing ratio lines up to 24, which are enough to illustrate this fact. The chart on page 43 only extends to 26^{0}C to fit the book page. The

original nomogram of the Weather Bureau extended to 50^{0}C.

The capacity of a given space (air) to store molecules of water vapor increases rapidly with only modest increase in temperature on the Absolute scale. That's because molelcules of gas gain kinetic energy (displayed as faster motion, which defines temperature). It was the faster motion that had broken the molecular bonds of liquid water causing the change of state to a gas (evaporation). If heat is lost, motion slows and some bonds are restored (condensation).

DEWPOINT-- A quaint useful term for ordinary temperature of air at saturation point (100% relative humidity). If temperature falls, condensation occurs. If it rises, relative humidity decreases from 100%.

VAPOR PRESSURE--Simply the pressure exerted only by the molecules of water vapor at that location. It can't be measured directly, but is easily computed from basic measurements of temperature, pressure, and relative humidity.

Laboratory techniques have established the precise relationships of those three measurements. Relative humidity deserves special attention because of its importance in forecasting, and the ingenious methods for measurement.

RELATIVE HUMIDITY -- In a given volume, the ratio of mass of water vapor to the maximum mass possible with existing conditions. In forecasting, temperature is the main factor, by far.

The processes of evaporation and condensation dominate many weather events. Because they involve molecular physics which is invisible, unnecessary mystery prevails.

Evaporation is the escape of individual molecules of water vapor from the electronic bonds of its liquid state. In liquid the molecules are extremely concentrated in space. One cubic foot of water weighs 62.43 lbs. One cubic foot of dry air weighs 1.22 oz. at sea level (Standard Atmosphere). If a cubic foot of air (at 1013 mb and 15⁰C) is *saturated* with a mixing ratio of 10 grams per kilogram, the water vapor in that space would weigh only 0.0122 oz.

Condensation is the reverse process from evaporation.

Although this discussion has focussed on the condition of saturation amid details of the adiabatic nomogram, the momentous change of state to and from water vapor is not limited only to the specific condition of 100% RH (relative humidity). Evaporation and condensation are nearly always going on at the same time at the same place. But the *rate* of such transition can be favored or hindered. We can't see the molecules themselves, only the net balance of contrary actions.

An explanation of the change in state is simplified by describing the escape of one molecule from a flat liquid surface into the space above. Such space may contain molecules of water vapor or other gases, but all are widely separated compared to a liquid.

Within a single substance such as liquid water, all molecules have the same mass. They are very near each other, but there is some free space because each has individual freedom of movement. The mass and speed of motion determines its kinetic energy. That energy is measured as temperature, based on the *average* molecular motion in a cluster of molecules. In this context, cluster means ten thousand or maybe a million.

In the chaotic jostling and bumping of each other in a cluster, each molecule does not always move at exactly the same speed. A single molecule at the liquid surface may be bumped upward by two others simultaneously, or almost simultaneously. It likely will overcome molecular bonds and escape to the greater freedom of a gas.

The total kinetic energy of the liquid has decreased slightly during the escape of a single molecule because it broke the molecular attraction which bound it to others in the liquid state. Compare with the force of gravity, which also is mysterious. We explain it simply by describing it. Thus evaporation removes heat from a liquid.

What favors the return of a water vapor molecule to liquid form? Any which wander close to a water surface, and any which slow down for whatever reason, such as head-on collision with other gaseous molecules (even those of dry air) or with cooling by radiation, or with a lowering of pressure (as in adiabatic expansion).

An increase in the density of water vapor molecules in a space increases the rate of condensation. At 100% RH the rates of condensation and evaporation become equal, assuming no other change in conditions.

Any vapor which returns to the liquid state, whether to a body of water on the earth or a droplet in the atmosphere, adds latent heat to that liquid just as it removed heat during evaporation. Again, compare with falling bodies on earth, the conversion of potential energy of position (latent energy) to the kinetic energy of motion.

There is very little mass of water in the atmosphere compared to the water and ice on the surface of the earth. But it is remarkably active in what we describe as weather. We try to learn how it works.

Water vapor can also condense on ice, the solid state of water. Such leap, and also the reverse leap from ice to vapor, is called sublimation. The molecular rearrangements during changes of state involve absorption or release of latent heat energy. The amount of heat energy does not change in an adiabatic process, by definition. However, temperature is a measure only of kinetic energy, not potential energy.

The molecular effect on temperature is greater for the vapor/liquid transitions than the liquid/ice transitions. The two unequal effects on temperature, even during the "leap," are additive.

The concept of relative humidity is greatly involved in forecasting, and its measurement needs discussion. Amid the modern development of electronics, I assume that type of measurement is becoming predominant, even for surface observations. In 1946 at Great Falls, Montana, I barely learned how to launch a radiosonde and translate the data received by radio. The female observer instructors were much more quick witted.

Such method of upper air observation still continues. RH is measured by the flow of electricity across a strip of plastic, the surface of which is coated with a substance (lithium chloride in 1946) that attracts water vapor in proportion to its density in the atmosphere. The conductivity across the strip varies with the accumulation or dissipation of those molecules.

I assume any 1994 device, even for hand-held observations, is similar. I also wonder to what extent atmospheric pollutants might adhere to the coating, and alter the conductivity. For radiosondes, even those recovered and repaired, that piece is replaced after one use.

I can't vouch for electronic humidity instruments, but I can explain the old-fashioned, reliable, and very accurate wet-bulb psychrometer. It's a marvel of ingenuity. You can easily make your own for the cost of two glass thermometers which can be read quickly.

From Greek, psychrometer means a cold meter. When water vapor cools to the dewpoint, dew (evidence of a change in state) forms on the exposed surface of the object being cooled, such as a blade of grass. In a laboratory, the temperature of the beginning of condensation can be detected precisely, obtaining a dewpoint temperature by eye observation.

The wet-bulb thermometer is pref-

erable for field conditions, requiring only a quick reading of two similar thermometers. One has a bulb covered with a thin muslin sleeve fully moistened with water. Both thermometers must be sheltered from any "extra" heat, even from nearby human skin or exhaled air. The two are usually mounted rather close to each other but that isn't necessary.

The wet-bulb thermometer must be "ventilated" by a gentle flow of ambient air, to remove the vapor molecules evaporating from the muslin. Such ventilation does not affect the dry-bulb. The muslin must not dry out.

The wet-bulb reading will decrease because of evaporation, and stabilize at the wet-bulb temperature. The maximum difference between the two thermometers is the wet-bulb depression.

A mathematical formula defines the fixed relationships of dry-bulb and wet-bulb temperatures to relative humidity and dewpoint. Pressure is a very minor factor. (Note the almost vertical solid lines on the overlay, page 45.) Tables are available, but weather observers are equipped with a circular slide rule.

The *rate* of cooling of the wet-bulb decreases for two reasons: (1) cooling molecules on the wick have less kinetic energy for escape to the gaseous state, and (2) heat from the ambient air replaces heat lost during the evaporation. Soon, heat gained by conduction and radiation equals heat lost via evaporation.

Very clever. It's nice to know how weather works. Also to know why.

On the next page is a homemade nomogram for the relationships between dry-bulb temperature, wet-bulb temperature, relative humidity, and dewpoint.

In constructing this nomogram I was surprised that all lines were straight. Although the abcissas and ordinates are obviously linear, the slanting lines are variable in slope and spacing, from each other and among themselves. But all seem closely related to a psychrometer.

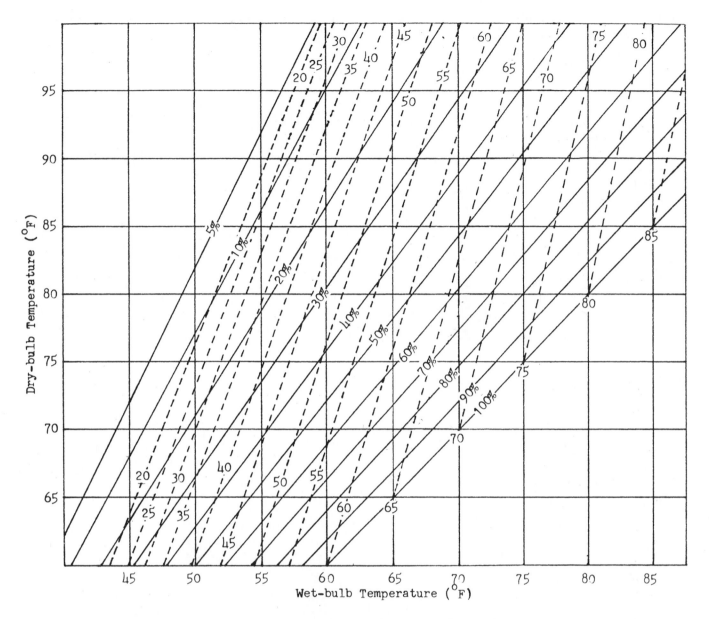

Nomogram for dry-bulb temperature, wet-bulb temperature, relative humidity, and dewpoint. Solid sloping lines show relative humidity. Dashed sloping lines show dewpoint. Plotted from psychrometric tables of National Weather Service, form WSTA, B-O-6C (5-72), for use at elevations between 1900 and 3900 feet above sea level. May be used with negligible error from sea level to 6000 feet elevation. However, the correct procedure for obtaining wet-bulb temperature should be followed carefully.

Chapter 8. Buoyancy

In most books or lectures this topic is usually called "Stability." Such sources also emphasize instability, which is more of a problem. When a local airmass is unstable, parts of it are buoyant, and such condition can develop very quickly. Pages 27 and 29 introduce the closely related topics of density and gravity. One must remember that within liquids and gases (both are also described as fluids), the force of gravity pushes a mass up or down (makes it float or sink) with equal ease. Within the atmosphere, these motions are mostly invisible. A forecaster must strive to recognize both and to predict them.

The handy-dandy nomogram called the adiabatic chart makes this so easy. The main problem is making sure what you plot on the chart is accurate and up-to-date. The less your confidence, the more you have to make a subjective estimation.

Those last two words are almost a summary of the world of a forecaster. That world often is strenuous, but filled with opportunity. You ought to know by now there are not many good forecasters.

You also know I'm trying to coax you, in addition to inform you. The task is actually easier than the selfish elite claim it to be. That group wants to maintain its monopoly.

Later I will explain how to plot raobs from the standard codes reported every 12 hours (at 00Z and 12Z, which means midnight and noon at 0^0 longitude which is the meridian at Greenwich, England). Such times are 0400 and 1600 on the 24 hour clock in Pacific Standard Time at Salem, Oregon, the nearest raob station to Portland where I live.

In the next column is a simplified adiabatic chart, using elevation above ground instead of pressure levels. The purpose is solely to illustrate and interpret common "lapse rates" in the atmos-

phere especially those near the ground. The rate refers to the variation in temperature along an upward scale, where temperature usually decreases, or lapses. If temperature increases upward through a layer of air, the layer displays an "inversion."

The graphical plot of T with altitude (pressure on a real chart) is a "curve," even when portions are a straight line. A separate curve is plotted for dewpoints. Our attention is on the "dry adiabats" which means T versus pressure only, and no change of state involving water.

The conditions described here are almost never presented on TV. Although this discussion may appear involved, after a little experience it's quite simple.

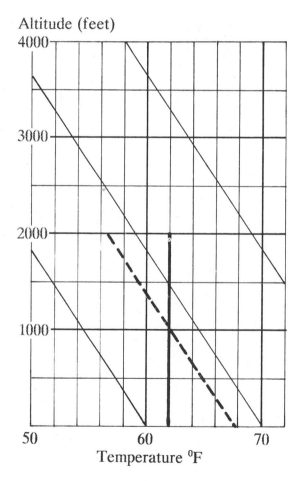

Altitude (feet)

Temperature ^{0}F

Consider an imaginary layer of air from the ground up to 2000 ft. The T is 62^0F throughout, as shown by the heavy vertical line. Such a layer is described as isothermal. Also it is said to be very stable. That means gravity has pulled the heavier air (more dense and non-buoyant) to the bottom of the layer, which means the lighter air (less dense and buoyant) has floated upward.

In slightly more technical words, although the T is the same all through the layer, P (pressure) is greater below altitude of 1000 ft, and less above 1000 ft. The molecules of air are closer together where each air parcel is more compressed.

For brevity and to avoid ambiguity, I will introduce some maverick labels. These are not used in academic texts.

T will now be called OT, for ordinary temperature. Potential temperature, displayed by the dry adiabats, will be labeled DAT, meaning dry adiabatic temperature.

In the isothermal layer, OT scale, plotted as a heavy vertical line on diagram on previous page, gravity has already arranged the layer with "colder" air (lower DAT) underneath, and "warmer" air (higher DAT) floating above.

When we measure OT with a thermometer or a radiosonde the numbers are on the Celsius scale and we plot them on the chart using the vertical lines of OT. Then we must keep in mind those sloping lines of DAT, which soon becomes as natural as breathing.

Mentally we can "move" a parcel of air upward or downward anywhere in an isothermal layer (defined by OT) but it must move diagonally on the nomogram, along a line parallel to the dry adiabats. A parcel moved upward will expand but its density will remain greater than the surrounding parcels because its DAT was lower at the starting level. Conversely, a parcel moved downward in an isothermal layer will retain its buoyancy (less density than surrounding parcels).

Hence, any parcel in an isothermal layer is restricted from any up or down motion, unless conditions change.

Imagine that we change the conditions. We will mechanically mix the entire layer, with a giant fan or eggbeater, such as a helicopter. The lower parcels with lower DAT will blend among upper parcels with higher DAT, until they all have the same DAT. The new plot on the chart is the heavy dashed line on the nomogram. Note that the "mean" OT of the layer is still 62°F, where altitude of the curve is 1000 ft. But the entire 2000 ft layer has the same DAT (not labeled).

The mixed layer now has a dry adiabatic lapse rate, which academic texts define as "neutral" because there is neither encouragement nor hindrance for vertical motion of any parcel. This lapse rate is the boundary condition between stable and unstable air. However, the mixed layer has now lost all stability.

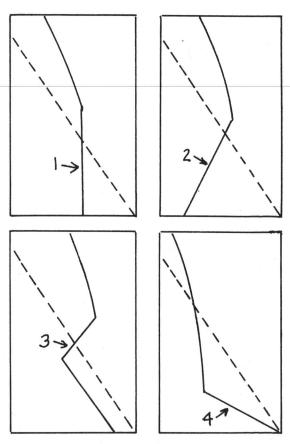

In these simplified examples of plotted curves, No. 1 shows an isothermal OT layer next to ground. No. 2 is an OT inversion, which is extremely stable. No. 3 is an inversion layer aloft with a dry adiabatic layer below. No. 4 shows an unstable layer common during surface heating, which is a non-adiabatic process. Daytime heating from solar radiation, nighttime cooling of air near the ground, and events in the atmosphere above, are everyday problems in forecasting. That's why we need frequent "soundings" to measure OT, P, and RH, and display them on an adiabatic chart.

Because of the complex interaction of such factors, the changes are not always linear (in straight lines). However, with the linear design of dry adiabats, the horizontal lines can be labeled with altitude instead of P with only very small error, at least up to 4000 ft, as on page 55. In everyday U.S. units, the dry adiabatic lapse rate is approximately 0.55°F per 100 ft. Keep in mind that is only 0.055°F per 10 ft, which you would hardly notice. That is our pocket tape measure for a dry adiabat.

There is another significant lapse rate, called the auto-convective lapse rate, which is 0.187°F per 10 ft, a little over three times the dry adiabatic rate. Air becomes extremely unstable in this condition, but it occurs only in shallow layers near heated ground.

The relationships between OT, P, RH, and also DAT, altitude, and density are precisely described by mathematics. This book strives to simplify the factors of buoyancy to aid comprehension, at least for the needs of local forecasting.

There is one little complication we can dispose of here, because it's very minor. And it's always part of the computations in radiosonde observations.

Air is a mixture of gases which do not combine. There is no such thing as a molecule of air. However, by combining the molecular weights of each component with the proportion of each (not counting water because it varies so much), we can invent a molecular weight of 28.966 for dry air. The molecular weight of water vapor, H_2O is only 18, because the molecular weight of H is only 1.

Thus moist air is lighter, meaning less dense, than dry air because for every molecule of water vapor added to a fixed volume of dry air, one molecule of dry air is crowded out, and those weigh an average of almost 29. Most of the atmosphere, even below 18,000 ft, is usually less than 1% or 2% water vapor.

For the computation of "thickness" between pressure levels, T must be converted to VT, "virtual T," a slightly higher number. You may now forget this detail, knowing it is not overlooked.

Back now to buoyancy. The pressure measured at each elevation results from the weight of mass of air above. Pressure always decreases upward because if not, adjustment will be almost instantaneous.

In a layer of air through which the lapse rate is dry adiabatic (even though the air contains water vapor) there is still buoyancy equilibrium. The air may be without motion. Density still decreases upward. If vertical motion is imposed, buoyancy remains neutral, meaning without effect. Such motion is not encouraged. The layer has lost stability, but it is not yet absolutely unstable.

However, if the lapse rate exceeds the auto-convective rate, density does increase upward. Gravity will soon take care of that no-no. This happens very frequently when the sun shines strongly on the surface of the earth.

When you read about the "overturning" of a layer of unstable air (as I did as a beginner) don't envision the flipping of a pancake. Think of thousands of hot air balloons. Air is gaseous, and without cohesion. Each parcel does its own thing, quickly, according to existing forces.

Don't be dismayed. You seldom will need this particular information. But we might need it for the many unsolved problems. Few seem to have been solved in the last thirty years.

The next diagram attempts to describe the diurnal progression of daytime heating and nighttime cooling as

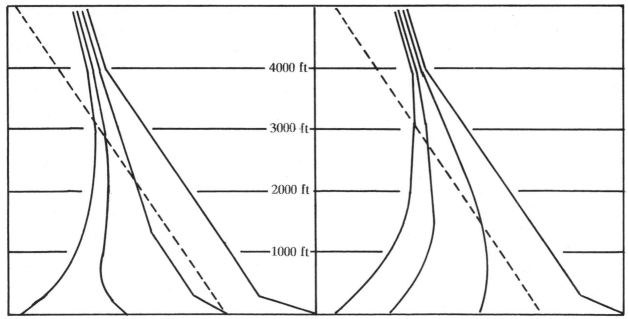

Daytime Heating →   ← Nighttime Cooling

shown by hypothetical plots of temperature versus altitude. Actual radiosonde observations seldom show such detail because they occur only every 12 hours, and the instruments rise too rapidly for detailed measurements near the ground. The diagram is adapted from "Fire Weather" (1970) U. S. Forest Service, Agriculture Handbook 360.

These plots are only to illustrate the effects of surface heating and cooling on the layers of air near the ground. They are generalized because of variations in the character of the surface, season of year, geographical location, altitude, and existing synoptic pattern.

The lack of diurnal change above 4000 ft above ground (such number is arbitrary) demonstrates that although the earth is heated by the sun, the atmosphere is heated almost entirely by the earth. The clear atmosphere is nearly transparent to sunlight, called short wave radiation. Also the atmosphere, composed of low density gases, cools slowly. Water vapor loses heat rapidly, but it's a small component of air.

With clear dry air, the T at or near the ground varies significantly during daynight sequences. Clouds reflect sunlight away from the earth, but also hinder the escape of its heat. The combinations are too numerous to discuss here.

Obviously the marked changes in lapse rates near the ground generate or suppress up-and-down motion of air, because of variation in buoyancy. Also, a forecaster must anticipate variations in horizontal air flow. It gets complicated.

Such diurnal variation in lapse rate results from gain or loss of heat, which of course is non-adiabatic by definition. It introduces another important branch of physics called heat transfer.

To review a few definitions: heat is a common form of energy. Energy is the capacity for doing work. Work means movement against an opposing force. Our need is to understand at least the elementary processes of how heat flows from a warm zone to a cool zone. Classical physics lists three basic modes.

One is conduction, where the molecules of mass are "touching" each other, which you soon learn if you try to shower with water that is too hot. Another mode is convection which means a movable mass, such as a liquid or gas, flows from one location to another, and thus transfers heat. The hot air register from your furnace is an example. Another is when parcels of air aloft, with a higher DAT, subside and are compressed under increasing layers of air, and add to the hot air being heated by the sun at the ground.

Those are the engineering definitions. In meteorology, convection is often defined more narrowly, meaning only upward motion of air. Downward motion is usually called subsidence, unless pronounced, as in thunderstorm downdrafts. Horizontal broadscale motion is advection.

The remaining process is heat transfer by radiation. Radiant heat energy is continually emitted from all substances that contain heat energy, which includes all substances on earth. Everyday examples are solar energy, which is mostly in the form of light, radio waves which bring sound and pictures to your TV, and the heat from flames. This last kind can bring warmth to you even though air is moving away from you and rising up the chimney. How radiant heat is actually transmitted is beyond my understanding.

For example, as radiant heat moves away from its source, in the form of electromagnetic waves, it needs no medium or substance for transfer. It actually travels best in "empty" space. Also, it can pass through, without any loss by absorption, any substance which is fully transparent to its particular characteristics.

Radiant energy may be loosely described as a sort of kinetic energy in transit between bodies, but not requiring contact. The tranmission is extremely fast, at the speed of light, about 669,600,000 miles per hour.

Radiant energy is classified on the basis of differences in its electromagnetic wave lengths, just as TV stations are tuned to different wave lengths. All bodies radiate energy at a spectrum of wave lenths, but not in equal amounts at each wave length. The rate of radiation peaks at a specific wave length, depending on the T of the radiating surface. As T rises, that peak wave length decreases.

Radiation from all surfaces of the earth are classed as long wave radiation. Solar radiation, from a surface about 10,000°F is called short wave radiation.

Everyone knows that the hotter an object becomes, the faster it radiates heat. The rate of total radiation from a body, whatever its T, is called its emissivity (from the verb, to emit). However, the emmissivity of a body varies with its atomic structure (or something).

There is an upper limit for such emissivity at each T (regardless of the nature of the substance). Physicists have invented a imaginary body which they call a black body, but the concept does not refer to color. A black body has an emissivity of 1.00, and everything is rated somewhat lower. Water is 0.96, ice and snow are 0.96.

The imaginary blackbody has another characteristic; it will absorb all radiant energy which reaches it. None will be reflected, or pass through because of transparency.

If substances are good radiators of heat, they are equally good absorbers of heat. At any given temperature, any substance has the same rating for both emissivity and absorbtivity compared to a black body under similar conditions.

If a body receives a fixed rate of radiant heat, its temperature will adjust until it emits radiation at the same rate as it absorbs radiation, thus reaching a heat equilibrium.

The radiation processes for gases are much more complex. Gases have no surface as do solids or liquids. Molecules are comparatively far apart. Much empty space exists.

Frank Kreith in "Principles of Heat Transfer" 1973 states:

Elementary gases such as oxygen, nitrogen, and dry air have a symmetrical molecular structure and neither emit nor absorb radiation unless they are heated to extremely high temperatures...

Hence, such gases in nature are transparent to radiation and have no emissivity. However, Kreith explains that water vapor, and carbon dioxide have polar molecular forms. They absorb and emit radiation in limited wave length ranges called spectral bands.

You may consult texts on physics. But you may not need all the details. Everyone who drives a car knows to slow down around sharp curves, without knowing much about centrifugal force. But the more you know, the better driver you are. So it is in forecasting.

The next chapter turns attention to wind, which especially interests me. That seems more important than T, which fascinates TV viewers. Maybe they are getting what they want, or maybe they only seem to want what they are getting.

Chapter 9. Myths, Errors, and Distortions

I'll start out with a big one to maintain your attention, but explain it in Chapter 11. Tornadoes don't "touch down" from a parent cloud. They "spin up" from the surface. The maximum intensity is within a few hundred feet of the ground, and weakens where the "funnel" appears to widen at higher elevation.

At first I planned to entitle this chapter Local Winds. In some earlier books and training courses, such category was a catch-all for low level winds seemingly unrelated to broadscale synoptic patterns (sea level and upper air).

Instructional material often is too structured, divided into many pieces. In some ways it may make knowledge more digestible. But the learning process is not killing prey and feasting. It's a sort of grazing. Gradually we gather new ideas and blend them with older ones. Often one plus two plus three adds up to ten.

The atmosphere near the ground where we live is always adjusting to multiple influences, exhibiting variety of action, which in turn produces new action. This book strives to explain the more important topics of physics. Such tools will help solve a reader's own forecasting problems.

Man's effort to anticipate weather events obviously began with eye-observations. But many atmospheric processes are invisible. Not surprisingly, existing weather lore includes many myths, errors, distortions, and omissions.

This chapter will review some of those, and some were promoted by me, until I gradually became aware of the inconsistencies in my own tree of knowledge. That tree will always need pruning.

Local weather has its own complexities, comparable to the personalities of individuals. Accurate forecasting can only be attained by focussing on one location. Local forecasting is the logical path for technical effort, even though superimposed on the broad background of synoptic patterns.

#1 The "Lid" of Warmer Air over an inversion layer of colder air at the surface-- The lid holds in pollutants in a shallow stagnant layer near the ground, hindering their dispersion. Prominent distortion in the late 1950s when Los Angeles was striving to curb pollution.

A lid implies a barrier. The only force holding down the cool layer is the force of gravity, as it holds water in a bucket. Compare with the absence of a lid over a bin of frozen food in a supermarket. The cold air does not spill out. The warm air above is a poor radiator of heat, and radiates little heat into the bin.

A layer of cold air at the ground can be a shelter from strong winds, if the inversion is strong, and the winds above do not persist too long (because frictional eddies may gradually sweep away the cold layer). In early January 1880, Portland OR with a population of about 15,000 suffered the worst windstorm of its history. The local newspaper, The Oregonian, crowed that Seattle, a smaller competitive city, must have suffered even more, especially its larger fleet of ocean-going boats.

Communications lagged because a train was stuck in snow between cities. The Puget Sound area was covered with 3 to 4 feet of snow, roofs were collapsing from the weight, but what windstorm was Portland complaining about? No boats lost. PDX had no snow. What a pity, no synoptic maps for that date, no news photos, only dramatic journalism.

Fast forward to 1964, Winds Over Wildlands, U.S.Forest Service, condensed: "Cool, gently moving winds aloft sometimes prevent winds from developing in poorly ventilated basins, even with strong heating. Nighttime inversions form in the basin. In the cooling process the air aloft settles down onto the upper slopes. If upper air is dense, heating the following day, even though intense [within the poorly ventilated basin], may not lift [the dense upper air] back up above the ridge-tops. This creates a very strong super-adiabatic lapse rate and a potentially explosive situation in the trapped air below [the hot air in the poorly venti-lated basin]." (insertions in brackets)

In 1970, in Fire Weather, Agri-culture Handbook 360, the same topic appeared, with same illustration (caption and text condensed):

"Strong heating may produce a pool of superheated air in poorly ventilated basins. If upper winds are unable to pro-vide a triggering mechanism to overcome inertia and release the instability in this superadiabatic layer, a potentially explos-ive fire-weather situation develops. Such pools persist until released, and they may move out violently."

Here's a better explanation. The cool clean marine air arrives as a sea breeze in Los Angeles. Pollutants are not trapped by a "lid" of warm air which floats passively above the marine air. The cool surface layer merely hinders the rate of dispersion of pollutants. The sea breeze is shallow, soon becomes polluted, warms in its new environment, and in turn gets lifted gently by fresh marine air.

Keep in mind, this "lid" was warm air over cold air, "trapping" pollutants.

Switch now to poorly ventilated valleys, filled with superheated air which is trapped by colder air above. It may become explosive, and "move out" violent-ly. [Be wary of superheated air]

How can any valley, open to the sky, without any roof or lid, be poorly ventilated? Answer: Only at night, by radiation of heat upward. Next day, from radiation downward from sun, air rises and floats upward in "convection col-umns," whenever it becomes buoyant. Same as over flat land.

#2 What causes Wind Gusts?
Answer: Faster winds from above swoop

down like an aircraft making a landing. What makes them swoop? : Turbulence (which means mixed up-and-down motion of air parcels) combined with horizontal wind. As a preliminary, consider the path in space of a "mark" on the tread of a tire,

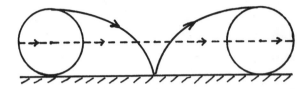

of a car moving at a given speed, say 30 mph. The axle also is moving 30 mph, and the bottom of the tire, in contact with the roadway, is momentarily stationary. Therefore the top of the tire must be moving 60 mph, or twice the speed of the axle. I was impressed to learn this in a shop class for mechanical drawing in 10th grade, 1929. Saved it for this very day.

It's easy to bridge the gap from the diagram above to the one below.

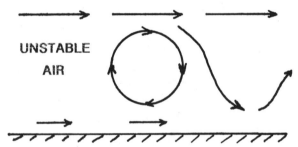

UNSTABLE AIR

In stormy weather, in a layer of air from the ground up to 5000 ft or even more, it should be expected that the layer will develop an adiabatic lapse rate. Air will move up or down with the greatest of ease, as part of "rolls" carried in the horizontal flow.

The rolls have a horizontal axis, like wheels, because the horizontal component of the wind is slowed near the ground by friction. A descending parcel of air, say one million cubic feet weighing 76,000 lbs (page 27) can knock you over before it slows down. Many air parcels are much larger than that. As a thumb rule, during storms peak gusts are about 50% higher than the average windspeed near the ground.

The topic of wind gusts on the surface of the earth is included here because it has only recently emerged from almost total obscurity in public weather forecasts. The order of importance seems to be temperature, the attainment of "new" record highs or lows, sky cover (clouds), rain or snow, and finally wind.

For many years the official anemometer was a wind odometer, not a wind speedometer. Each 1/60 "mile" of air was counted for one minute. As a solitary Junior Observer in 1941 in Des Moines, during a thunderstorm, I counted 60 buzzes in 1 minute (average speed, 60 mph).

The definition of duration of a gust must be arbitrary, but even a good instrument has a certain lag in response time. From the standpoint of damage to structures, vehicles, and vegetation, each must take several seconds to yield to the stress, so maybe we should use 5 as a minimum.

The main point is that wind flow during storms is not all horizontal. Some of the real punches arrive on a slant from above, as shown above. Some come straight down, in what are labeled mysteriously as "microbursts, or wind shear." However, the most destructive winds of all are essentially horizontal, namely those in hurricanes and tornadoes. Those are a very special category which in simple language are whirlwinds, but which are now labeled "vortices."

The singular form is vortex, and dictionaries give preference to the plural form of vortexes, which will be the title of Chapter 11.

High winds surely are scary. Maybe we should be glad air is invisible. Also, we ought to understand how something invisible (except for the rain or dust or flying debris) can be so destructive.

The average person cannot stand erect in a wind of about 60 mph. If one leans into the wind, its pressure removes weight from the feet, and traction become inadequate. At Crown Point in the west end of the Columbia Gorge near Portland, an estimated east wind of 65 during a fair weather episode, circa 1957, forced me to crawl on hands and knees back to my car.

The Columbia Gorge is a remarkable gap, almost down to sea level, in the Cascade Mountains of Oregon and Washington. They blend with the Rocky Mountains in British Columbia, and extend southward to the Sierras of California. In summer the west winds of the Gorge, an unusual extension of a sea breeze, create a newly discovered environment for wind surfers, reportedly of worldwide fame.

In winter the east winds reaching Portland often interrupt the relatively mild semimarine climate. Portland also is at the north end of a rather broad and fairly long Willamette (Wil-lam'et) Valley.

The Pacific Northwest, and most of the large western states, are characterized by rough terrain. Obviously, wind flow near the ground tends to be "channeled" in the lower parts of such terrain. The common horizontal rolls in the "friction layer" immediately above ordinary flat land can be modified or disrupted by large ridges, mountains, canyons, and gorges.

Certainly the friction layer extends farther upwards from the ground. In general, we should assume horizontal motion of air is slowed if such friction increases. Thus we come to another distortion in weather lore:

#3 The "Funnel Effect." We can't see air, but we can see water and how it flows across the land in streams and rivers, and in pipes and conduits to our cities and homes.

We have great faith in what we see. The four most repeated words among TV weathercasters are: "As you can see."

But air is a gas, not a liquid. The physics of hydraulics pertain to closed systems in pipes, or partially closed (by the enormous force of gravity) in streams and rivers and blocked by dams. I've emphasized the force of gravity on air, but we still call it the "free atmosphere."

A funnel is defined as a conical utensil with a narrow tube at the apex, used to channel the flow of a substance into the narrower channel. For liquids the apex points down, in the direction of gravity. Also, a funnel is a flue or stack for the passage of smoke, as of a ship or locomotive. Smoke is buoyant, and noxious, to be channeled up-up-and-away. So the apex of the cone points up, to confine and concentrate heat (which creates the buoyancy) and accelerate the dispersion.

In the world of weather lore we know tornadoes look like a funnel, with the apex pointing down. Destruction occurs when the funnel touches "down".

Almost everyone has a kitchen sink and a bathroom washbasin, and in the time of my childhood, also had a bathtub. In those appliances the drain develops a miniature whirlpool, with a vertical axis.

Does air drain down and develop a whirl in a tornado funnel cloud? Is that why destruction occurs when the funnel cloud touches "down?" Where does all that dust and debris and descending air go after the touchdown?

Weather lore also warns us about horizontal funnels, meaning those with a horizontal axis. The air flows fairly straight through such funnels, with no apparent whirlpool action. It's more like the nozzle on a garden hose. The aperture becomes smaller, and the fluid flows faster.

But a river valley or a river gorge is not a closed system. Rivers are filled with dense water, flowing downhill to sea level. Our discussion is about thin air above the water surface, or dry river bed. Such air is open above to the whole out-of-doors. It can quickly move up or down according to its buoyancy, or horizontally according to the horizontal pressure gradient.

My experience at Crown Point in 1957, probably in late autumn, was caused by a very strong pressure gradient in a comparatively shallow layer at the bottom of the Gorge, between cold air at the east end, and warmer air at the west end (plus falling pressure probably from a storm approaching from the Pacific). Clear sky over arid land during long nights allows substantial surface radiation.

The Columbia Gorge was only a limited outlet for air to move horizontally from high pressure to low pressure. It was a partial relief valve for a pressure imbalance. The gradient was caused by the Cascade Mountains, heat transfer, and a synoptic scale pattern, not by a horizontal funnel "accelerating" a horizontal flow.

Fast forward to 1987, to an article in *The Oregonian*, reviewing the Columbus Day storm of 10-12-62 for its 25th anniversary (see Chapter 12 this book). Authors were the top leaders of the NWS in Oregon, one was the Chief Forecaster, probably following orders from Washington D.C. Possibly the article was ghost written by an "expert" back there. The pile of distorted propaganda from that source over recent years is almost unbelievable. Anyway, NWS management is responsible for this story, as per these linked excerpts: [photocopy available]

Why was it [the storm] so terrible? Could it happen again? Yes, but first, a fast-moving storm would have to form close enough for violent winds to be funnelled northward through the state. That is exactly what happened to create the Oct. 11-12, 1962 storm [actually, there were two separate storms about 36 hours apart].

A particularly strong jet stream moved the remains of Typhoon Freda [which earlier had] winds of more than 100 mph, quickly eastward, making it reach full force near land rather than at sea. The fast speed intensified the low air pressure associated with the storm.

When the storm's path turned northward, the natural geography of the Willamette Valley [see page 41] functioned as a funnel to intensify the wind.

Freda [now a new developing storm in a new environment, not a reviving corpse of a typhoon. "Freda" sounds more exciting than "Columbus Day"] invaded the domain of cold air just off the Oregon coast. Its warm, moist air began rising.

When air is forced aloft into the atmosphere, it must be replaced by air at the surface. If air doesn't flow into the vacated region fast enough, the surface pressure begins to fall. The pressure at the surface was falling rapidly off the coast Oct. 12, 1962. Meanwhile, there also was a strong jet stream to result in even lower air pressure.

As air accelerates through the jet stream, it also creates lower pressure, similar to air flowing over the top surface of an airplane wing.   The faster it moves, the lower the pressure.

There was a strong jet stream present over the Pacific Ocean in early October of 1962. All three main characters--the cold air, the warm moist air and the jet stream--met at center stage just off the Southern Oregon and Northern California coasts on Oct. 11 and 12, 1962.

Destructive storms, such as the Columbus Day Storm, develop rapidly as they approach the coast. As they curve northward along the coast, the surface pressure is falling rapidly ahead of them and rising rapidly behind them. This effect creates a large difference in pressure. The greater the difference in pressure between point "A" and point "B," the stronger the wind.

While the majority of storms that strike Oregon and Washington come from the west, Columbus Day-type storms arrive from the south. The key to the destructive power is that their track, or path, also must take them between the coast and 130 degrees west longitude.

Geographical features help create strong wind. The Willamette valley is oriented north-south with the Coast Range to the west and the Cascades to the east. Air accelerates as it passes through a constriction. In this case, the Willamette Valley is the constriction.

[Send a self-addressed stamped envelope for a free photocopy of the above NWS explanation offered to the public six months after publication of my first book, The Weather Tomorrow, in April 1987. (book for sale, $10 + $2.) It describes the failure of NWS to predict a similar but slightly more distant storm in Nov. 1981. See Chapter 12 of this book about the 1962 storm.]

The first diagram in next column shows how a constriction in a closed sys-

tem can accelerate the speed of water in that constriction. But the diameter of the pipe is smaller, so the volume of water per unit time doesn't increase, assuming the pressure in the pipe remains the same.

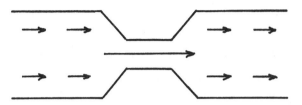

Beyond the constriction, where the pipe is larger again, the water speed slows. I'm not a hydraulic engineer, but I suspect the increased friction of the restriction has lowered the pressure downstream, actually slowing the rate of flow. Friction is an opposing force to any motion, and a smaller pipe must surely increase the friction.

When one realizes that valleys or even gorges are not closed conduits, and that during storms the winds aloft are always stronger than near the ground, and that a dry adiabatic lapse rate overhead "opens" any invisible lid to those strong winds, we can skip the imaginary danger of horizontal wind funnels. But if you do live at either end of the Columbia Gorge you should keep track of the local pressure gradient through the gorge.

On flat open ground, even in the Willamette Valley, the main indicator is how isobars move across your local landscape (to be discussed in Chapter 12).

#4 Wind Over Mountains.   This topic is about air flow over, but close to the tops of the ridges or mountains. For winds more than about 5000 ft, maybe sometimes 8000 ft, above the mountains, there probably is little or no adjustment unless the crossing winds are unusually strong. But the winds in the extended friction layer can be extremely complex.

Consider the gross oversimplification in this next diagram. The airflow is shown by "streamlines." In steady state flow the steamlines illustrate the trajectories of the air parcels, a sort of smoothing if the details are unimportant. But a diagram like this often appears in elementary books. Smoothing of streamlines is useful, but if overdone it offers distortion.

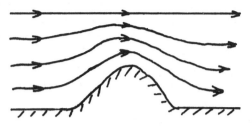

While living for six winters in "central" Oregon, at an elevation of 2600 ft, 26 miles east of Mt. Jefferson in the Cascades, I noted something interesting. In midwinter, there were times when Portland was under a layer of clouds, with a daily max temp of 40-45. I would be enjoying about 60 with sunshine.

A thick layer of mild Pacific air was arriving from the W or SW. The lowest part was partly stopped by the Coast Range, and the rest sailed over the cool cloudy stagnant air in the Willamette Valley, extending upward to about 3500 feet MSL. The average elevation of the Cascade Mountains is about 4000 ft. Mt. Jefferson is a 10,495 ft peak. Mt. Hood is 11,239 ft. (I climbed Mt. Hood, alone and unwisely, seven weeks after moving to PDX in 1949. Mountains fascinated me.)

My point is that an entire layer of moving air approaching a mountain or ridge does not necessarily slide smoothly up and over and down the other side. Much of it may just stop and stagnate.

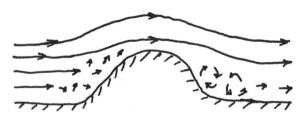

What about the air that seems to flow down the leeward side? Well, if so, it need not be the lower part that I claim might have been stopped by the barrier. It might be air that was already at or above the barrier upon arrival. Air that already had a higher heat content per unit mass, which the books call potential T, and I have called DAT. Which is what you nearly always find on plots of raobs which extend several thousand feet above your terrain.

I don't see how zillions of tons of air can be lifted several thousand feet against the force of gravity because its horizontal motion unlikely has that much inertia to coast up and over.

Unless of course we can add some heat to it, making it buoyant, and then gravity will actually push it up, indirectly. Air arriving from the Pacific, especially in winter, always contains some water vapor. With a little uphill coasting from momentum, some of it will cool below the initial dewpoint, and rain or snow will occur. That air, minus some water vapor, now has a higher DAT, and can float up. And if it doesn't float up, it probably sinks to help push up the air that rises.

Also, the streamlines which do rise slightly over the bump ought to spread apart slightly as the layer expands in the lower pressure at the higher elevation.

This bit of rambling is to explain that multiple simultaneous actions in the atmosphere are often complicated. A forecaster can never anticipate all of them. But he ought to eventually learn to cope with the main actions in his local environment that happen over and over and over.

I've been intrigued with the weather in the Pacific Northwest since 1949, and I'm still learning slowly.

No one can write a manual for all local forecast problems in North America. A do-it-yourself forecaster must review past episodes. These sometimes are called postmortems, but those episodes are not really dead. They will be back to challenge you again and again.

Chapter 10. Convection, Thunderstorm Downdrafts

In engineering, convection means the transport of liquid or gaseous mass, without moving the containers, such as air into or out of your furnace, or water to your kitchen or bathroom. In meteorology the definitions are a little more specific. The horizontal winds are advection, and localized upward air motion is usually classified as convection.

Subtle upward motion over a large area is often called convergence, because horizontal pressure gradients create an inward spiral of motion. Subtle downward motion over a large area is called subsidence. Pronounced downward motion in a local area is nearly always under a thunderstorm, and formerly was simply called a thunderstorm downdraft.

The main topic here is the very common localized upward motion of air that has become buoyant, for whatever reason. This is an important and neglected topic, at least in public understanding.

Older instruction manuals refer to the overturning of an air mass. Judging from the accumulated diagrams over the last 60 years, the details of such overturning must surely be complex, and I won't contradict. Neither do I ridicule some of early explanations of convection. Some of the peculiar ones I accepted, and even "taught" to others.

For example (to encourage modern students to open their minds), note the concept of upslope and downslope winds. At night, a land surface radiates heat upward, especially if sky is clear. Air itself is a poor radiator, but water vapor in air is a good radiator. A shallow layer of air near the ground (which nearly always contains more vapor than air above) becomes cooler, and more dense, and tends to flow downhill, as does rain. Okay so far.

Next day, sun shines, ground warms, and air next to ground becomes buoyant. Situation is *reversed*. Heated air flows back uphill. In "Compendium of Meteorology" (1951, 1334 pages, page 662) Friedrich Defant is quoted, as of 1949, in article "Local Winds" :

. . .air heated over the inclined mountain slopes. . .causes the phenomenon of air rising in daytime along the slopes of mountains, well known to every mountain climber. These winds start at one fourth to three fourths of an hour after sunrise, and flow uphill in daytime. They. . .reverse their direction in the evening (about one fourth to three fourths of an hour after sunset).

As an avid mountain climber 1950-1963 I never noticed any upslope winds, only winds arriving horizontally, day or night.

Colder air (denser air), if on a slope will flow downhill, even in daytime because of deflection by terrain. Gravity acts vertically, straight down. Warmer air, having comparative buoyancy, and no terrain overhead, will float straight up, unless it is deflected and/or mixed with other air already moving horizontally.

Whether the sun rises or the sun sets, or night changes to day, the physics of gravity and buoyancy do not "reverse." In this example, only the density changes.

I have respect for writers and researchers, but even more respect for logic. When adding new ideas, and revising and rearranging old ones, a student must constantly test for logic.

The earth is heated by the sun, but the atmosphere is mostly heated by the earth. We strive to keep track of comparative heating by measurements of OT, ordinary temperature, which is not the same thing as heat, but much more conveniently measured, and usually meets our needs. The transfer of heat from earth to air is by conduction, convection, and radiation, the routine big three. In meteorology we add another big one, the condensation of water vapor. Such change of state adds huge amounts of heat to air.

This diagram is compiled from *Smithsonian Meteorological Tables* and adapted from a graph in *Atmospheric Science,* J. M. Wallace and P. V. Hobbs, Academic Press 1977. The plot is for OT according to the Standard Atmosphere, from MSL to somewhere near heaven. The altitude and OT scales are linear. As airline passengers, many readers remember how smooth the ride becomes after reaching the stratosphere, which often is lower than defined here.

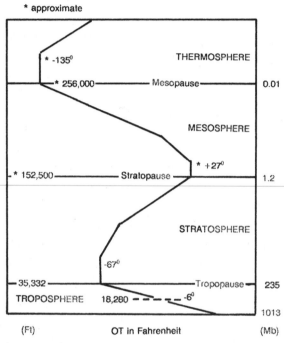

* approximate

THERMOSPHERE

* -135⁰

* 256,000 — Mesopause — 0.01

MESOSPHERE

* 152,500 — Stratopause — * +27⁰   1.2

STRATOSPHERE

-67⁰

35,332 — Tropopause — 235

TROPOSPHERE   18,280 - - - - - -6⁰

1013

(Ft)   OT in Fahrenheit   (Mb)

Note the lapse rate in the lower segment of the atmosphere. A dry adiabatic lapse rate is even greater than that of the SA. The horizontal dashed line is the 500 mb level, the very top of the adiabatic work chart on page 43. Recall that one-half of the mass of all air remains below the dashed line. A local forecaster seldom has to look at any data above that line. We have narrowed the problem, sort of.

Why is the average lapse rate large in the troposphere? Because there is so much up-and-down motion in that layer. Parcels of air expand or shrink as the ambient pressure varies, and the OT changes according to the dry or moist adiabats. One must pay attention both to

OT, and DAT (which in formal books is called potential temperature). Indirectly, we are keeping track of buoyancy, which is controlled by omnipresent gravity.

I never did learn why it's so warm at the top of the stratosphere, but that would be filed under unimportant information. It helps to remember that our usual concept of warm and cold is more dependent on net rates of radiation than on conduction. The tranfer of kinetic energy to human skin is tiny when the blows from those invisible molecules are infrequent.

Although we can narrow our focus on convection away from the vastness of the upper atmosphere, there is plenty of action below 500 mbs (18,000 ft). Also, we can set aside the tiny disordered motions of small air parcels. If those begin to organize and coalesce, pay attention.

Whether very small parcels become buoyant and rise as bubbles, or form gentle "convection columns" is not important. But when such a column is topped with a type 1 cumulus cloud, and soon swells to a type 2, and then develops an ice crystal top, a thunderstorm has developed.

Eye observations are useful, but a forecaster must widen his view. He needs weather maps, raob plots, and hourly airway reports. Satellite "imagery" and radar displays are of value. At present they seem exaggerated, distorted, and unduly mysterious. What they have added is less than we have lost, by less availability of, and attention to, earlier weather data. One thing for sure, they are presumed to be entertaining.

Small disordered air motions occur when air parcels are essentially in equilibrium with gravity and nearby pressure. Absolute equilibrium results in calm air. It doesn't take much to create small imbalances in thin gases.

The forecaster must recognize as soon as possible any factor likely to cause significant change. In distance, vertical motion usually creates more change than horizontal motion. However, the physics of both are intermingled. Atmospheric processes are three-dimensional. Early technology, even up to World War II, did not provide much data for the vertical dimension. Even today, with the expanded data base (which still has serious shortcomings) there is inadequate attention to the air aloft. Not far aloft, just up to 18,000 ft, the lower 50% of all air.

One neglected topic is to recognize the latent heat available in water vapor. That heat is stored in air parcels when conditions favor evaporation from water source surfaces, such as oceans or vegetation. If those parcels rise, and water vapor condenses during adiabatic cooling, it's something like tapping a reserve fuel tank, to hinder the adiabatic cooling. Adiabatic cooling at the "moist rate" is slower than cooling at the "dry rate" because of the latent heat released during condensation (gas to liquid or solid). Always remember, *moist air has much more potential for upward motion than dry air* at the same T and P. It has hidden energy. The word "latent" is too mild.

A mathematician can precisely define the quantity of such release. An easy insight can be gained from the moist adiabats on page 45. Overlay them on the dry adiabats on page 43. That should impress you, at least in warm air masses. (In cold air the moist adiabats become more like the dry adiabats because cold air at 100% RH contains less water vapor than warm air at 100% RH.)

Another neglected topic is called entrainment in the textbooks. Buoyant air rising in a column is not inside an isolated tube or chimney. It's exchanging position with denser air. Air is thin stuff, and a little mixing takes place along the sides of the column. We don't know exactly how much, but it's a significant amount. The rising column gradually entrains some of the non-rising air. The surrounding air also absorbs some of the rising air, but that is of little concern. The surrounding air also must sink slightly during the exchange of vertical positions, which warms it and may lower its humidity, a small but stabilizing influence.

What is neglected about the physics of entrainment? The quantity of the water vapor in the air surrounding the convecttion column. Just as the surface of the earth is the main source of heat energy, it is the *only* source of water vapor. All WV is carried upward in the atmosphere by rising parcels. The parcels lose WV by condensation. If large enough, the products of condensation immediately fall earthward. If too small, they semi-float, until later when they evaporate or grow larger and fall.

Whatever, the rate at which air in a convection column gains or loses WV depends not only on the moist adiabats on the nomogram, but to some extent on the flux of WV during entrainment. If the surrounding air is dry, the rising parcels empty their fuel tank sooner. Conversely, if the entrained air is moist, either by WV or water molecules compacted in droplets or crystals, the buoyancy persists longer.

Here in Oregon thunderstorms in summer are not common because the air aloft from the Pacific High is usually dry. In the Midwest, thunderstorms are common because air from the Atlantic High, after moving westward over subtropical waters and curving northward after crossing the Gulf of Mexico, is loaded with water vapor, especially in the lower and intermediate levels. The fuel tanks of convection columns are nearly full even when they reach the Canadian border.

Returning to generalized physics, convection columns often create new imbalances which intensify local action, at least temporarily. A stable layer above surface heating may become unstable, encouraging more convection columns. Convective-type clouds may form. Precipitation may begin, and some events are not friendly gifts from Mother Nature.

Thunderstorms are extreme convective columns that also produce lightning, which defines a thunderstorm. Thunder is the sound created by lightning, a shock wave from very quick heating.

Among the total vertical motions in a cross section of invisible layers of air, the masses of *up* and *down* must be equal. But the vertical speeds are not equal. Rising air is channeled into localized columns. Updrafts are faster. Descending air, over a much larger area, sinks more slowly. That is, except the unusual event under a downpour below thunderstorms.

My homemade explanation is that air pressure increases rapidly during descending motion. Parcels must be squeezed into smaller space. We are accustomed to think of air moving horizontally in the direction of lower pressure (unless deflected by the coriolis force). Sinking air (which is warming because of the squeezing) slows down over a cushion of slightly denser air.

Why is rising air channeled? Someone has already suggested that when masses adjust to imbalance, they adjust in the easiest, most efficient way. *Channeling* usually means directing fluid flow from small shallow streams into wider and deeper streams. Although rivers are dense liquids confined to the earth by gravity, they are not in closed conduits like pipes. Channeling doesn't mean funneling (which is directing a stream of large volume through a narrow closed conduit). There are none of those in the atmosphere.

Convection columns are not closed conduits. Convection begins when low level parcels become buoyant. If certain ones start upward first, there must be others nearby almost as buoyant, and needing only the slightest nudge. To achieve the "overturning" of a layer of air heated from below, it probably requires less energy to develop a few larger columns than many smaller ones.

These various ideas are not meant to be a clerical checklist, or a "decision tree," to explain how forecasts are made, or should be made. Such an attitude is akin to automation. These ideas are stored in the mind of a real forecaster, to be used subjectively and subconsciously.

The forecaster is focussed on the deadline ahead, the final decision. He is checking the changes in synoptic maps and raob plots (a light table helps), and the changing local pressure (monitoring his barometer, and the hourly airway reports).

Both this chapter and the next one are about convection. Although all convection columns probably rotate slightly around their vertical axes, this chapter is limited to those columns in which rotation is insignificant.

The thunderstorm is the king of convection columns (without significant rotation) for at least three reasons: 1) greatest intensity (including buoyancy, size, turbulence, rain, hail), 2) lightning, and 3) the remarkable ability to develop *downdrafts* reaching the surface of the earth with destructive force.

The very important electrical processes are beyond my ability to understand. Years ago I tried, unsuccessfully. Like everyone I'm awed and fearful.

Although I also fear destructive downdrafts, they are easier to understand. My awe is redirected to the recent "rediscovery" of downdrafts. The actual physics is almost elementary. The politics is awesome, and revealing.

Because I'm involved in reporting the present-day brainwashing of the public amid the "modernization" of the National Weather Service, I'll include extra detail in the explanation. A brief review of texts in my modest library may help.

1940. At top of next page is an illustration, enlarged from 1.00x to 1.54x, from page 355 of *Physics of the Air* by William J. Humphreys, C.E., PhD, copyright by the author. This is a third edition, 676 pages, of an unusual book for its time; the first edition was in 1920.

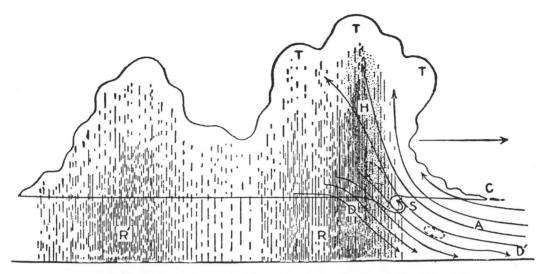

Ideal cross-section of a typical thunderstorm. A, ascending air; D, descending air; C, storm collar; S, roll scud; D', wind gust; H, hail; T, thunderheads; R, primary rain; R', secondary rain.

Chapter 17, The Thunderstorm, filled 49 pages, and Chapter 18, Lightning, filled 34 pages. The author extensively discusses the abrupt and violent gusts which usually accompany thunderstorms, and clearly links them to the cooling of air aloft by the process of evaporation.

For a thunderstorm of July 30, 1913 at Washington, D.C. he presents a graph of rapid drop in temperature (about 30^0F), and rapid increase in rainfall, pressure, and windspeed (to 70 mph). After considering the descent of "originally potentially cold air", and the chilling of air by cold rain falling from above, he declares, "Evaporation, therefore, appears to be both necessary and sufficient to produce all, or nearly all, the cooling of a thunderstorm." He later adds, ". . .and a consequent downrush of cold air."

Although Humphreys draws the column of descending air (downrush) in the vertical, between two obscure dashed lines, his streamlines of flow blend with the horizontal motion of the thundercloud itself. The wind gusts are shown only on the leading edge of the thunderstorm.

Humphreys presented many "details." The main one, evaporative cooling by falling rain, still persists. Apparently, he never used the simple word "downdraft." World War II had already started by October 1940, date of his preface. People in meteorology had other things on their minds, including this SP-3 Junior Observer, after seven months in a new job.

1941. Aeronautical Meteorology, by George F. Taylor, Ph.D., Air Corps Technical School, Chanute Field, Illinois. 455 pages. Revised and enlarged edition. Copyright by Pittman Publishing Corp.

Thunderstorm downdrafts are not mentioned, except a minor reference to *mammatocumulus* clouds, usually observed on the underside of an anvil cloud. These often have been listed as danger signs, which is true for the nearby convection column. But such clouds are evidence of only slight sinking, from the evaporation of ice crystals falling slowly from a cirrus layer.

1943, Meteorology for Pilots, by B. C. Haynes, Senior Meteorologist, U. S. Weather Bureau, Civil Aeronautics Bulletin No. 25, 2nd edition.

The illustration at top of next page shows more detail than the one above, but lacks a net gain for understanding. Chapter 13, Thunderstorms, 17 pages, includes

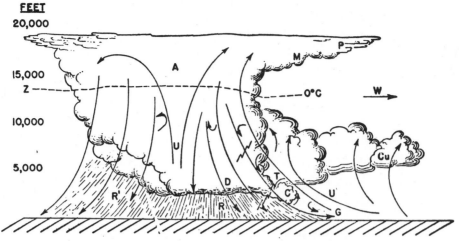

Figure 77.—Vertical section through a "thermal" type thunderstorm.

Figure 77 illustrates the air currents in a typical air mass thunderstorm. *A.*—anvil; *C*—roll cloud; *C_u*—advance cumulus clouds; *D*—descending air; *G*—strong gusts; *M*—mammatocumulus; *P*—protruding portion of anvil (false cirrus); *R*—primary rain or hail area; *R'*—secondary rain; *T*—severe turbulence; *U*—updraft; *W*—wind direction; *Z*—zero isotherm.

classification according to cause, theories of condensation, hints for forecasting, comments from pilots, guidelines for determining flight paths, a section on tornadoes, and two pages of test questions. Haynes warns of turbulence, with emphasis on upward velocities (probably exceeding 200 mph in severe storms).

The next sentence states, "The strong upcurrents alone are not hazardous but when they are associated with adjacent down drafts [two words], exceeding-[ly] high velocity gradients are created."

Earlier he had written, "The rising currents within the cloud are associated with *compensating down currents* [italics added] both within and without the cloud. Vorticity results and visible curls are produced . . ." No mention of the evaporation factor which Humphreys emphasized.

The recent attention to thunderstorm downdrafts is focused on the hazard of aircraft landing during a "downburst," which is more violent than the older concept of "first gust" preceding the leading edge of a thunderstorm.

Haynes included a topic of "Encountering Wind Shift on Landing," which obviously pertains to the jazzy new label for thunderstorm downdrafts. But

the fledgling technology of meteorology had not yet comprehended the physics of the evaporative cooling of air after it sank below the base of the cloud, after it was initially cooled by chilly rain falling from colder regions above, and partly dragged down by friction of descending rain-drops. Humphreys had the idea, but others were slow to develop it. Haynes wrote:

One of the most disconcerting and often dangerous phenomenon that pilots have to deal with is the wind-shift line that crosses the landing area just as a landing is being effected.

A wind shift is said to occur when the wind suddenly changes direction. As an example the wind may be south and suddenly change to west or it may be west and suddenly change to north. Usually the wind change occurs along a line which is followed on a weather map as a front or "wind-shift line" as it is often called.

The cross wind and added tail-wind effects are the most dangerous and may produce disastrous results if the pilot is caught unaware. The effect of changing of the wind to a tail-wind component during landing is to experience a sudden loss of lift, which may force the plane down outside of the airport or . . . there is a danger of striking obstructions near the edge of the field. . . The drop may damage the landing gear. The cross-wind effect is always dangerous. . .   [end of quote]

Note the offhand inclusion of "added tail-wind effects" at beginning of third paragraph (the first two are completely quoted). Until that addition, the "most disconcerting and dangerous phenomenon" had been the wind-shift line which "crosses" the landing at a 90⁰ angle.

A tail-wind during landing is a 180⁰ *reversal* of surface wind. My quote covers the first 15 lines of Haynes' topic. In the remaining 32 lines the idea of tail-winds was not mentioned again. He did advise that "In the northern hemisphere the direction of a cold front wind-shift is always from your right if you are landing into the wind before it has shifted." (In 1943 synoptic meteorology was blooming, and I was in the enlisted forecasting school at Chanute Field.)

In the diagram on page 72 there are 7 downward arrows within the cloud, all associated with falling rain, and only 3 upward arrows in the main cloud. Everyone knew thunderstorms were a convective (upward) type. How could a downward circulation produce so much rain, and a cloud base at 2500 ft above ground?

Maybe this offhand "added effect" was the first notice to the aviation world that meteorologists were really pondering the mystery of thunderstorm downdrafts.

Haynes is listed as author. One may guess the final editing of a book published by the government involved more than one individual. This reference seems to prove that some pilots already knew of such hazard before 1943. Maybe this was a turning point in scientific research. My unfolding of the Downburst Mystery continues.

1944. Descriptive Meteorology by Hurd C. Willett, Associate Professor at M.I.T., 310 pages, copyright by Academic Press, Inc. He stated it was not a reference textbook. I found no mention of "downdrafts," but after becoming involved in fireweather forecasting in 1949 in Oregon, I admired his expansion of the concept of evaporative cooling of air below the cloud base, as per Humphreys (1940). This quote is edited for brevity:

> The feature of the thunderstorm circulation that distinguishes it is *the cooling by evaporation of the air between the cloud base and the ground* in the area of falling precipitation. The cooling which is possible depends on the relative humidity of the air [under the cloud, which] is almost proportional to the vertical distance beneath the cloud base. This accounts for the very large fall in temperature at the ground [under] convective showers in the semi-arid western mountains where thundershowers [have] an exceptionally high cloud base in quite dry air.
>
> Sometimes all of the rain is evaporated before it reaches the ground. [These] conditions occasionally start forest fires [from] lightning. Since the shower is caused [partly] by strong heating at the ground [also by the arrival of high level moisture which replenishes the comparatively tall narrow convective cloud by entrainment] the surface air is usually dry enough [to cause] a sharp drop in temperature at the ground.

1944   General Meteorology, by Horace R. Byers, ScD, 645 pages. Copyright by McGraw-Hill Book Company, Inc. (Well worn after hundreds of hours of my striving to learn how weather works.) Haynes (1943) had begun his chapter on thunderstorms by classifying the types according to presumable causes: air mass, frontal, orographical, and horizontally converging currents.

Byers began his 28-page chapter: "A thunderstorm is no different from an ordinary convection shower, except that it is accompanied by thunder and lightning." He included a small simplified sketch of a convective cloud with almost vertical streaks of rain underneath, but with no streamlines of wind within the cloud, probably to distance himself from the assumptions of earlier writers. He was a leader in the 1946-1947 U.S. Thunderstorm Project, reported in a federal publication in 1949.

Foreword

Important advances have been made during recent years in man's knowledge of the weather. Much of this new knowledge is of direct concern to flying.

Ten years ago the term "clear-air turbulence" was almost unknown. The jet stream—a narrow band of very high speed winds near the tropopause that offers astonishing tail winds—had scarcely been penetrated. Recent years have brought forth new knowledge about aircraft icing. A two-year project of planned probing flights into thunderstorms has revealed knowledge about the structure of thunderstorms and their hazards that previously was hardly more than theory and speculation.

These and many other developments, plus the changes that have been necessary in weather reporting methods to meet the needs of the aviation industry, have finally made the old CAA Bulletin No. 25, "Meteorology for Pilots," published in 1943 obsolete. This completely revised edition gives the pilot the authoritative source of information needed to prepare for the CAA pilot qualifications examinations and, more important, to help the pilot cope safely with the weather problems he encounters. An attempt has been made to keep the technical treatment as nonmathematical as possible and to relate physical concepts to the pilot's experience.

"Pilots' Weather Handbook" was written as a joint project of the U. S. Weather Bureau's Training Section and Domestic Aviation Section. The actual writing was done by J. T. Lee, Meteorologist and Training Specialist, and Carl M. Reber, Meteorologist and Commercial Pilot. However, many individuals gave of their time and effort toward the completion of the book. Major contributors, each a specialist in a particular field of Weather Bureau operations, were:

LeRoy Clem, Project Leader, Clear-air Turbulence Research;

DeVer Colson, Project Leader, Standing Wave Research;

Dwight B. Kline, Weather Bureau-NACA Icing Research Project;

Conrad Mook, Research Meteorologist;

Parke Starke, Observational Procedures Specialist; and

Jack C. Thompson, Meteorologist in Charge, U. S. Weather Bureau Station, Los Angeles, California

Recognition for contribution to the chapter on Sailplane Weather is given to glider pilot Nicholas Goodheart, Commander, H. M. R. N., and to Colonel Floyd J. Sweet, U. S. A. F., and Chairman, Technical Committee, Soaring Society of America.

All material for the book was reviewed by a special committee of Weather Bureau personnel experienced in aviation, consisting of: D. M. Little, Assistant Chief of Bureau; B. C. Haynes, who was Acting Chief, Station Facilities and Meteorological Observations Division; R. H. Simpson, Aviation Weather Specialist; Arthur C. Peterson, Chief, Domestic Aviation Section; and George F. Brewster, Weather Bureau Pilot and Chief of the Field Inspection Program.

All material was reviewed from the training value aspect by A. V. Carlin, Chief of the Weather Bureau's Training Section. Review for technical accuracy was done by James E. Caskey, Chief of the Weather Bureau's Editorial Section, and editing by Ira L. Smith, of the CAA Office of Aviation Information. Illustrations were prepared by the Staff of the Weather Bureau's Daily Map Unit.

1954. Pilot's Weather Handbook, C.A.A. Technical Manual No. 104, 143 pages. This was an exhilarating time. The ordeals of the Great Depression, World War II, and the Korean War had ended (with respect to calendar). The U. S. was the world's superpower, and television had arrived. Aviation had invented the third dimension of the atmosphere. People were being introduced to the "science" of meteorology. This obscure individual had just abandoned a GS-7 job in the Weather Bureau, partly to avoid mental breakdown, and partly to live in the new world.

The world of politics also expanded. This revised handbook for pilots was not written by one author, or two or three. See photocopy of Forward on facing page. Here was a modern popular text, dramatically illustrated, for only $1.25. Even for $50 I wouldn't sell my only copy.

I was fascinated then, and also now. My gadfly comments in this 1994 book are not disparagement of meteorology; they are an effort to develop it faster, to explain the obstacles erected by selfish elitists, and suggest ways to work around them. That is the path of progress since the beginning of civilization.

Most of the contents of this 1954 book I believed, or tried to understand. In 1994 I'm offering useful revisions, and warning you of the unnecessary barriers ahead.

There is much talk nowadays about the forthcoming information highway. But many of the older roads are also good, such as the invention of oral language, the written word, the printing press, and the U.S. postal service. Twelve years ago I could not have published this book. Also I wasn't motivated.

An older technician, like me at age 80, has a small advantage called perspective. After the 1962 Columbus Day storm in the Pacific NW (see Chapter 12), I realized my career in public forecasting had no future (explained in my 1987 book, $10.00 + $2.00, for sale by mail only).

Gradually a trend developed to separate the academic part of meteorology from the operational part. "Descriptive" texts were taken over by federal handbooks, including those prepared within, and for, the armed services. Academia took over "dynamic" meteorology, as contrasted to "synoptic" meteorology.

In my opinion, while maintaining respect for theoretical science and its preferred language of mathematics, the academic world isolated itself, to better develop its own hierarchy and access to federal appropriations. Success has been remarkable.

Academic textbooks rose beyond my ability to comprehend, or to afford for a personal library. Also, the popular books offered little in the way of technical knowledge. Retirement in 1974 provided leisure to learn more about my neglected education in economics and politics.

This book has two parts, not separate, but blended: technical, and political. Ideas should not be categorized, except maybe for convenience in filing.

The recent propaganda exaggerating the importance of Downbursts even hints a vague relationship with tornadoes. I'm guessing this is a studied part of the modernization program of the nation's public weather services. That includes huge sums for Doppler Radar installations. The flag they are waving behind the scenes, to the selfish elite, appears to display F M P M T, which is my acronym for "you can Fool Most of the People Most of the Time." That's all it takes to win on Capitol Hill.

To the power structure I plead: Only a few will read this book. Only some will agree with me. Please don't shoot. You have won the war. That is, until the part of the population that votes becomes sufficiently educated for 51% to move above the present majority that are still being fooled.

In the last part of my adult years I managed to cross the great divide. With the help of modern opportunities enough voters will eventually make it. But that may take 10 to 20 years. Wish I could be here to see it.

I hear rumors the NWS reached an appropriation of one billion dollars this fiscal year, for the first time. The total for the entire weather business: Dept. of Commerce, Military, Academia, and behind the scenes sale of weather services probably is 6 or 7 or 8 billion.

I haven't forgotten this is still a chapter about Convection. I'll limit technical discussion to what the 1954 Handbook offers about thunderstorm downdrafts, including its preliminary comments. I forgot to mention the List of Figures, page vii, has 174 entries (for 143 numbered pages). Some diagrams don't make much sense, or even any sense. Maybe those are intended to hide what the monopoly boys don't want you to see, such as their ignorance.

Paste-ins from photocopy of PWH 1954 are in 10 pt serif type. My comments are in 10 pt Helvetica, san serif.

Characteristics of Thunderstorms

This chapter deals in detail with the thunderstorm—a phenomenon which occurs when an air mass becomes unstable to the point of violent overturning.

The text and diagrams lack detail. The early-day term "overturning" tends to imply equal speeds for up and down. In the atmosphere the ups tend to be channeled, hence narrow and faster. The downs are not channeled (except when created by a plume of rain or hail) and hence much slower, and difficult to discern.

In recent years a great deal of new information on the structure of the thunderstorm has been accumulated, principally through a joint U. S. Weather Bureau—Air Force—Navy—N. A. C. A. project conducted during the years 1946–1949. Much of the descriptive material which follows has been taken from the final report on that investigation. In this project, more than 1,300 flights were made through thunderstorms at altitudes ranging from 5,000 ft. to 26,000 ft. with F–61 "Black Widow" aircraft. These investigations were carried out

in Florida and Ohio, but it is believed that the conclusions listed below are generally representative of many (but not necessarily all) thunderstorm conditions in other parts of the Nation.

When an unstable condition is formed in the atmosphere, such as may occur if the air is heated from below or forced to ascend the side of a mountain or frontal surface, the resulting buoyancy forces will tend to cause the air which is warmer than its surroundings to rise as convection currents. The thunderstorm represents a particularly severe and, for the aircraft operator, dangerous form of atmospheric convection. Here, the upward motions of air are accompanied by compensating downdrafts both within and outside of the thunderstorm cloud. These currents form separate units of convective circulation which are called thunderstorm cells. Within the cells, strong turbulence is associated with the vertical currents and is accompanied by thunder, lightning, heavy rain, and occasional hail, while the cell boundaries are characterized by relatively smooth cloudy air.

The life cycle of a thunderstorm cell may be conveniently divided into three stages, depending upon the nature of the predominating vertical motions. These stages are:

1. Cumulus stage—characterized by updrafts throughout the cell.
2. Mature stage—characterized by the presence of both updrafts and downdrafts at least in the lower half of the cell.
3. Dissipating stage—characterized by weak downdrafts prevailing throughout the cell.

When something gets too complicated, and you can't explain it, one trick is to divert attention. Divide the problem into parts or stages, and emphasize the classification. The student is happy to move on to the next topic.

On the facing page are diagrams of the life cycle of a thunderstorm, summarized from those 1,300 flights or more, by Black Widow aircraft, gee whiz. One wonders how they can be so sure of these details, from measurements made at such high speeds while penetrating those flimsy clouds consisting of liquid droplets, ice crystals, snow pellets, and maybe some hail.

Cumulus Stage

The main feature of the cumulus stage of the thunderstorm cell is the updraft.

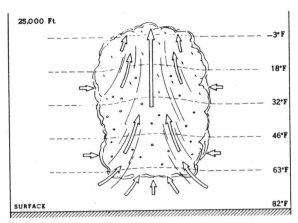

Figure 91. Idealized cross section of a thunderstorm cell in the cumulus stage.

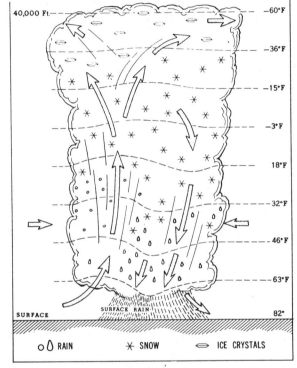

○◊ RAIN   ✳ SNOW   ⬭ ICE CRYSTALS

Figure 92. Idealized cross section of a thunderstorm cell in the mature stage.

In this stage, as a rule, the maximum vertical speed occurs at higher altitudes late in the period—speeds as great as 3,000 feet per minute are not unusual.

Figure 91 shows a vertical cross section through a thunderstorm cell in the cumulus stage of development.   The difference between the temperature of the cloud and the surrounding air increases with time, reaching a maximum at the end of the cumulus stage of development.

At the beginning of the "cumulus" stage, the amount of visible water and the size of the cloud droplets is small, but these continually increase with time as the cloud develops.

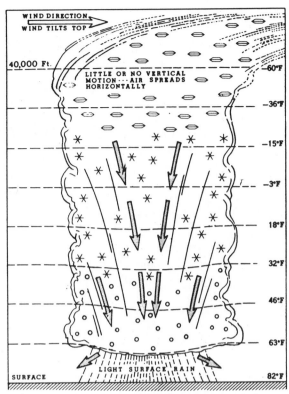

Figure 93. Idealized cross section of a thunderstorm cell in the dissipating stage.

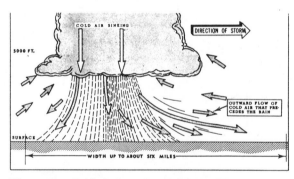

Figure 97. Cold air dome beneath a thunderstorm cell in the mature stage. Arrows represent deviation of wind flow. Dashed lines indicate rainfall.

The cumulus stage of development varies considerably in the length of time required for the change from a small cumulus cloud to the time when the mature stage begins.

Mature Stage

With the continued updraft during the cumulus stage, more and more vapor condenses; the water droplets and ice crystals within the cloud become more numerous and increase in size. When the size of individual drops or ice particles increases to such an extent that their weight can no longer be supported by the existing updraft, they begin to fall out of the cloud. The beginning of precipitation at the earth's surface indicates the change from the cumulus to the mature stage of development.

Simultaneously with this event, certain significant changes take place in the circulation pattern within the thunderstorm cell. In a portion of that region where formerly an updraft was found, there now occurs a movement of air in the opposite direction. The downdraft, which at first is found only in the middle and lower levels of the cell, gradually increases in horizontal and vertical extent throughout the duration of this stage of the thunderstorm development.

Figure 92 shows a vertical cross section through an average thunderstorm cell at about the middle of its mature stage. In general, the speed of the remaining updraft still increases with altitude and some of the strongest updrafts in thunderstorm cells occur early in the mature stage, when speeds may locally exceed 6,000 feet per minute. The downdraft speed is more nearly constant with altitude, except near the earth's surface where the ground affords a solid barrier which necessitates a gradual decrease in downward speeds in the lower 5,000 feet. Above this lower region, downdraft speeds of 2,000 feet per minute are not uncommon.

The moving air of the downdraft does not come to rest at the surface of the earth, but spreads out as would any fluid striking a solid barrier. This produces one of the most characteristic of the surface phenomena associated with thunderstorms—the gusty surface wind that flows outward from the area of rainfall. The onset of this horizontal outflow is usually marked by a sharp increase in windspeed, occasionally to destructive force, accompanied by a sharp drop in surface temperature and a sharp rise in pressure.

The region of the thunderstorm cell where temperatures are lower than the surrounding air grows larger and more intense during the mature stage. As illustrated in figure 92, this cold portion of the cloud occurs in the downdraft area, with the lowest temperatures accompanying the strongest downdrafts. The gradually decreasing updraft is still associated with temperatures warmer than the environment.

At this stage, rain is found in the lowest levels, snow and rain mixed in the middle levels, and usually only snow at the highest levels. With very strong updrafts, however, the liquid water may be carried up to very high sections of the cloud before it can freeze. It is during the mature stage that hail occurs, although hail

is not found in every storm.

Heavy turbulence is encountered in both the cumulus and mature stages of a thunderstorm cell, but it is during the mature stage that it reaches a maximum. It is strongest in the regions of maximum updraft and downdraft speeds, with definite zones of decreased turbulence between adjacent cells. It is least severe in the lowest altitudes, but even there heavy turbulence may be experienced at some points.

As the rainfall continues throughout the mature stage of the cell, the downdraft area increases in size until, in the lower levels, it extends over the entire storm cell. This is considered to be the end of the mature stage, which usually lasts for a period of 15 to 30 minutes, but may, in an extreme case, last much longer.

Dissipating Stage

During the dissipating stage the downdraft spreads over the entire area of the cell at successively higher and higher altitudes. This process continues until the entire cell contains only downdrafts, or air with little or no vertical motion. As the downdraft expands, the updraft is gradually cut off. This results in a progressively smaller amount of liquid water being released, a reduction of the amount of precipitation, and, finally, the gradual stopping of thunderstorm activity.

Figure 93 shows the principal characteristics of the thunderstorm cell in the dissipating stage during the period when the downdraft is still well defined. As the downdraft decreases, temperatures within the cell slowly return to values near to those of the environment, precipitation diminishes, and the wind near the surface assumes a direction and speed more nearly the same as that in neighboring areas not affected by the storm.

Other Modifying Effects

The preceding discussion of the stages through which the thunderstorm cell passes in its life cycle presents a somewhat idealized situation in which a single cell develops and goes through a life cycle without additional cells developing in the adjacent area. While this frequently happens, it is seldom that such a single cell attains a height comparable to a cell that is one of a group; and consequently, the weather phenomena—such as rainfall, draft speeds, and high surface winds—associated with the single cell, are usually less intense than those associated with storms which develop as members of a group. As the multi-cellular storms develop, it has been found that each successive cell attains a greater height than did previous ones.

Where there is a marked increase with height in the horizontal wind speed, the mature stage of the cell may be prolonged. In addition, the increasing speed of wind with height produces considerable tilt to the updraft of the cell and, in fact, to the visible cloud itself. Thus, the falling precipitation passes through only a small section of the rising air; it falls thereafter through the relatively still air next to the updraft, perhaps even outside the cell boundary. Accordingly, since the drag of the falling water is not imposed upon the rising currents within the thunderstorm cell, the updraft can continue until its source of energy is exhausted. The cell may then dissipate without going through a period when the principal vertical motion is downward. Furthermore, precipitation falling from the tilted cloud may produce a downdraft, or an area of sinking air, in the clear air outside the cloud boundary.

I have reproduced all of the text from PWH 1954 about the life cycle of a thunderstorm. A revised edition with a new title, *Aviation Weather* was published in 1965. Another revised edition in 1975 was completely rewritten by new authors, "streamlining it into a clear, concise, and readable book." In both books many illustration are in dramatic color. However, details in printed language, which students formerly read, are increasingly superseded by pictures.

My copy of 1975 Aviation Weather, reprinted 1988, was purchased for $8.50 on 3-1-93 at a Government Printing Office Bookstore. The preface states: "The text will remain valid and adequate for many years." A companion manual, Aviation Weather Services, Advisory Circular 00-45C, now supplements Aviation Weather. It will update "changes brought about by latest techniques, capabilities, and service demands." Price $8.50 as of 3-1-93 for 1985 edition.

In my opinion, the revised editions of *Aviation Weather* since 1954 have less value than the PWH of 40 years ago. They are more entertaining, but more superficial. The grade-level is lower. Since 1954 aviation has developed rapidly. Meteorology has developed slowly even at the academic level. The popular understanding of the physics of weather is deplorable, which should be obvious to any serious reader of this book.

PWH 1954 had defects also. Its jumbled text about thunderstorms is difficult to criticize in orderly fashion.

In 1994 thunderstorms seem almost as mysterious as in 1954. The multiple displays of violence are complex: turbulence with both updrafts and downdrafts, heavy precipitation (often with hail), wind gusts at ground level (some destructive), and dangerous lightning (with frightening noise).

Figures 91, 92, and 93 from 1954 PWH are copied on page 77. The writers divided thunderstorms into stages, and also into cells. The first stage shows a visible cloud with updrafts only. Figure 92 is a taller cloud, of which half is updraft, and half is downdraft. In Figure 93 the downdraft arrows are darker and 8 in number instead of 4, and no updrafts remain. Also the isotherms (about 5000 ft apart) are almost horizontal and nearly unchanged from Figures 91 and 92.

The text for the Mature Stage is long and lacking in clarity. Simultaneously with precipitation reaching the ground, *"certain significant changes take place in the circulation pattern within the thunderstorm cell. In a portion of that region where formerly an updraft was found, there now occurs a movement of air in the opposite direction."* [a downdraft]

Updrafts formerly existed everywhere in the thunderstorm cell.

"The region of the thunderstorm cell where temperatures are lower than the surrounding air grows larger and more intense. . . This cold portion of the cloud occurs in the downdraft area, with the lowest temperatures accompanying the strongest downdrafts."

The pedantic text for the mature stage is limited to description, with no physical explanation of the remarkable reversal from updrafts to downdrafts. Under the topic of Other Modifying Effects, a seemingly offhand clue appears, about precipitation falling from a cloud tilted by horizontal winds aloft. (See final paragraph of paste-in at top of left column.)

Rather than a piece-meal criticism, I will abbreviate my understanding of how precipitation creates downdrafts within a cloud which was created by rising air. The air floats upward because of buoyancy, because heat energy has spread the molecules apart, decreasing density. Atmospheric pressure decreases upward. Molecules spread still farther apart if expansion is adiabatic. Ordinary temperature, OT, decreases as P decreases. RH increases, condensation begins. Latent heat is released, partly offsetting adiabatic cooling, as per moist adiabats on raob graph. Rain, or ice crystals (snow, hail) have much more density than air, hence always lack buoyancy. Their rate-of-fall to the earth depends on the speed of any updraft, just like headwinds hinder aircraft, called "drag."

The drag acts both ways; the updraft is hindered by the precipitation. But the motion of air also depends on other factors. The original factor was the lower density of the updraft compared to the surrounding air. The latent heat process also acts both ways. The moist adiabats on page 45 assume RH remains 100%, with condensation continuing during upward motion of air.

If air motion is downward, meaning P is increasing, OT increases, RH decreases, and many raindrops or ice crystals present in downdraft will evaporate. Heat becomes latent (disappears), meaning OT of downdraft follows moist adiabat on nomogram. If surrounding air has a lapse rate at or near dry adiabatiac, one big reason for the conversion from ascent to descent is obvious.

Another good reason exists. Rain or snow, condensed amid cold OT aloft, and with drops or crystals having enormous mass compared to an equal volume of air, is a refrigerant, like ice in ice water.

The drag of falling precipitation is probably a minor factor for causing downdrafts, and even this factor disappears when the speeds of each become equal. Refrigeration seems much more important. Evaporation is a strong factor if the cloud base is high, and the air below is dry. This is common in the western states in summer. The source of water vapor is mostly from Gulf of Mexico, arriving at middle and high elevations. The thunderstorms are relatively slender, but lightning often reaches the ground, even when cloud bases are at 10,000 ft MSL.

Downdrafts seem complicated when described in words by using a 26-letter alphabet, but they appear logical after one learns the ABC's of weather physics. The language in this book is about the 12th grade level.

My comprehension of thunderstorms is directed at the movements of air and the vapor content. Hail and lightning are extremely important, but my understanding is already burdened. A lot of things are still unexplored, meaning the physics of the atmosphere.

(Back now to normal font) The above material discussed the 1954 PWH, and subseqent revisions entitled *Aviation Weather*. In this informal and incomplete review of source material about thunderstorms and downdrafts, the next notable

text is *Natural Aerodynamics* by R. S. Scorer, copyright by him (1958), publisher Pergamon Press. The book is about fluid mechanics. He was explaining air motion in Nature, via elementary treatment, (meaning in English rather than mathematics). He also wrote, "The dynamics of unbalanced flow are not usually given the emphasis due in ordinary textbooks." In spite of his help, there is much I still don't understand.

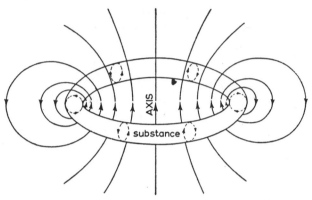

This diagram is copied from page 67. It should be considered in the public domain. He wrote, "A vortex ring is an isolated closed (or re-entrant) vortex." It clearly illustrates the idea of entrainment around the outer surface of a convection column of buoyant air. A smoke column from an active fire often seems to be turning inside out. This was the first time I ever heard of a vortex ring.

In an offhand way in another part of the book he mentioned the stretching of a vortex with a vertical axis, as in a dust devil. That was an astounding idea for me, which explained much of the mystery of tornadoes, to be discussed in the next chapter about vortexes with vertical axes.

Both of these ideas were slow to be picked up by meteorologists. My interest in the profession waned after 1963, and I retired in 1974. My interest revived in 1983 after another big windstorm in Oregon in late 1981 and a shameful coverup by the NWS. That involved old fashioned synoptic weather maps (see Chapter 12).

Because I live in a region where

thunderstorms are relatively infrequent, compared to regions east of Rocky Mountains, I have neglected to keep fully informed on research about such storms during the last 20 years. So I'm no expert, especially on the subject of downbursts. Assuming you are also a student, we can review this together. Logic, which means common sense, should be our guide.

As I write this, the newspaper this morning shows a large diagram of "How a microburst causes dangerous wind shear." An aircraft crashed at Charlotte, N.C. on July 2, 1994, 4 days ago, killing 37 people and injuring 20.

At bottom of page is a diagram to illustrate the motions created when a downdraft reaches the surface of the earth. It's copied from *Microbursts, A Handbook for Visual Identification,* by Fernando Caracena, Ronald L. Holle, and Charles A. Doswell III, 2nd edition, 1990, published by U. S. Dept. of Commerce, 42 pages, $6.00, 38 illustrations in color.

Every pilot should own a copy, and maybe every airline passenger. I bought my copy from a Printing Office Book Store in Portland. They will mail it postpaid. Maybe the government doesn't realize what I see. Here is a book filled with color photographs to identify and explain the hazard of downdrafts. I can imagine a jet liner with persons at a window seat during take-offs and landings, on watch for rain plumes emerging from the bottom of a convective cloud.

On next page is a dramatic diagram from a paper presented by Tetsuya Theodore Fujita, December 5, 1983, entitled *Andrews Air Force Base Microburst*, Satellite and Mesometeorology Research Project, Research Paper 205, 43 page photocopy.

On back of title page is an acknowledgement: "The research work presented in this paper has been sponsored by three government agencies: National Science Foundation under Grant No. ATM8109828, National Aeronautics and Space Administration under Grant No. NGR-14-001-008, and National Environmental Satellite, Data, and Information Service under Grant No. NA80AAD00001."

Dr. Fujita is a recipient of many scientific awards, and an authority on tornadoes and thunderstorm downdrafts. His research at the University of Chicago began in 1953; from 1956-1962 he was Director of Mesometeorology Project, and in 1962 he became Director of Satellite and Mesometeorology Research Project (SMRP). He was a co-principal investigator of the Northern Illinois Meteorological Research on Downbursts (NIMROD 1978), and a co-investigator in the Joint Airport Weather Studies (JAWS 1982).

The University of Chicago has a longtime interest in meteorology. During World War II it trained Weather Officer Cadets. Later, many famous researchers

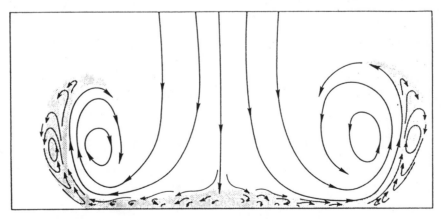

Figure 4. Cross section of a conceptual vortex ring model of a microburst (Caracena, 1982; 1987). The shaded portion is the friction boundary layer that contains vorticity opposite to that of the descending ring.

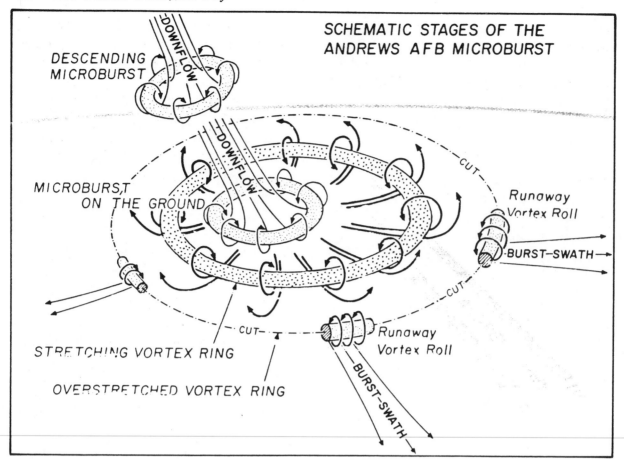

DESCENDING MICROBURST

DOWNFLOW

SCHEMATIC STAGES OF THE ANDREWS AFB MICROBURST

DOWNFLOW

MICROBURST ON THE GROUND

CUT

Runaway Vortex Roll

—BURST—SWATH→

STRETCHING VORTEX RING

CUT

OVERSTRETCHED VORTEX RING

CUT

Runaway Vortex Roll

—BURST—SWATH→

emerged from U of C, or assisted in its investigations.

In addition to the Research Paper 205 by Fujita (sent to me by a friend in early 1984) from which the above diagram is copied, I have two hardbound books purchased in late 1987 from the University of Chicago for total of $23.00 postpaid, entitled *The Downburst, Microburst and Macroburst*, Report of Projects NIMROD and JAWS, copyright 1985 by Fujita, 128 pages, full color, and *DFW Microburst,* on August 2, 1985, copyright 1986 by Fujita, 160 pages, full color. DFW means Denver-Fort Worth (TX).

The episode at Andrews Air Force Base, (Wash. D.C.) was on August 1, 1983.

The five references involving the concepts of a vortex ring and a "downburst" are recommended for the personal library of any serious student. But in my role as aging pathfinder through the maze of publications, science mixed with propaganda, I try to expose the differences as I belatedly come to understand them.

Propaganda is defined as the systematic propagation of a doctrine or cause or of information reflecting the views and interests of those people advocating such a doctrine or cause (American Heritage Dictionary, 3rd edition 1992).

Part of this book is a short course in the physics of weather. The other part is about the propaganda effort of the power structure in weather (see Preface). Each group in that structure is promoting its self interest. I'm promoting the self interest of SFU's. I hope the lopsided "contest" remains limited to civilized discussion, but any reader of newspapers is aware of quicker roads to success.

Keep in mind I am not intending personal criticism of any individual, but only the logic of his promotion. I have yielded to many convincing proofs of my temporary misjudgments.

The 1958 explanation of Scorer about a vortex ring appears much different than the 1976 model of Fujita et al.

Scorer was diagramming the non-violent eddies at the circular walls of a buoyant convection column of air or smoke. Attention was on vertical motion, either up or down, parallel to gravity, with no conversion to an *acceleration* of motion in the horizontal.

Fujita renamed a downdraft a *downburst,* probably borrowing from the connotation with the word cloudburst which needs no definition for anyone over age 12.

No one should belittle the danger of a downburst (they were known and feared at least 60 years ago), but neither should the danger be exaggerated, such as distorted claims of actual measurements, technical language inappropriate for the public, or subtle connection to the universal fear of tornadoes. I have been studying the success of the hyper self interest propaganda of the weather bureaucracy for a long time. The present crescendo for Dopplar radars has been building for a least 15 years.

One need not study fluid mechanics to understand a downburst. A mass of air becomes more dense than the air around it. Gravity pulls it downward. For varied reasons the descent rate may increase, but probably not as fast as pilots measure if using an aneroid pressure altimeter. Those are designed for semi-level flight in the Standard Atmosphere.

The downburst soon will collide with an immovable object, which will absorb most of the kinetic energy created by the conversion of its former potential energy of position aloft. The air in that downburst, excluding any fallout products, makes its own cushion near the ground. Creating the cushion temporarily stores some of the kinetic energy lost in the collision (compression of air parcels).

Such compression creates a horizontal pressure gradient in all directions, redirecting motion from downward to outward, the well known gust front even before the book by Humphreys in 1940.

Perhaps there was too much emphasis on the movement of the thundercloud, which did increase the gusts in that direction.

The idea of outward gusts from site of impact, seen as a horizontal ring, is logical and also the idea of eddies spreading outward. A cross section view of an eddy shows circular motion around a horizontal axis. If eddies develop in all horizontal directions, the axis of each whirl in cross section blends into a circular ring in the horizontal. But such circulation is opposite to the ring of Scorer (1958) which rises in the center and is non-violent because it doesn't stretch significantly. Fujita's ring sinks in the middle and is violent because it stretches.

The diagram on the opposite page (82), is copied from page 34 of Fujita's SMRP Research Paper 205. That event in 1983 included a peak gust of 150 mph which he reported as the strongest microburst wind ever documented.

Perhaps there is an oversight in the documentation. That microburst was accompanied by very heavy rain and hail up to 1/4 inch. A propeller anemometer recorded a trace-line with a brief peak at 150 mph during the "fallout" (a more accurate term than precipitation, which is borrowed from chemistry).

Liquid water, snow pellets, and hail have enormous density compared to air. The propeller was bombarded with projectiles of ice and liquid water. It was not merely measuring the kinetic energy of moving air, for which it was designed.

Maybe the violence of the outflow from a downburst has been exaggerated. Maybe the stretching of Fujita's vortex ring is a weak theory. Below the diagram he divided his description into four stages, reprinted in italics here:

During the 1st stage, the microburst was descending.... The 2nd stage was the contact stage in which the microburst hit the ground.... During the 3rd stage, the vortex ring was stretching rapidly.... The wind speeds reached their peak values during this stage.

When the vortex ring overstretched, the ring was cut into small vortex rolls called in this paper "runaway vortex roll." It is speculated that such a fast-moving vortex with horizontal axis could induce damaging winds beneath its path.

I don't know where Fujita first learned about a vortex ring. Everyone knows about an ordinary vortex with a vertical axis, as in a dust devil or tornado. It was from R. S. Scorer (1958) that I learned about the stretching of that vortex as the cause of intensification. His introduction of a vortex ring seemed merely an explanation of entrainment in an updraft.

The idea of horizontal rolls of air, with horizontal axes, which often develop because of ground friction, and also aloft between layers of air moving in different directions or speeds, seemed quite natural. But those axes were straight, not curved.

All students should recognize the difference between a horizontal axis in a circular loop with no beginning or end, and a vertical axis with two open ends.

The diagram below is copied from the same Research Paper 205, from page 28. It also appears on page 14 of *The Downburst*. The caption says:

Similarity between "Tornado" and "Microburst." The inflow wind in a

tornado increases the wind speed during its approach toward the vortex core with the vertical vortex axis. The downflow in a microburst increases the wind speed during its approach toward the vortex core with horizontal vortex axis. In both storms, the stretching action of the vortices provides the mechanism for the spin-up rotation.

The spin-up rotation is ambiguous to me. This two-dimension diagram, even when drawn in oblique perspective, shows no upward motion for the tornado, although we know the air spirals upward, lengthwise along the axis, in a presumably symmetrical pattern.

In Fujita's pattern there is no spiral motion lengthwise along the axis. The air speeds up while moving outward, and slows down while moving inward. The only part of the whirl ascending is the outer half. The inner half is descending. The whirl itself was created instantly, in a doughnut shape. It is turning inside out, around an axis which remains near the ground. The bottom is braked by friction.

Keep in mind that the area of a circle (such as the area involved in the outflow from the impact site) increases much faster than the circumference (79% of the square of the diameter), which in this event provides rapid dispersion of kinetic energy.

A tornado is an inverted funnel, in

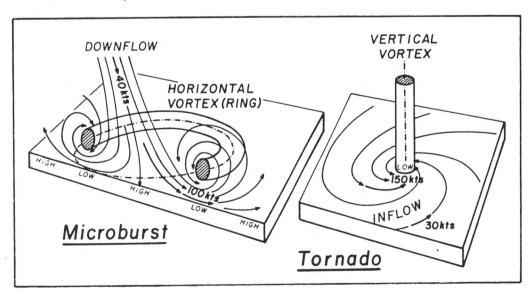

which individual parcels of air already rotating slowly around a vertical axis because of their curved horizontal path near ground level, converge toward an updraft. The rotation increases as the small multiple axes merge into a single axis. Many slow rotations become one intense rotation.

In a downburst the rotation of the "ring" is not the *combining* of similar small whirls for intensification. It's a mechanism for *dispersion* of concentrated kinetic energy at the impact site. There is no cohesion in the horizontal vortex. A better image is a doughnut, sliced into segments, each like a wheel, each rolling away from the site on its own axle (axis) with *"backspin"* ! Each wheel disappears in the distance as its individual angular momentum spreads over the landscape.

There is more in this review than Fujita's version of physics. I'm not a scientist. But I'm becoming more expert in recognizing self-serving promotion by the power structure in meteorology.

Dr. Fujita is very successful. He also has a great sense of humor. In *The Downburst*, page 104, he even included a picture of an anteater at the zoo, in color.

Not only are weather events sometimes impressive, but so is the ingenuity of the tabloid journalists and graphic artists working in the Halls of Science. They are the wizards of the "Ah"s murmured by the crowds of awe-struck taxpayer tourists entering those Halls via television, radio, books, magazines, and theme parks.

On page 75 I referred to an imaginary propaganda flag being waved by the power structure in meteorology (PSM), displaying the acronym FMPMT. As a background image we ought to add the outline of a Dopplar radardome.

Anyone reading this book is aware of the vigorous campaign called the Modernization and Restructuring Demonstration (MARD) of the NWS. The NWS is under the National Oceanic and Atmospheric Administration (NOAA) in the Dept. of Commerce. The national implementation plan (NIP) for MARD, March 1990 edition, 164 pages, lists 113 sites for Dopplar radars for NWS and 24 supplemental sites for Dept. of Defense. Work is underway at a site 23 miles northwest of my home in Portland.

The NWS says the cost of each unit is $2.5 million. Hence the cost for 137 units will be $342,500,000. That doesn't include future costs for operation and maintenance.

The propaganda story in our local paper, planted of course by the NWS, promised readers the new radar would increase lead time for tornado and winter storm warnings, improve detection of severe thunderstorms at sea and ashore, [plus] earlier, more accurate flood warnings using current ground saturation together with predictions of additional precipitation, and improved weather advisories and routing around hazardous weather for pilots and mariners.

We can hardly wait.

In Research Paper 205, nearly 11 years ago, with presumably a straight face, Fujita recommended:

In order to issue timely warnings of microburst winds, it is necessary to detect microbursts during their descending stage, not after the contact stage. Since a microburst can descend directly to the runway area, it must be monitored by a Dopplar radar located 5 to 20 miles outside the airport. The author urgently recommends that a Dopplar radar be placed at a strategic location in the Washington D.C. area, capable of scanning Andrews AFB, Washington National, Baltimore, and Dulles Airports. Meanwhile, the helicopter route between the White House and Andrews AFB should be monitored by such a Doppler radar.

We gotta safeguard those gold mines in Washington D.C. (End Chapter 10)

Chapter 11 Vortexes

In earlier days this category was simply called whirlwinds. Nowadays, instead of the singular form vortex, we also have dust devil, fire whirl, waterspout, tornado, cyclone, hurricane, typhoon, and probably some others. Some academic types like to talk about vorticity, defined mathematically as the curl of the velocity vector, which is the product of the velocity and the del operator.

I will describe my understanding of air rotating around a vertical axis. Although there are countless everyday examples of rotation, the elementary physics of rotary motion is a neglected subject. Part of the neglect is the difficulty of drawing simple diagrams of rotation.

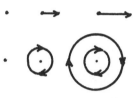

If a tiny dot represents a particle of mass in space, linear motion can be indicated by an arrow, with obvious direction in the plane of the paper, and speed suggested by its length. If the dot merely represents a point in space it's meaningless to consider rotation. Strictly speaking, a point only has position, but no dimension. If the dot represents a small thin disk on the paper, rotation can be suggested by a circular arrow, but the rate of rotation is unknown. A longer circular arrow implies a larger disk.

Two concentric arrows reveal the longer path of a particle on the rim compared to one nearer the axis of rotation (a straight line into the page). The rate of rotation is the same for both.

It's handy to think of the *plane of rotation*, in which the curved motion can be displayed (clockwise or otherwise). But always remember the *axis of rotation*. It's useful to draw patterns on paper to illustrate an idea, somewhat like arranging letters of the alphabet in printed language. We need only to guard against illustrations which deceive.

A vertical vortex is a whirling *and rising* column of air, not a solid disk. A cross-section diagram shows curving motion but it fails to reveal the "spiral staircase" of the upward component of motion. That's the motion described by language--the stretching of the vortex.

There is another common image to help understanding--the small whirlpool above the drain in a kitchen sink or bathroom washbasin. Gravity is removing water from one end of that vortex, the output end which is the sewer pipe. We look down on the input end, where the whirlpool is created, an example of converging currents of a liquid.

All atmospheric vortexes, especially the local vigorous ones, are similar, except they are transporting buoyant air upward, instead of heavy water downward. Gravity energizes both systems.

The concept of *motion* pertains to the movement of a particle of mass from one place to another place. The simplest form of motion is the shortest distance from point A to point B, straightline motion or linear motion. Another simple form is motion in a perfect circle, rotary motion. If the curvature varies, the idea becomes more complicated. Such motion is *curvilinear* and may have random characteristics.

If a particle of mass is "at rest," it has no motion. But all mass always has *inertia* which means it will continue it's present motion, zero or more, unless kinetic energy is added or subtracted. This describes only the visible form of kinetic energy, not internal molecular motion.

Any motion of mass, starting at zero, begins as linear motion in a specific direction. Any change in direction results from a *deflective* force, meaning a force with a component in some direction other than forward or backward. If the deflective force is constant, the motion becomes circular, because the radius is constant. A diagram can illustrate some of the differences between linear motion and rotation.

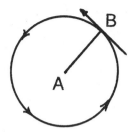

Let A be the center of a disk rotating counterclockwise. At B on the rim is a tangent perpendicular to the radius. The arrow represents the *instantaneous* direction of motion at B, which is constantly changing as B moves in a circle.

A particle of mass at B (assume it has shape of a tiny arrow almost too small to see) will rotate once during each rotation of the disk. At the same time it will move around the circumference. If the length of the circumference is divided into segments too small to see, each will have microscopic length. In language slightly less precise than mathematical symbols, the arrow moves linearly in each segment, for the total distance around the circle. Rotary motion is superimposed on linear motion. We can call it *curvilinear motion.*

Another part of comprehension is to remember the circumference of a circle is 3.1416 times the diameter. Speed is distance divided by time. RPM is a common reference to revolutions per minute. All particles in a rotating disk have the same rpm, but those at the rim are moving much faster, along a curved path, than those near the axis of rotation.

As a bizarre example, if you drive a stake in the ice one foot from the North pole, in 24 hours it will move 6.2832 ft in a small circle. During the same time, a stake in the ground at the Equator will move 24,875 miles (assuming a mean radius of 3959 miles) not counting orbit of earth around the sun. Make that about 26,000 miles. Earth is not an exact sphere.

Keeping in mind our goal involves revolving air, temporarily we will move from plane geometry to solid geometry, meaning volume instead of distance and area. Instead of a thin flat disk, consider a rotating cylinder. (Also, I'm not a graphic artist. This is a low budget show.)

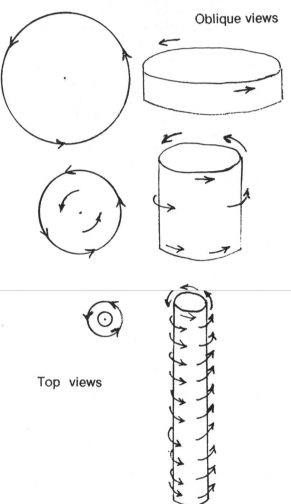

Oblique views

Top views

Starting with a flat cylinder rotating slowly, and assuming the kinetic energy of the composite linear and rotational motions within such volume remains constant while its shape elongates, the rpm of the vertical cylinder will increase. The curvilinear speed of the outer rim will greatly increase.

This is what R. S. Scorer meant in 1958 in *Natural Dynamics,* page 180. He was describing the stretching of a vortex in dust devils. The idea seems to apply to any fluid vortex, including tornadoes. What difference does size make?

So far this discussion of rotation in vortexes presented elementary diagrams in two dimensions, suggesting a thin disk, and oblique views of a solid cylinder which elongated, something like an event during an old-fashioned "taffy pull." The volume remains constant, but the dimensions can be revised. Such is easy with a column of air, either stretching (usually upward), or spreading out (usually downward).

Air is gaseous, of very low density. Its molecules can move in response to very small forces compared to liquid or solid masses.

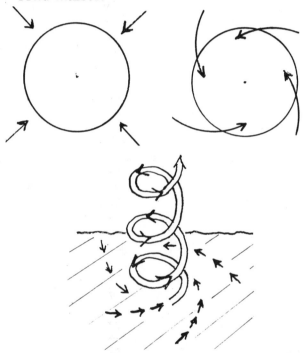

What makes the air in a vortex rotate, and why does the vortex stretch?

Keep in mind the water whirlpool of the sink drain. That vortex drains water downward by the force of gravity. An atmospheric vortex is an upside-down whirlpool. Buoyant air rises over a "hot spot," but gravity still is in control. Nearby air, not quite as buoyant, is converging horizontally to push it up. Remember Archimedes and why boats float.

With air converging from all directions at ground level, it's virtually impossible to keep converging streamlines aimed exactly dead-center into the bottom of a convection column. Even one streamline off-center would deflect the others. Counter-clockwise curvature is almost certain to appear in the spiral inflow. Even stagnant air at the surface is rotating slowly because the earth is rotating. Also a weak surface Low may have already developed over the warmer area.

When such units of rotation begin to merge (units of both single molecules and tiny parcels of air) the rotation is quickly intensified, a concentration of rotation and kinetic energy (but not of molecules). The kinetic energy of motion will not disappear until it is opposed by some equal force. (Usually there are no thick brick walls handy.)

The curving motion is deflected into a spiral of shorter radius. But that spiral path is now a "staircase," in which the curving motion is accelerating *very rapidly*, both horizontally and vertically. Think of it as Nature's vacuum cleaner. All such machines only produce partial vacuums. Man-made machines have internal fans. Nature uses centrifugal force to produce a partial vacuum in the stretching vortex.

Centrifugal force is ~~exactly~~ *nearly* the same as the Coriolis Force explained earlier. It exists in all rotating masses, but we usually are not aware of it in solid objects like wheels, where centrifugal force on one side is balanced by an opposite centrifugal force on the other side. One awareness is when our car slides off the road during a tight turn with too much speed. It shows in a laundry spin dryer, and sparks from a grinding wheel.

A very old example is a stone tied to a string, and whirled in a circle, the weapon that killed Goliath. In a vortex of air, the straight-line inertia of each molecule (free to move independently) creates a partial vacuum in the center along the axis.

If this explanation makes sense to you, why is general public perception so different? In the last part of this book

I will present an assortment of excerpts and photocopies of propaganda and "educational" material produced by the leaders of the monopoly in local weather forecasting. They are trying to reach you with their federally supported efforts. I'm trying to reach you via comparatively simple means such as a word processor, self financed book printing, U. S. Postal Service, and the goal of "free speech" supposedly supported by citizens.

The leaders are so blinded by recent successes they are indifferent to the need for better public understanding of local weather processes. Part of that indifference may be a subconscious realization that a loss of the existing monopoly would reduce their P P, power and profits.

Almost everyone is aware of the ominous report, "a tornado has touched down!" However, nearly all meteorologists admit air is rising in such vortexes. But I have never come across an explanation as to how a column of whirling air rising upward, can spread destructive winds *downward* from a cloud, to the surface of the earth where humans live, where initially all the kinetic energy of wind must be horizontal.

Are we to believe a tornado is a huge atmospheric screw boring its way downward against the upward stretching of the ascending vortex?

In Federal Meteorological Handbook No. 1, April 1988, price $13.00, page A7-8, paragraph 2.2.21: *"Funnel Cloud.* A violent, rotating column of air which does not touch the ground, usually a pendant from a cumulonimbus cloud."

Paragraph 2.2.20: *"Tornado.* A violent, rotating column of air, forming a pendant, usually from a cumulonimbus cloud, touching the ground. -- It nearly always starts as a funnel cloud, and is accompanied by a loud roaring noise."

If it looks like a duck, and quacks like a duck, it is a duck. This weather duck looks like a funnel. Propaganda is poured into the funnel from "above." It

really acts like a "duct" (sic). If our leaders are mixing the physics we can mix a metaphor once in awhile. Our mixing is for fun, theirs is for power, which also means money.

Let's think in our non-professional way, while being an SFU, or a wanna-be SFU, about the physics in this elementary book. We all have seen cumulus clouds Type 1, the little puff-balls, with flat bases where the rising air in a gentle convection column reveals the abrupt onset of condensation of water vapor. (The CCL, convective condensation level.) Such abrupt onset occurs merely from the gentle approach to the dewpoint because of the dry adiabatic lapse rate of expanding air, as it rises slowly.

If a convection column becomes a vortex worth noting, it happens where the stretching is at a maximum. Air rising from the surface initially has no vertical component. If that component accelerates quickly (violently), the logical location is near the ground, where upward motion increases from zero.

Logic seems to explain that a "funnel cloud" is merely a cumulus type convection cloud, which never reached a cooling to the dewpoint near the ground. And when it did, higher up, the updraft weakened and expanded, which also is called divergence.

If such is correct, it brings up another subject which seems to be one of the most bizarre oversights in our surprisingly primitive body of knowledge about tornadoes. *The visible base of a tornado (touching down) may contain water droplets, but mainly it contains solid particles of dust, dirt, sand, gravel, and debris.* Anything picked up by Nature's vacuum cleaner.

Now I reminisce. Although I lived in the midwest until age 25, I never saw a tornado, except the scene of one about two hours later. In Minneapolis, in the summer of 1928, or possibly late spring of 1929 (I moved to Little Rock in June), a local radio bulletin (no TV in those days) reported a tornado in the southwest part of the city. Our family of five piled into the Essex to go see the unbelievable destruction.

At least three homes in a row had essentially disappeared, except for brick foundations, and the basements below ground. Most of the nearby homes had little apparent damage. I particularly remember one vivid impression. A hedge-row across the path of the tornado was stripped of all branches and *even the bark*, with only the main stems, about 1 1/2 inches in diameter, remaining intact. The species was Osage Orange, which is part of the yew family.

I was an avid Boy Scout, learning about archery, and how to make your own bow. Yew was the choice of Robin Hood because of its toughness. flexibility, and availability. Those stems had not been broken from their roots!

But I was puzzled about the missing bark. Many years later I realized the Osage Orange hedgerow had been *sand-blasted!* Minnesota has a lot of sandy loam soil.

The missing houses? Everyone assumed they were blown away by the terrible winds of the tornado. No one explained the lack of severe damage nearby. And at age 14 I didn't know about centrifugal force, and the partial vacuum in narrow whirlwinds. Those houses exploded when the vortex passed over.

About three weeks ago the newspaper, in plot previews of the Soap Scene, for "All My Children," warned of the tornado to rip through Pine Valley, leaving some residents trapped and injured. Tad is buried alive when the Martin home *implodes !* So I watched that episode. Very dramatic. Excellent staging.

As we know, low altitude pressure is about 29.90 inches Hg, or 1000 mbs, or 14 lbs per sq inch. That is 2016 lbs per sq ft. Using arithmetic, if outside pressure suddenly decreases 10%, and the inside

pressure only has time to decrease 5% because of limited outlets for air, a 1200 sq ft house would have a total outward force of about 120,000 lbs to blow off the roof, plus an outward force of 100 lbs per sq ft to blow out the outside walls.

Another thing, friction from flying particles would generate static electricity, so I can imagine a lot of noise from miniature lightning as well as the sounds of countless impacts from airborne particles. Everyone should hope never to see a tornado, let alone be in one.

However, we should remember that tornadoes come in assorted sizes because of the variations in the factors which cause them. Those include the lapse rate in the lower atmosphere, the water vapor content, and the curvature and horizontal pressure gradient in airflow near the ground. In the Pacific Northwest there are countless whirlwinds, but only rarely does one become an obvious tornado. I'm sure conditions never attain the imbalances which occasionally occur east of the Rocky Mountains, even to the Atlantic coast.

We do have big dust devils, which can be defined as whirlwinds which develop in a shallow layer near the ground, and soon dissipate in more stable air above. I can reminisce again.

It was July 10, 1949, while westbound on U.S. Hwy 30, now I-84, rolling downhill from the Blue Mountains toward Pendleton, Oregon. Moving to my first "professional" job in Portland, in a Willys station wagon, with wife, two boys ages 3, and 9 months, loaded with luggage, ice chest, folded crib, top speed 45 on level road, sometimes low gear on hills, temperature about 95, time near noon.

Ahead I saw what first appeared to be smoke plumes from fires in a grain field. A closer view showed giant dust devils, estimated 300 ft high, and 100 ft in diameter, with 2 or 3 visible at one time. But I didn't stop to take pictures. I was straining to reach PDX that night, which succeeded after "wearing out the steering wheel" in the old, only, scenic highway in Oregon through the Columbia Gorge.

I want to alert you about possible distortion of fact in published pictures of tornadoes. I can't prove anything, but a picture in Parade Magazine, a Sunday paper supplement May 22, 1994 showed three students from U of Oklahoma tracking a nearby tornado with a portable Dopplar radar. A similar picture appeared on cover of Bulletin of AMS for December 1989. I would guess it was a big dust devil. I'm certain it helped the appropriations for the 137 Doppler radars now being installed.

Another vortex, relatively small, but *extremely intense,* is a fire whirl. They can occur with any very hot fire. As a former fireweather forecaster, and occasional instructor at fire behavior schools, I stand in awe, even though I never saw one. It's not merely the inflow of air to the vortex (fire creating "its own wind"), which supplies extra oxygen to stimulate the burning process. It's the lifting of burning brands from the fire, and spreading them around the nearby fuels not yet burning. Nature's vacuum cleaner applied to forest fires is a horrible disaster.

Fire "normally" spreads from one piece of burning fuel to another non-burning piece, such as lighting a cigarette. But when the exit end (top) of the vacuum cleaner is spraying burning matches as far as half a mile away, and in some cases known to be two miles away, the efforts of brave, straining fire fighters are overwhelmed.

An ordinary match soon burns out. Forest fuels include punky vegetative pieces, something like cork, or dry fir or pine cones. As a child I remember buying "punk" which would slowly glow for many minutes, to light firecrackers on July 4th.

Forest fuels, especially the evergreen species, contain an unusual proportion of oil. When burned, the heat produced is almost unbelievable.

The significance of "dry" fuels is seldom understood. One factor is that the major heat source is among the "fine fuels" which means needles, leaves, twigs, and small branches, both living and dead. They have a large surface area compared to total volume of each piece. That's where oxygen can make contact with the molecules of carbohydrates already heated above the ignition temperature.

But if the fuel is damp, as after the winter rain or snow season in the Pacific Northwest, the water content becomes water vapor, which crowds out oxygen, molecule for molecule. Water vapor is Nature's own fire retardant. That's why they drop water on forest fires, to temporarily decrease the oxygen and slow the rate of burning. The addition of certain chemicals (colored orange to warn fighters below and to mark areas already sprayed) also helps to hinder ignition and the subsequent rate of burning.

Ordinary convection columns carry buoyant air upward, air heated at the surface by the sun, because the lapse rate becomes greater than the dry adiabatic rate. Fire whirls develop when the lapse rate above the fire becomes enormous, perhaps 1000 or 1500 or maybe even 2000 times the dry adiabatic rate. There is no mystery about fire creating its own wind, especially its own local tornado, which will endure as long as the fire burns like a blow torch.

That's why I included a little lecture about the physics of fire, which in turn depends very much on the physics of the atmosphere.

The next chapter will return to my favorite subject of synoptic meteorology, introduced in the first two chapters of the book. It will present details of the strongest extratropical storm to affect the Pacific Northwest since the one in 1880. Little about that one is known. I've studied the 1962 storm more than anyone. Some of the story has remained untold, until now.

Chapter 12 The Columbus Day Storm

The picture on the cover is a rare photograph of an uncommon optical phenomenon called anticrepuscular rays. The word crepuscule comes from Latin, meaning dusky or dark, defined in English as twilight. Most people have seen the occasional crepuscular rays after a sunset, looking toward their source, the sun.

The rays seem to diverge because of perspective, usually disappearing even before reaching overhead. Sunlight is reflected, not refracted as with rainbows, from tiny particles of dust or water droplets in the field of view.

This picture was taken across the city of Portland, Oregon a few minutes before the onset of destructive winds on October 12, 1962. But the rays are *converging toward the eastern horizon!* The sun is *behind* the camera, temporarily appearing during a break in the clouds.

The picture was taken by Gertrude E. Myers from her high apartment window, near the campus of Portland State University, camera aimed toward ENE. She gave me a complimentary 8x10 inch enlargement. Paul Nichols, a retired engineer from KOIN-TV, and nephew of Mrs. Myers, told me the picture is not copyrighted.

I never have viewed a sky like that, because I was trembling with fear alone in the Forest Service weather office, hurrying to prepare for my weathercast in less than an hour in the studio about 2 miles distant. The wind began before I started the hectic drive.

Such "anti-" rays were caused by the enormous cloud of dust arriving from California and southern Oregon, above the shallow warm front approaching PDX, but not yet obstructing horizontal vision.

Only a few people saw this ominous display, and even fewer were aware of the impending disaster. A wind warning had been issued by the Weather Bureau at approximately 10 a.m. Pacific Daylight Time for local winds of "20 to 40 with gusts to 60." The units of speed were not mentioned. I'm quoting from indelible memory. Public forecasts were always assumed to be in miles per hour, except in knots for marine or aviation forecasts. Later, some sources claimed the forecast was in terms of knots. I never learned of any updates for that forecast. The winds began in Portland about 5:00 or 5:15 pm daylight time.

To explain necessary details here, I began seasonal employment with the Forest Service in May 1960, as a fireweather forecaster, to augment a small staff from the Weather Service on detached duty from airport station. The FS allowed me to retain the part-time freelance job with KOIN-TV as "Mr. Weatherman" from 1960 to 1968, when the FS job became year-round.

I had worked the early fireweather shift beginning at 4 a.m. PDST Oct. 12. Went home at 10 a.m. because of only 2 hours sleep the night before, and the afternoon Weather Bureau forecaster was already on duty. Returned about 3:30 p.m. to prepare for the 6 p.m. TV show. The crisis by then was worse than anything I had expected.

At 7:30 a.m., earlier that day, astounded at developing events, I had written fire weather forecasts for the 6 forests in my area of responsibility (Cascade Mtns), predicting winds (not merely gusts) of 70 mph in all 6 forests. I had never heard of any FW forecast for winds that strong. This was put on the FS teletype network to supervisors of the 19 forests of Region 6 at 7:45 a.m. Because of semitropical air moving into the storm from SW, I also expected substantial rain, bringing an end to fire season about 3 weeks early. Everyone in fire control was weary. My forecast: too much for rain, too little for wind.

Why didn't I stay on duty and update the forecast during the day? That question involves politics and concerns for one's career. I'll answer later, but first I'll review the physics of the 1962 storm. There has already been another one like it, in 1981, the path of which was about 110 miles farther off the coast of the Pacific NW. My reaction after that one was the writing of my 1987 book, still in print and which has been recertified to public domain.

During the years 1960-68, and even earlier, I worked during the off-fire season parttime and intermittently for Owen Cramer, a research meteorologist at the Pacific NW Forest and Range Experiment Station in Portland. He persuaded his Director to authorize a detailed analysis of the physics of that storm.

A semi-technical paper on the results of our project was published in the Monthly Weather Review for February 1966, Vol. 94, No. 2. The entire text (but not all of illustrations) is reproduced here.

1. INTRODUCTION

The windstorm of October 12, 1962, caused more destruction in the Pacific Northwest than any other windstorm in recorded history. In Oregon and Washington, 31 persons were killed, and property damage was estimated conservatively at $225 million to $260 million. Numerous accounts [2, 4, 7, 9, 14, 17, 18, 19] describe events during the storm, details of destruction, and maximum winds; a few include a brief synoptic description. The blowdown of timber in western Oregon and western Washington amounted to more than 11 billion bd. ft., approximately equal to the annual cut in the two States. Nearly 98 percent of the blowdown was on the west side of the Cascade Range [13]. Wind damage to forests is a serious problem in this area where the forest industry is foremost in the economy. In addition to the immediate destruction of timber, there are associated longer term problems of increased fire danger and bark beetle epidemics [1, 5, 15].

Despite their impact, the meteorological features of previous windstorms have received scant investigation. The descriptions of past storms are vague. No detailed synoptic analysis of a violent windstorm in Oregon or Washington has heretofore been published. Even statistics on maximum winds are extremely limited [20] as a result of the sparse distribution of wind gages, most of which are located in valleys protected from the strongest

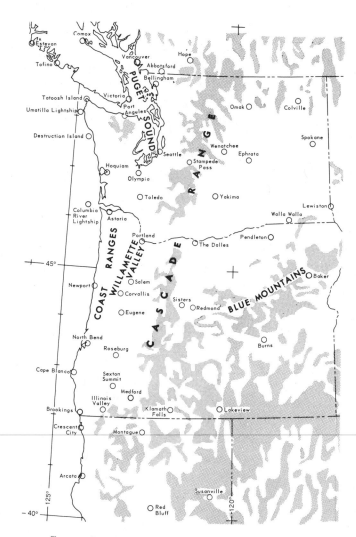

Geography of the area struck by Columbus Day storm, 1962. Shading indicates elevations over 5,000 ft.

wind. Wind records seldom include the speed of peak gusts. Furthermore, during violent storms, instruments are often damaged by flying debris or become inoperative because of power failure.

Why was the Columbus Day storm so violent? Was there some unusual characteristic that needs to be identified? Decker et al. [3] wrote: "Meteorologists will long study and puzzle over the storm's structure." They listed as unusual the double minimum of some barograph traces and the abrupt onset of high winds. They also mentioned the warming in eastern Oregon prior to the time of lowest pressure contrasted with the abrupt warming in western Oregon accompanying the pressure rise.

Immediately after the storm, forest agencies requested advice on the probable location of greatest blowdown. To locate the areas of strongest pressure gradient and to estimate the maximum wind, a series of sea level pressure maps was prepared for Oregon and Washington from airway teletypewriter data. The detailed structure of

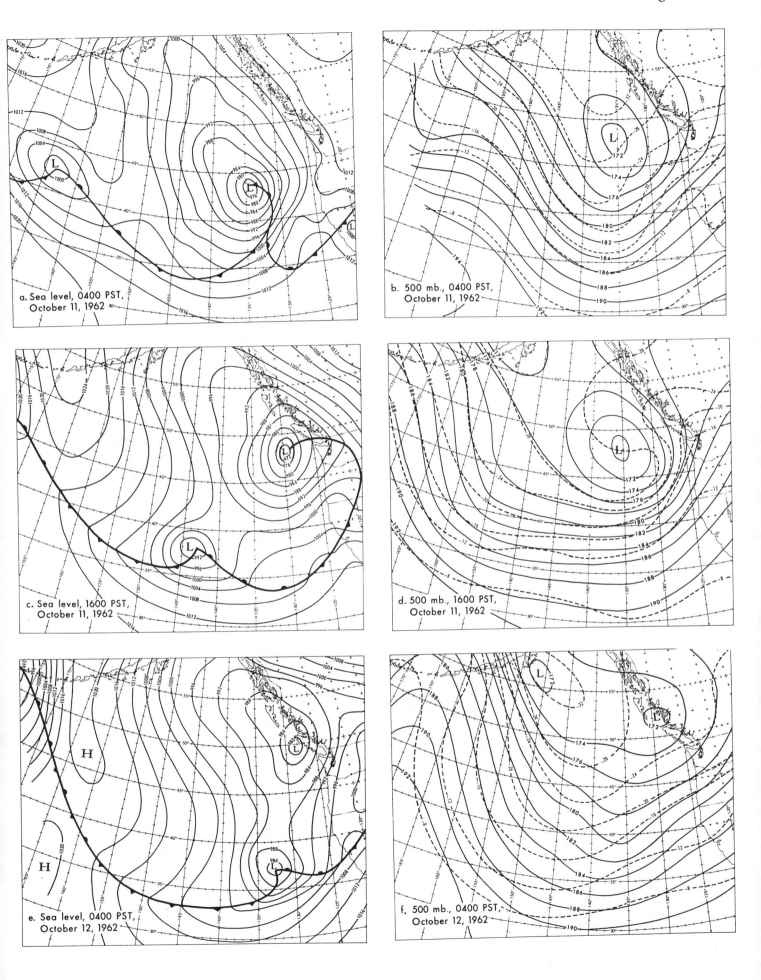

a. Sea level, 0400 PST,
October 11, 1962

b. 500 mb., 0400 PST,
October 11, 1962

c. Sea level, 1600 PST,
October 11, 1962

d. 500 mb., 1600 PST,
October 11, 1962

e. Sea level, 0400 PST,
October 12, 1962

f. 500 mb., 0400 PST,
October 12, 1962

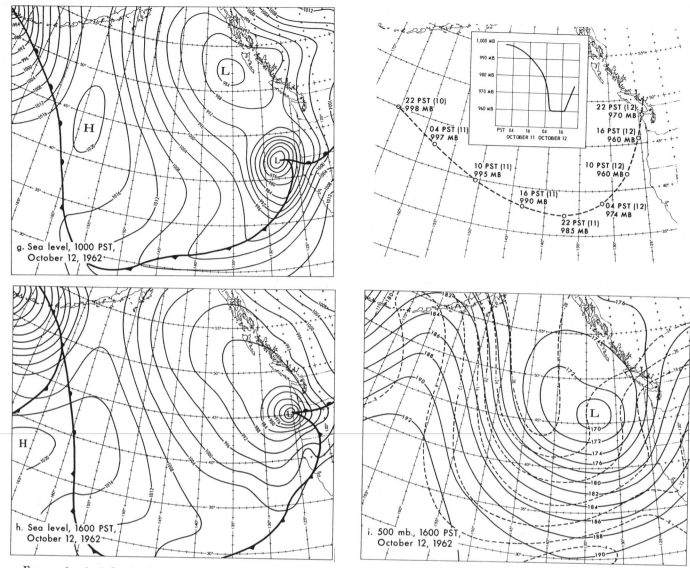

FIGURE 2.—(a–i) Sea level and upper-air charts for October 11 and 12, 1962 (PST), from microfilm by San Francisco Weather Bureau Office. (j) Path of low center across eastern Pacific (time, date, and central pressure); inset: graph of central pressure vs. time.

the storm was not clear from the preliminary analysis. Some teletypewriter reports were missing because of transmission difficulties during the storm, some data had poor fit, and the frontal positions seemed uncertain. A more detailed analysis was needed.

In addition to questions about this particular storm, there was another incentive for an intensive case study. Forest fire meteorologists have long been concerned with detailed weather conditions over rough terrain. The synoptic macroscale analysis is too coarse to meet many needs. A mesoscale network is not available. For investigative purposes, the intensive reanalysis of important cases is the best method to improve understanding of local weather structure. A reconstructed analysis can be refined by using all available data, including some not at hand for immediate analysis, such as microbarograph traces. Continuity can be improved by working backward as well as forward in time. Errors in observation can be corrected by systematic checking and comparing of data.

2. SOURCES OF DATA AND PROCEDURE

The National Weather Records Center provided photocopies of original surface and upper-air observations from both land stations and ships of the United States in the area shown in figure 1. Microbarograms from most of these stations were included. Unfortunately, original observations were not available from ships of foreign registry. The Weather Bureau Office at San Francisco provided a microfilm copy of manuscript sea level and upper-air charts [21].

Sea level maps of limited area were prepared for intervals of 1 hr. for a period of 14 hr., beginning at 1000 PST October 12, 1962. For these, pressure values were checked with microbarograph traces. Weather elements changed so rapidly that even a 10-min. error in observation time produced significant distortion of the pressure analysis. Records of observations were checked carefully, and a correction was made only if there was strong evidence that the reported value was incorrect.

(Text continues on page 100)

Sea level, 1000 PST,
October 12, 1962

Sea level, 1100 PST,
October 12, 1962

Sea level, 1200 PST,
October 12, 1962

Sea level, 1300 PST,
October 12, 1962

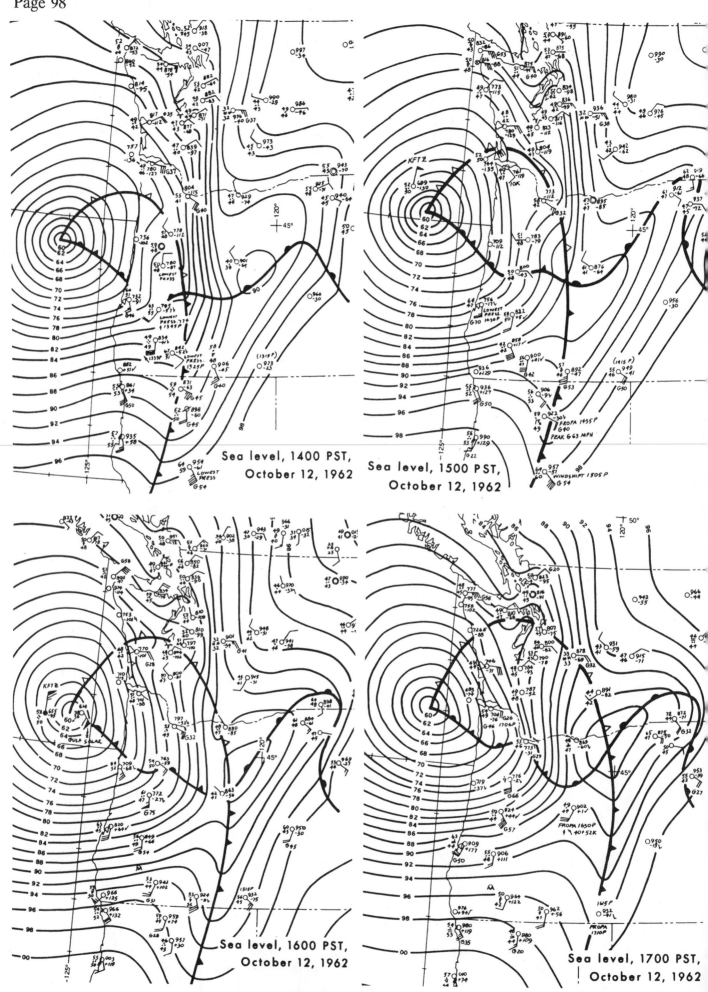

Sea level, 1400 PST,
October 12, 1962

Sea level, 1500 PST,
October 12, 1962

Sea level, 1600 PST,
October 12, 1962

Sea level, 1700 PST,
October 12, 1962

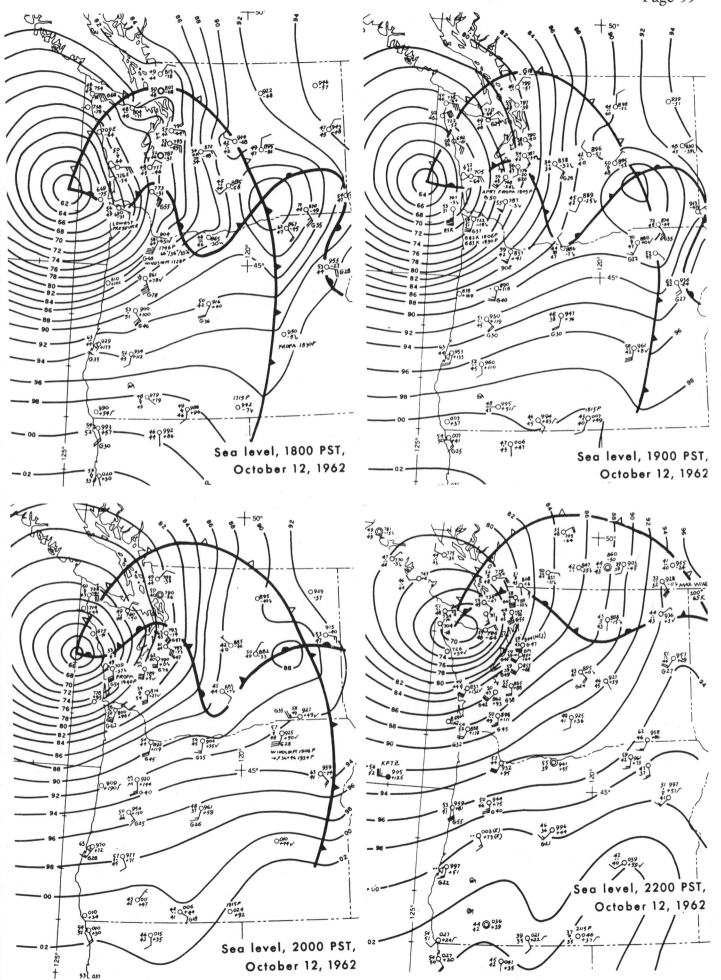

Sea level, 1800 PST,
October 12, 1962

Sea level, 1900 PST,
October 12, 1962

Sea level, 2000 PST,
October 12, 1962

Sea level, 2200 PST,
October 12, 1962

A vertical cross section from north to south across the storm was made for 1500 PST. Fortunately, the fast-moving fronts were in a position that permitted sampling at mid-afternoon radiosonde observation time.

3. CHRONOLOGY AND STRUCTURE OF STORM

The Columbus Day storm was the second and the strongest of three storms which reached the Pacific Northwest on successive days. The first one, on October 11 (figs. 2a and 2c), caused damage to buildings and powerlines at Gold Beach, Oreg., estimated at $750,000. In some instances, damage from this storm may have been credited to the storm of October 12.

The relationship between the Columbus Day storm and earlier tropical storms has been reviewed by Green [6] and Namias [11]. First, typhoon Emma appeared in the western Pacific on October 3. Typhoon Freda developed about 1,000 mi. to the east of Emma on October 4. The huge cyclonic circulation, associated with these typhoons in the western Pacific during the period October 2–11, responded downstream in the next long wave, contributing to an abnormally strong upper trough near 135° W. during October 9–13.

After its formation near 23° N., 165° E., Freda moved northward for four days, then northeastward for two days. By 0400 PST October 10, Freda had weakened to less than typhoon intensity, and the remaining depression was at 45° N., 180° W. The depression moved eastward and southeastward as a moderate frontal wave at the surface and as a short-wave trough aloft (figs. 2a to 2i).

As the surface wave moved under the major trough near 135° W., it intensified rapidly as an extratropical storm and developed a central pressure of 960 mb. The storm followed a curved path (fig. 2j) quite similar to the mean wind flow aloft. The center passed very near picket ship PS 25 at 40° N., 130° W., at 0700 PST October 12. At that time, the pressure at the ship was 962.6 mb. and the 3-hr. pressure tendency was −22.5 mb. Hourly observations at the ship aided in the determination of the path and central pressure of the Low in that vicinity.

It is noteworthy that the maximum deepening of the storm had occurred by 0700 PST (inset, fig. 2j) near 40° N., 130° W. This location is nearly 300 n. mi. southwest of Brookings, Oreg. During the next 11 hr., until the center passed near Astoria, there was no evidence of any significant change in central pressure. After 1800 PST, the storm filled rapidly.

Detailed sea level patterns of the storm were prepared for each hour from 1000 to 2300 PST October 12 (figs. 3a-n). The warm front and cold front progressed into a warm-type occlusion. The cold front moved uniformly (fig. 4), whereas the warm front moved irregularly as local terrain aided or retarded the retreat of the shallow layer of cold air (fig. 5).

The low center on each map was located along a smoothed path between reasonably reliable fixes at 1000, 1600, and 2200 PST. The precise locations and central pressures cannot be determined, but any error depicted here is probably small. Reports from ship ZXJG, off-shore from Brookings, were finally omitted because of several unresolved inconsistencies in five teletypewriter reports received over a 3-hr. period. Observations at ship KFTZ at 1500, 1600, and 2200 PST were assumed to have been taken somewhat early.

Notable conditions and events, with reference to the hourly sea level maps, are discussed below in chronological order:

1000 PST (fig. 3a).—The storm center, 160 n. mi. west of Crescent City, was moving toward the north-northeast at approximately 42 kt. A shallow layer of cold air covered Washington and nearly all of Oregon. Isobars over the land were oriented north to south. Wind flow in the cold layer near the ground was from the east, hindered by the north-to-south Coast and Cascade Ranges. Winds aloft were strong from the southwest or south-southwest, a direction 90° to 135° different from that of surface winds.

1100 PST (fig. 3b).—A pilot reported southerly winds of 100 kt. at 9,000 ft. between North Bend and Crescent City.

1230 PST.—Seattle relayed a report from a U-2 pilot at 55,000 ft., position not reported, "Most severe turbulence ever experienced." Crescent City reported a frontal passage with pressure rising rapidly.

1300 PST (fig. 3d).—According to a letter from Marcus L. McGhee, in charge of the Cape Blanco Loran Station, the wind was estimated at 150 kt., gusting to 170 kt.; the anemometer had already been broken.

1400 PST (fig. 3e).—The pressure was rising rapidly at Roseburg and the temperature had suddenly risen 8° F. with the passage of the warm occluded front.

1440 PST.—A pilot reported downdrafts of 2,000 ft./min., 5 mi. west of Portland. The upper cold front had just passed.

1500 PST (fig. 3f).—Three-hour pressure tendencies showed remarkable contrasts—for example, −12.9 mb. at Hoquiam compared with +12.9 mb. at Brookings. Temperatures at Pendleton and Walla Walla rose 6° and 7° F. from the previous hour as wind moving downslope from the Blue Mountains scoured out the shallow, cool air. The wind at Eugene was from the east at only 8 kt.

1600 PST (fig. 3g).—As the warm occluded front passed Eugene, the wind shifted to south and increased to 55 kt., gusting to 75 kt., and the temperature rose from 50° to 61° F. The front had not reached Salem where the wind was only 15 kt. with gusts to 25 kt.

As the warm occluded front passed each location, extreme winds began abruptly. The lack of strong wind until this climactic moment was deceptive to anyone unaware of the frontal structure. In the area north of the warm occluded front, the isobars were still oriented north-south and surface winds were from the east. However, southward from the front, the isobars had rotated almost 90°. In the latter area, the surface wind was blowing from the south or south-southwest, from the same direction as the free-air wind. The two mountain ranges offered no important obstruction to wind from this direction. No longer was there any shallow layer of cold air shielding the earth's surface from free-air wind of 70 to 100 kt. Turbulent eddies could carry this wind downward to the surface for the first time.

1700 PST *(fig. 3h)*.—Shallow, cold air in the Columbia Basin was pushed westward against the Cascade Range as water against a dam. An east wind over the Cascades produced a lee trough in the Puget Sound area (figs. 3 e–i). The secondary low center east of the Cascades had reached its maximum development. It was partly caused by the intersection of two fronts—a "point-of-occlusion Low"— and partly by the lee trough effect of southeast winds blowing down from the Blue Mountains. This secondary Low probably increased the wind in its own southeastern quadrant and probably decreased the wind in the Cascade Range in its northwestern quadrant.

1746 PST.—With the passage of the warm occluded front, the telepsychrometer at Portland recorded a temperature of 66° F., a rise of 10° F. in 10 min. During the same time, the relative humidity dropped from 72 percent to 33 percent. The warming and drying were only temporary, apparently caused by downdrafts. The temporary warming and drying observed with the frontal passage at Portland occurred at many other locations. Hygrothermograph traces at Illinois Valley in southwestern Oregon and Sisters Ranger Station in central Oregon (fig. 6) show abrupt warming accompanied by a change in relative humidity from saturation down to 50 or 60 percent.

2000 to 2300 PST *(figs. 3 k–n)*.—Strong winds spread through the Puget Sound area. A "fastest mile" of 65 (56 kt.) was measured in downtown Seattle at 2057 PST.

Peak gusts were reported as follows: Renton tower, 87 kt. at 2000 PST; Whidbey Island, 78 kt. at 2142 PST; and Bellingham, 85 kt. at 2358 PST. The storm weakened rapidly as it moved into British Columbia, although additional destruction occurred there.

Additional types of analysis were used to show the structure and character of the Columbus Day storm. A vertical cross section (fig. 7) shows a north-south slice of the lower atmosphere across western Oregon and western Washington shortly before the extreme winds hit the Willamette Valley. The marked stability below the 900-mb. level which existed temporarily at Salem was due to

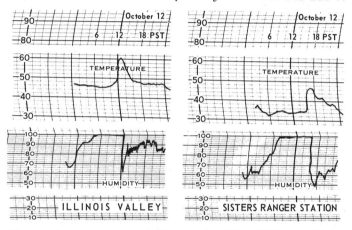

FIGURE 6.—Hygrothermograph traces for Illinois Valley and Sisters Ranger Station, October 12, 1962.

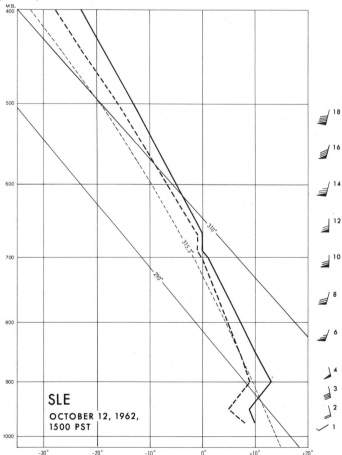

FIGURE 8.—Pseudoadiabatic diagram for Salem, Oreg., 1500 PST October 12, 1962. Temperature in °C.; dry and moist adiabats in °A. Wind: half-barb=5 kt.

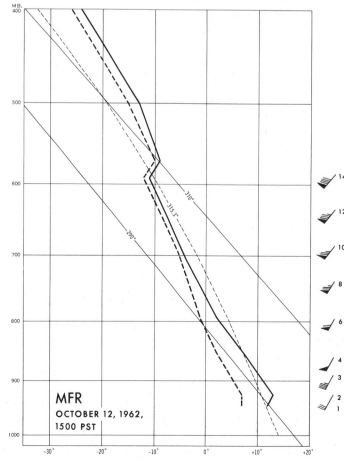

FIGURE 9.—Pseudoadiabatic diagram for Medford, Oreg., 1500 PST October 12, 1962. Temperature in °C. dry and moist adiabats in °A. Wind: half-barb=5 kt.

the overlying warm front. Winds over Medford were blowing parallel to the cross section. The slope of the isentropes in this portion of the cold air mass indicated strong cold air advection. This slope and the increase in wind speed from 30 kt. at 2,000 ft. to 74 kt. at 8,000 ft. were conducive to strong downslope motion.

Neither the sounding for Salem nor for Medford (figs. 8 and 9) indicates at first sight the low relative humidity temporarily observed at Portland and elsewhere. However, if a point on the Medford sounding at 800 mb. is moved dry adiabatically down to 980 mb., it will show a temperature of 66° F. and a relative humidity of 32 percent, almost identical to values which occurred at Portland after the passage of the warm occluded front. Downdrafts of this magnitude probably were common.

Microbarograph traces during the period of lowest pressure are shown in their relative geographic positions in figure 10. The striking differences between stations suggest the complex details of the storm's structure. Frontal passages are quite evident at some stations (Salem, Portland) but are almost obscured at others (Baker, Stampede Pass). Times of frontal passages, as derived from the hourly maps (figs. 4 and 5), have been indicated on each trace. The nearby passage of the deep low center overshadows frontal passages at a few coastal stations (North Bend, Hoquiam). Early development of a lee trough in the Puget Sound area decreased the slope of the falling trace at Bellingham. A double minimum was pronounced at Eugene, Salem, Portland, and The Dalles. It was caused by the successive passages of the upper cold front and warm occluded front. The most rapid pressure rise observed anywhere during the storm was at Destruction Island where a 3-hr. tendency of +22.1 mb. was noted. Only a portion of that pressure trace is shown. Many trace variations remain unexplained; they were probably caused by structures too small or too transitory to be disclosed by the technique used here.

4. EVALUATION OF MAXIMUM WINDS

After the storm, there was an urgent need for accurate information on maximum winds for insurance companies, the legal profession, forest agencies, and even for the design of structures to replace those destroyed by the storm. Reports of highest winds on October 12 were compiled by Harper [7], Phillips [14], and Sternes [18].

It is improbable, however, that these reports represent the true maximum winds over the area. With respect to the Oregon reports, Sumner [19] remarked: "In practically every case there were periods of power failure. . . . It is quite likely much higher speeds occurred but for which no measurement was possible." Futhermore, very few anemometers are self-recording, and amid the confusion of the storm, observers could not devote constant attention to wind-speed indicators. Many of the published reports were only estimations and, for wind speeds exceeding previous experience, observer skill is questionable. In some cases, personnel safety took precedence over complete observations. Weather stations at New-

port, Mount Hebo, and Corvallis were abandoned during the storm, possibly before the maximum wind occurred. The Troutdale tower was occupied only intermittently.

Under such circumstances, it is proposed that a careful analysis of sea level pressure gradients offers a conservative and sound basis for an approximation of true maximum winds. The locations and magnitudes indicated by pressure gradients supplement and revise the incomplete measurements and estimates which are available. Pressure gradients at 2-hr. intervals were measured from detailed sea level maps and drawn on a composite diagram (fig. 11). Measurements of isobar spacing were made across pressure differences of 10 mb. and applied to a simplified geostrophic wind scale (fig. 12). Not all the zones of maximum pressure gradient were included. For example, extreme pressure gradients appeared across the Cascade Range from east to west. Although easterly winds did blow across ridges and through passes in the Cascades, none was destructive because of blocking by the terrain and because this direction was dissimilar to that of the wind aloft. Also, areas covered with a layer of cold air, under the warm front surface, were protected from gusts and squalls in the faster wind above. Hence measurements of isobar spacing were limited to areas south of the warm occluded front and to areas where the direction of the surface pressure gradient was within 40° of the direction of the upper wind, or approximately between 150° and 230° from the low center. The isotachs (fig. 11) show those areas where the strongest winds probably occurred.

The isotachs were labeled in units of indicated geostrophic wind. Adjustment from these values depends upon the particular need for maximum wind data, such as the highest 1-sec. gust, the highest 1-min. wind, or the wind at different elevations above the ground. Also, the individual exposure of any specific location will influence the maximum wind produced by any specific pressure gradient. For estimating the maximum wind at the standard elevation of 20 ft. at locations where no significant obstruction exists, the following ratios appear reasonable: The highest 1-min. wind will be 50 percent of the indicated geostrophic wind. The highest 1-sec. gust will be 70 percent of the indicated geostrophic wind. These ratios are in general agreement with the ratios described by Myers [10] and Sherlock [16].

5. SIGNIFICANT FEATURES AND COMPARISONS

The significant features of the Columbus Day storm are listed below:

(1) The broad pattern was unusually favorable for storm development. A strong upper trough covered the area off the west coast.

(2) A new storm appeared as an open wave under this upper trough. The central pressure decreased to about 960 mb. and the spacing of the isobars indicated geostrophic winds of at least 100 kt. The new storm was fully developed by the time it neared the coasts of Oregon and Washington from the southwest. It remained at peak intensity as it moved north-northeastward along the coast.

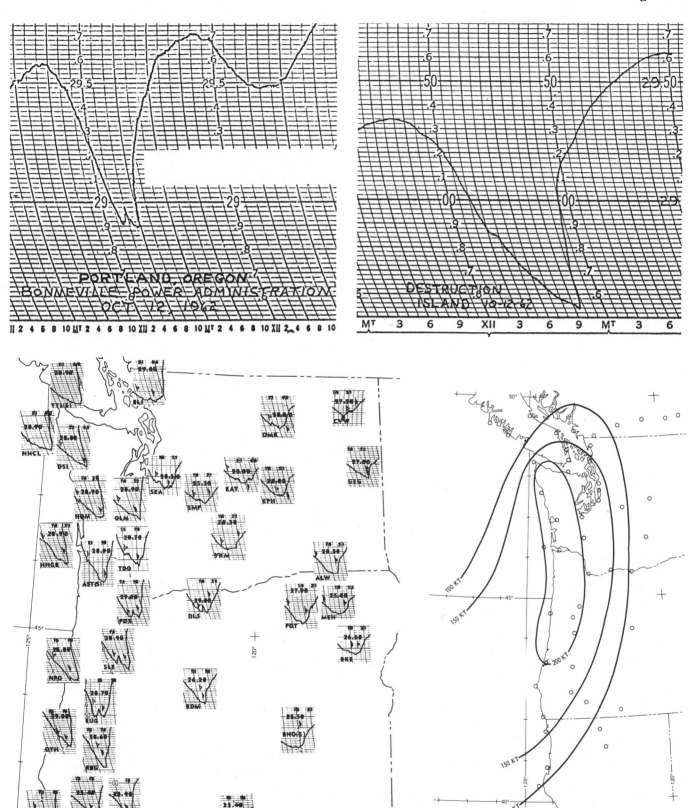

FIGURE 10.—Microbarograms for lowest station pressure on October 12, 1962. Horizontal lines for intervals of 0.02 in. Hg. Time is PST. Traces "shortened" from faster charts are labeled "S." Eugene trace partly estimated. Time of frontal passages indicated by symbols: |▶, cold front; |>, upper cold front; |◗, warm front or warm occluded front.

Composite isotach chart of indicated geostrophic wind, derived from sea level isobars, derived from sea level isobars, between 1300 and 2300 PST, October 12, 1962. (See text for restrictions imposed)

(3) The upper wind at 700 mb. and 500 mb. was 100 kt. from about 230° over western Oregon and western Washington. As the storm approached, the wind direction backed slightly to about 190°. The surface storm center, steered by this upper wind, moved almost northward just off the coast, and reached the mainland near Tatoosh Island (fig. 13).

(4) The surface isobars across southwestern Oregon became oriented from west to east, or from southwest to northeast, creating a southerly wind. This wind blew between the north-south ranges of mountains with no significant blocking by terrain. The surface wind, from the same direction as the wind above, was reinforced by a transfer of momentum downward during squalls.

(5) Three-hour pressure tendencies of +12.0 mb. appeared in southwestern Oregon at the same time −12.0-mb. tendencies appeared in western Washington.

A *detailed* comparison of the Columbus Day storm with notable windstorms of earlier years was not undertaken. However, a limited search in files of Northern Hemisphere Historical Maps and printed *Daily Weather Maps* showed other windstorms of similar general type but of lesser intensity. Specific dates include November 14, 1953, April 14, 1957, February 24, 1958, and March 27, 1963. The sea level pattern of the famous Olympic Peninsula "hurricane" of January 29, 1921, was that of a storm moving northward just off the coast, but upper-air charts are not available for that date.

Some of the windstorms of the past, affecting western Oregon and western Washington, were significantly different from the Columbus Day storm. However, all storms not of the Columbus Day type appear to fall into a single category. This other type (fig. 14) approaches from the Gulf of Alaska and moves eastward across the area under the steering of a westerly wind aloft. Maximum surface wind also is from the south, but occurs ahead of the cold front, is of shorter duration, and is not reinforced by the upper wind. The cold front trails southwestward from the eastward-moving low center. Pressure rises behind the low center while pressure is still falling in southwestern Oregon ahead of the cold front. The south-to-north gradient between the mountain ranges immediately decreases as the low center reaches the Cascade Range. Surface wind in the wake of the storm is from the west or northwest and is hindered by the Coast and Cascade Ranges. Notably severe storms of this type occurred February 28, 1955, and December 16, 1961.

Even with limited investigation, it seems certain that no windstorm in the Pacific Northwest during the last 80 yr. equaled the Columbus Day storm in intensity and area of destruction. The storm of January 21, 1921, may have been nearly as strong; the 5-min. average wind at North Head, at the mouth of the Columbia River, was 110 kt. But the center of the storm was farther offshore and heavy timber blowdown was limited to the Olympic Peninsula.

The storm of January 9, 1880, probably was of comparable intensity. A newspaper of that date [12] reported widespread destruction in the vicinity of Portland, Oreg. The sea level pressure of 28.56 in. was the lowest ever observed at Portland, where the sequence of barometer readings showed a pressure rise of 22.8 mb. in 3 hr., equal to that observed at Destruction Island in 1962.

Two additional features about the Columbus Day storm should be remembered:

(1) It followed by only 30 hr. a destructive windstorm which also formed under the upper trough and moved northward along the Oregon-Washington coast.

(2) Its strongest wind occurred *after* the time of lowest pressure, after the frontal passage, and continued for 2 or 3 hr. Surface wind in advance of the storm center was generally from the east and deceptively weak, even along the immediate coast.

Because unusual 3-hr. pressure tendencies were observed during the storm, the concept of isallobaric contribution to wind was investigated. It was found that the existence of such an effect, or at least its relative importance, is subject to academic debate. Haurwitz [8] states: "The theoretical as well as the observational basis of the isallobaric wind is so unsatisfactory that this concept has to be abandoned." Isobaric gradients alone appeared adequate to explain the maximum winds of the Columbus Day storm.

After viewing each characteristic of the storm separate from the others, we found only one that was truly unusual—the appearance of a surface low center with a central pressure of 960 mb. in the vicinity of 40° N., 130° W. This location is far southeastward from the usual location of deep Lows. Other factors admittedly contributed to the violence of the storm, including the northward path close to the mainland and reinforcement of the surface wind by the upper wind. However, at least four other windstorms between 1953 and 1963 had similar characteristics, except that of such low central pressure.

6. CONCLUSIONS

In view of the economic havoc of severe windstorms in Oregon and Washington, it is regrettable that previous storms have not been more thoroughly analyzed and documented. The Columbus Day windstorm of 1962 was obviously worthy of the intensive analysis carried out in this study. The features of this storm should be compared with future storms.

The extreme intensity of the storm resulted from an unusual combination of circumstances. Primary among these was the formation of an abnormally strong upper trough near 135° W. This trough appeared to be linked dynamically with a huge typhoon circulation west of the dateline. The deepening of an open wave to a central pressure of 960 mb., off the coast of California, was a remarkable event. However, the subsequent path of the storm along the coast of Oregon and Washington was similar to several other notable windstorms in recent years.

This storm demonstrates that the occurrence of one intense storm beneath a persisting strong upper trough does not preclude the development of another intense storm in the same area within a short time interval. Hence, waves on trailing cold fronts, if beneath major upper troughs, should always be closely watched.

A detailed pattern of sea level isobars accurately indicated areas of maximum wind. During the Columbus Day storm, severe wind damage occurred in areas where four conditions were fulfilled:

(1) Major terrain features did not block surface wind flow.

(2) The indicated geostrophic wind was 150 kt. or more.

(3) Both surface winds and winds aloft were from similar directions.

(4) No inversion or stable layer existed between the strong winds aloft and the surface winds, permitting the strong winds aloft to reinforce the surface winds by turbulent eddies.

The described procedure for estimating both the location and magnitude of maximum wind is recommended for any future windstorm investigation, especially severe windstorms which render many anemometers inoperative by damage or power failure. However, the procedure cannot be applied to mesoscale windstorms such as tornadoes. The publication of isotach patterns for specific storms would be useful in the same way that isohyetal patterns of total storm rainfall are useful.

REFERENCES

1. J. S. Boyce, "Deterioration of Wind-Thrown Timber on the Olympic Peninsula, Wash.," U.S. Dept. of Agriculture *Technical Bulletin 104*, Feb. 1929, 27 pp.
2. J. Capell, "The Terrible Tempest of the Twelfth," Pioneer Broadcasting Co., Portland, Oreg., 1962, 2 pp.
3. F. W. Decker, O. P. Cramer, and B. P. Harper, "The Columbus Day 'Big Blow' in Oregon," *Weatherwise*, vol. 15, No. 6, Dec. 1962, pp. 238–245.
4. Dorothy Franklin, *West Coast Disaster Columbus Day 1962*, P.O. Box 7217, Salem, Oreg., 180 pp.
5. H. J. Gratkowski, "Windthrow Around Staggered Settings in Old-Growth Douglas-Fir," *Forest Science*, vol. 2, No. 1, Mar. 1956, pp. 60–74.
6. R. A. Green, "The Weather and Circulation of October 1962, A Warm Month with a Mid-Month Circulation Reversal," *Monthly Weather Review*, vol. 91, No. 1, Jan. 1963, pp. 41–46.
7. B. P. Harper, "Report on October 12 Wind Storm," U.S. Dept. of Interior, Bonneville Power Administration, Portland, Oreg., Oct. 31, 1962, 13 pp. (Mimeographed.)
8. B. Haurwitz, "On the Relation Between the Wind Field and Pressure Changes," *Journal of Meteorology*, vol. 3, No. 3, Sept. 1946, pp. 95–99.
9. E. Lucia, *The Big Blow—the Story of the Pacific Northwest's Columbus Day Storm, Storm Book*, 1835 N. Highland St., Portland, Oreg., 64 pp.
10. V. A. Myers, "Characteristics of United States Hurricanes Pertinent to Levee Design for Lake Okeechobee, Florida," *Hydrometeorological Report No. 32*, U.S. Weather Bureau and U.S. Corps of Engineers, 1954, 106 pp.
11. J. Namias, "Large-Scale Air-Sea Interactions Over the North Pacific from Summer 1962 Through the Subsequent Winter," *Journal of Geophysical Research*, vol. 68, No. 22, Nov. 15, 1963, pp. 6171–6186.
12. *The Oregonian*, Portland, Oreg., Jan. 10, 1880.
13. P. W. Orr, "Windthrown Timber Survey in the Pacific Northwest 1962," Pacific Northwest Region, Forest Service, U.S. Dept. of Agriculture, Mar. 1963, 22 pp.
14. E. L. Phillips, "Special Weather Summary," *Climatological Data, Washington*, vol. 66, No. 10, Oct. 1962, pp. 170, 180.
15. R. H. Ruth and R. A. Yoder, "Reducing Wind Damage in the Forests of the Oregon Coast Range," *Research Paper* 7, U.S. Forest Service, Pacific Northwest Forest & Range Experiment Station, July 1953, 30 pp.
16. R. H. Sherlock, "Variation of Wind Velocity and Gusts with Height," *Proceedings, American Society of Civil Engineers;* vol. 78, Separate No. 126, April 1952, 26 pp.
17. G. L. Sternes, "Summary of the 1962 Columbus Day Storm in Oregon," U.S. Weather Bureau, Portland, Oreg., Nov. 23, 1962, 11 pp. (Mimeographed.)
18. G. L. Sternes, "Columbus Day Wind Storm," *Climatological Data, Oregon*, vol. 68, No. 10, Oct. 1962, pp. 174–175.
19. H. C. Sumner, "Pacific Coast Storm, October 11–13, 1962," *Climatological Data, National Summary*, vol. 13, No. 10, Oct. 1962, pp. 518–522.
20. U.S. Department of Interior, "Distribution of Extreme Winds in the BPA Service Area," Bonneville Power Administration, Portland, Oreg., May 14, 1964, 18 pp.
21. U.S. Weather Bureau, "Manuscript Maps for October 1962," San Francisco, Calif., microfilm reel No. 117.

Here are additional notes on the paper written by Owen Cramer and I, all of which is reproduced above. (If any reader wants a quality photocopy of the entire article, 13 pages, I can provide them, postpaid for $2.00.)

Bear in mind that the MWR was published by the Weather Bureau, now called the National Weather Service. In the 1960s, although the MWR maintained high academic and publication standards, the agency itself was unlikely to view kindly any criticism from another government agency, such as the Forest Service in Dept. of Agriculture. It probably was all right, marginally, for the FS to "analyze" the storm. However, because the forecasting of the storm was almost nonexistent, at least for Oregon and Washington, the FS knew it could not enter into any discussion of forecast accuracy. Not only was the project lengthy and tedious, publication was delayed until February 1966 because of lack of sufficient approval from reviewers (by custom such reviewers remain anonymous).

My account here also is handicapped by the disappearance of the files for that research project. Owen P. Cramer acquired an extensive collection of material on the historic storm. After his retirement, the files were sent to a government depository in Seattle. Some years later, when inquiring informally about that file, I was told it was "lost." Maybe those papers really are in a landfill or have been recycled, or merely lost to gadfly critics.

Our MWR report was addressed to forestry people, and only partly to meteorologists. This book is addressed primarily to would-be local forecasters. Extra comments may be helpful.

Page 95 Sea level charts are drawn every 6 hours, and upper air charts every 12 hours. The 1000 PST and 2200 PST surface maps are omitted, except for 1000 PST Oct 12. Few people remember the storm of Thursday, Oct 11 because its main force remained offshore. Note the rapid intensification of second storm west of San Francisco because of unusual contrast between cold air to NW, and warmer air to SE. The two 0400 PST charts Oct 12 were the last ones I saw before making my 7:45 a.m. forecast.

The difference between the central pressure on SFO surface map at 0400 PST, and our 974 mb on the inset map page 96, top right, is because of the advantage of post analysis which can work backward as well as forward in time, plus data received after map deadline. Ship observations, at least in those days, often were made a little ahead of schedule, because radio transmissions were not always easy.

The steering of 500 mb winds explains the curving path northward of the surface Low. These patterns, to one accustomed to looking at synoptic charts, "blow one's mind."

P 97-99 Detailed maps submitted to MWR were each full page size. Space limits required reduction, although print quality was very high. These photocopies are enlarged 200% (per photocopy notation), and then trimmed a little. Isobar interval is only 2 mb because of smaller area, to reveal details of pressure patterns. (A 5-inch magnifier is useful.) The 2100 and 2300 PST maps are omitted.

By far the most important items on these maps are the 3 hr pressure tendencies, often called the "a.p.p."s by those who used to plot and draw their own charts before the days of Difax maps. The app pertains to the weather codes still effective today for surface observations worldwide. I have never seen before or since such immense changes on surface maps, although I'm sure there are other examples. On page 103 are the barograph traces (from my incomplete files) for Portland and Destruction Island (near NW tip of Washington). A barograph often is called an isobar counter.

To merely say, as TV weathercasters usually do, that pressure is rising or falling, is worthless without reporting how much change is occurring. The present day public is almost unaware of pressure patterns, and the significance of the rate of change. Someday when you can get your hands on real weather maps, and related data, you can stop watching the childish stuff on TV.

Because this book does not require the approval of any government agency for its publication, I'm not constrained for that reason, or hindrance to my career, which concluded over 20 years ago. In 1987 I published criticism of forecasting of the November 1981 windstorm. Forecasting skill of the federal and corporate monopoly seems even lower today, maybe because my view has widened. Mainly, the opportunity for economical self-publishing has substantially improved.

My message now is not a hope that the AMS will regain control of the weather profession, wresting it from the weather bureaucracy. The AMS always has been the leader, and its power is stronger in 1994. Any hope for improvement in weather forecasting must come from amateurs, meaning individuals with career security elsewhere. Gradually, the brainwashed public may wake up, and by exercising an informed vote, reform the very profitable alliance between Congress and the long list of corporate members of the AMS, which is a costly burden on present taxpayers, on investors who will be paid off with devalued dollars, and on our children who will pay the interest on the deficit spending for the pseudo-scientific modernization and restructuring of the NWS. (That's a long sentence, but such must be effective, as I have learned reading some of the propaganda from the power structure in meteorology.)

There's more on the untold story of the Columbus Day storm. After resigning from the Weather Bureau in late 1953 to become Mr. Weatherman on TV (before the days of Chief Meteorologist) I tried to present the best possible local forecasts. Conditions were primitive, and my forecasting skill undeveloped (only 4 years in Oregon, under administrative restraints).

However, when the AMS introduced its Seal of Approval in 1960, something like the Good Housekeeping seal of approval, I didn't think it was worth the bother. Then my friend and competitor Jack Capell received Seal #19. His station promoted that as the only Seal in Portland. My TV job was only a half-time freelance job with no contract security (never a staff employee), and the FS job was during fire season only. So I applied for an AMS seal.

It was denied on the grounds that the required video tape for evidence of professionalism be on a kinescope, a negative-image non-color movie film, rather than a VCR tape. One member of the approval committee was a WB employee in Connecticut, without access to a video machine. My station had no kinescope equipment.

After 15 months, plus okay from council of Oregon Chapter of AMS (with its apology for the "tone" of my blunt letter to each member of the national AMS Council), I received Seal #39. Until leaving TV in 1968 I personally paid the annual fee for such seal.

It had become clear that the Weather Bureau wanted to "get me off the air" but I didn't fully realize its annoyance at my occasional contradictions of its forecasts. Its resistance to a Seal of Approval had not discouraged me.

During the fire season, approximately May 1 to November 1, I was able to get daily data at the FS office. Now the WB tried another tactic to bring my forecasts into line with its guidance and control.

Eckley Ellison, the boss at Portland Weather Bureau, instructed the Fireweather Supervisor who was also my supervisor, to lecture me.

"Too many times" I had departed from the continuity of fireweather forecasts from one shift to the next (mine began at 4 a.m. the next day), and had been in error in doing so. More consideration should be given to the ideas and opinions of others (meaning WB guidance). We talked for an hour, amid our longtime friendship and respect. He offered no specific examples of error. He was faithfully carrying out orders.

That night I typed a full page single-spaced memo to him, reviewing our discussion and my reaction. I admitted my intentional nonconformity, and the reasons for it. I welcomed any specific correction of error, and any advice about accuracy. Until then I did not accept any criticism. I explained the characteristics which I always tried to avoid.

Excessive fear of error discourages the act of forecasting. Tendency to "play it safe" by holding on to persistency, which means all changes are missed. Anybody can be a persistency forecaster. Following the crowd so individual errors are submerged in the group error (insecurity). Use of scatter-gun technique to increase chance for fragments to verify. Shortening the time period to minimize error. Use of hazy, deliberately ambiguous statements to make verification more difficult. Transfer of responsibility, such as quoting prognostic charts. Hesitancy to sign forecasts, revealing a desire for anonymity. Poor use of English which hinders communication.

The memo is dated June 25, 1962. The subject never came up again. We continued our mutual friendship and cooperation.

Another behind the scenes tactic by the WB also occurred during this general period, but I failed to note the date, and failed to make the connection. Because the one-a-day TV appearances (6 days a week, but 2 on Friday) had gaps in time, and I worked an early morning fireweather shift, several times I called the station with a special forecast.

Orally I was firmly told to stop such offers, that the station would never interrupt regular programming for a special weather bulletin from me. Just come in for my regularly scheduled appearances.

So at 10 a.m. Friday, October 12, 1962 I went home exhausted after 6 hours of unusual anxiety. And also I estimated the storm would not reach Portland until several hours after my 6 pm show. Little did I know, or even know now, about all that must have gone on during that day.

My forecast was distributed to all forests in Region Six at 7:45 a.m. Clock times were in daylight savings time on that date. At some time in late forenoon, apparently between 10 and 11 a.m., the Portland Weather Bureau office put out its special forecast for "20 to 40 with gusts to 60", burned in my memory, but lost with Cramer's files. Much local emphasis was later placed on this unusual warning. Most citizens remained unaware of it.

But it has some resemblance to my forecast of 7:45 a.m. daylight time. Maybe some FS personnel were calling the WB about that non-conforming forecast from the PDX fireweather office.

Then if all WB forecast offices at Seattle, Portland, and San Francisco were monitoring that terrible storm all day, why were no upgrades issued later in the day?

I even learned via the local grapevine soon afterward that information about wind damage in SW Oregon was coming into the airport FAA office all afternoon, but only the WB was permitted to make public such information. I never saw any of the communications that must have poured into the regional office of the FS that afternoon. And if I prudently avoided asking unnecessary questions, you know why. I had a family to support, and a career to continue. So did a lot of other people. see p 119

A New Solution to an Old Problem

In addition to Lynott's analysis of Columbus Day type storms, it is safe to say that the "mystery" behind their unprecedented violence is more than solved.

Any serious forecaster should be able to pick off and predict such a storm accurately with today's technology. Just how does a forecaster "tag" the windspeed as accurately as possible? The older method of synoptic meteorology involves map analysis and measuring the separation of isobaric surfaces with distance, which means the horizontal pressure gradient. Then gradient wind or geostrophic wind calculations could be made to determine how fast the wind would accelerate to its peak value.

My experience has shown that at middle latitudes the calulation of the geostrophic wind is as accurate as one of the gradient wind (which is a little more tedious) when predicting severe windstorms. The streamlines of air parcels in storms like, or similar to, Columbus Day storms follow a long enough trajectory over the earth's surface to be curved and balanced with the rotation of the earth.

Therefore if one substitutes a time relationship into these calculations, an easier way to determine this prediction can be made that is highly accurate. My new invention, the Weatherwise Windicator does exactly that.

This instrument is a precise objective aid to a skilled forecaster. It is also a first generation line of instrumentation that predicts a future weather event. The Windicator will be available for sale in near future to amateurs and professionals alike.

Chuck Wiese, Weatherwise Inc., 1515 SW 66th Avenue, Portland Oregon 97225, 503-297-8801

Chapter 13 Forecasts by a Robot

In the Preface and Introduction, written almost a year ago, I stated an intention to promote a better understanding of meteorology, or simply "weather." So far the theme has been on physics, how weather works. The remaining pages will focus on how the weather "business" works. I'll show how it's very successful for the power structure, and how it shortchanges the rest of us.

Every technology has a body of techniques, but it also needs a guiding philosophy. Remember, this book is about preparation for forecasting, both how to do it yourself, and how to judge what others are doing when you need to depend on them.

At age 80, with time running out, I'm trying to share what I've learned, and encourage you to move farther and faster. This requires advice about obstacles and roadblocks you are likely to encounter.

If you want a career as a forecaster, rather than an observer or administrator, the immediate opportunities are discouraging. This may change soon. Meanwhile learn all you can, and prepare for the positions which will open when the federal government is forced by public opinion to yield its monopoly on public weather forecasting. Who can afford one's own personal forecaster?

There's nothing wrong with mass production, such as bread, books, or advice from stock brokers, but we ought not accept a system where only a federal agency is the provider. The NWS claims the monopoly to "protect life and property," because otherwise, in a time of crisis there would be public confusion and panic amid conflicting advice. Better to wait until the destructive event arrives, and the NWS describes it for you.

The weather elite have brainwashed the public to believe that, and they are laughing all the way to the bank. Each reader should enjoy occasional humor.

Ridicule is a potent political influence. And we would be assured better public forecasts.

The NWS doesn't really make forecasts, it just pretends. After reading the following pages you may revise a few ideas.

Forecasting in the proper sense of the word must be done locally, and with subjective judgment. On the other hand, observing the weather, and collecting the data is a suitable task for the federal government, even a necessary requirement. The NWS does a creditworthy job on that, and should be properly paid.

What the public doesn't understand, and who can blame them, is that the so-called forecasting of the government is esentially based on persistency of conditions, meaning no significant change, but that requires only clerical skill.

If there are signs of an impending important change, they announce a "watch." Or the obedient weathercasters assure you they are following it closely. Then if it arrives they tell you about it.

If Big Brother really can make such important decisions for everybody, everywhere, it would seem we ought also to turn over some of our other important tasks, such as selecting an occupation, choosing a mate, our votes for leaders, oh yes, and a lot of other things, but not including how much taxes we are willing to pay (or borrowing money to be repaid with interest and interest and interest by our children.) Big Brother will spare us all our present day dilemmas.

Just go out and play, and amuse yourself to death. Those last words are part of my plug for a remarkable book, *Amusing Ourselves to Death* by Neil Postman, Penquin Books, 1986, which probably is still available in paperback for $6.95, or at least for an adjusted price. The subtitle is Public Discourse in the Age of Show Business.

Forecasting is an art because it is creative and imaginative, and not merely a mechanical calculation or routine. We can excuse politicians and lower grade managers for failing to understand. But we should criticize academia for silence, and self-serving approval of monopoly while seeking grants for research.

To deceive citizens, and reinforce monopoly, the government pretends that local forecasts emanate from 52 Weather Service Forecast Offices (WSFOs), about one for each state, and each has a staff of about 16 forecasters, not counting observers and support personnel.

Judging from results, about 90% of the intellectual effort of these forecasters is focussed on the guidance from the National Meteorological Center (NMC) in Washington D.C., the home of the electronic Robot Forecaster. Hence WSFO forecasters function mainly as clerks.

The national effort is directed at administrative control, not scientific accuracy. That means uniformity, lowest common denominator mediocrity, inflexibility for quick revision when needed, undue adherence to climatological averages, and absence of vital contributions from individual experience and subjective judgment.

Instead of increasing skill and enthusiasm among local forecasters, there is stagnation and low morale.

However, among upper echelon administrators there are top-heavy rosters, high salaries, and abundant time to talk to each other about grand plans for the Modernization and Associated Restructuring of the NWS. Such plans call for increasing automation of weather observing, an approximate doubling of the number of WSFOs, and a doubling of the clerk-forecasters at each.

The existing system fails to provide state-of-the-art local forecasts. The "watches, warnings, and advisories" are essentially reports of existing conditions. But if appropriations are doubled or tripled, and gadgetry is expanded accordingly, the Robot will perform brilliantly.

The watches, warnings, and advisories will multiply, but the weather for tomorrow will continue to be mysterious unless it is the same as that today.

Consider now the mechanical brain, the Robot, assigned the difficult job of weather forecasting, a job so difficult that qualified experts are nearly impossible to find. Presumably they have retired or switched to other more rewarding careers. Here are some of the reasons a Robot can't make local forecasts.

1. Variety and complexity of local geography. Robot must cope with many areas, not just one or two.

2. Multiple weather systems co-exist over a large area, such as an ocean or a continent. Each system poses individual problems.

3. Nearly all input data for prognostic charts occurs once during each 12 hr period, synchronous with raob data. Major computations cannot be revised by intermediate 6 hr surface maps, or 3 hr surface maps over the lower 48 States, or intermediate hourly airway reports. Hence the Robot is blind during the last 10 or 11 hrs between raob observations. It spends that time "processing" the input data.

4. The whole array of maps, progs, and data displays are not needed for local forecasting, such as for a state or small group of states. The WSFO forecaster must wait while the Robot strives to solve the problems in 5 million square miles.

5. Any competent local forecaster is aware of the complexities in his area, at least when significant changes are impending. Computers are marvelous for recording, sorting, and displaying data, but the burdens placed on the Robot are overwhelming. It must simplify, generalize, and give undue weight to persistence of existing conditions, and to climatology. Therefore, predictions by the Robot should be viewed properly as "quick and dirty," to use modern slang.

Why is this imitation forecasting foisted on the public? Because the federal monopoly is profitable to the weather bureaucracy. Local proficiency would transfer prestige and power from headquarters to the field. Politicians and sychophants will not relinquish the existing gold mine until voters awaken and insist on change.

The existing monopoly is absurd. When voters are informed, which may be soon because of new technologies for self-publishing, the present power structure in meteorology will look silly.

To the young, in years or spirit, keep on with your studies and do-it-yourself forecasting. A free market will create opportunities like those in engineering, law, and medicine.

Chapter 14. Nothing But Blue Skies -- The Art and Science of Weathercasting

[Reprinted from the "Express", The East Bay's Free Weekly, of November 6, 1992, Berkeley CA 94710, with permission of author, a freelance journalist, of Oakland, California 94610.]

By STEVE HEIMOFF

Bill Martin, standing in front of a blank green screen about the size of a large bath towel, watches intently for the floor director's arm to fall, a signal that he is on the air. He fidgets with his clip-on microphone, clenches his jaw, straightens his tie. The instant the director's arm plunges, Martin's face brightens, as if an electric switch had been thrown, filling his body with high voltage. His eyes enlarge to give the appearance of energy and connectedness, the mouth upturns into an engagingly boyish smile. The combined effect of these bodily transformations is to heat Martin up for a medium that might otherwise make him appear grumpy and cold.

Martin is doing what they call a "cluster-bumper" at KTVU-TV, Channel 2 in Oakland, advising viewers that he'll be back at five-thirty to tell them all about the day's weather. The cluster-bumper is a teaser inserted into midafternoon programming and designed to dissuade viewers from touching their remote controls.

An hour or so later, I accompany Martin as he returns to do his weather segment. We tiptoe into the studio where weekend anchors Leslie Griffith and George Watson are on the air, reading the news. I find a remote spot near a darkened wall, and remain quiet amidst a pile of coiled cables. During a network feed of Boris Yeltsin doing something or other in Russia--during which time everyone is off-air--Martin threads his way to the news desk and sits down beside Watson, who is studying notes for his next item and does not acknowledge Martin's arrival. Griffith does, flashing him her pleasant smile.

Back on-camera, Griffith introduces her colleague: "And now, Bill Martin with the weather." The next few moments of polished, easygoing newsroom banter sound as choreographed as anything from *Swan Lake*. Watson remarks on how unusually humid the day has been. Martin agrees that yes, the day has been on the humid side.

I have to smile. Martin knew that he would be called on to engage in on-air banter about the day's weather, but he never knows exactly what subject the anchor will spring on him. He had explained this to me earlier, out in the parking lot, where he was scanning the sky, feeling the wind and nosing the wind like a stag. He had drawn up a little list of possible subjects the anchor might broach: Hurricane Iniki, which had just struck the Hawaiian Islands, seemed likely, Martin told me; perhaps the heat; maybe even the fog. I had been noticing the humidity all day, particularly while jogging. It seemed weird for late summer, which is normally dry, and I told Martin so. Actually, he had replied, it's not that humid, according to the National Weather Service. Around forty percent, he said; it only *seems* humid. Well, apparently it had been humid enough for Watson to notice the same thing, and I smile.

Still live, Martin walks toward the blank green screen, which is called a "Chroma-keyer." On 50,000 television sets in as many homes across northern California, viewers are looking at satellite photographs of cloud bands on the screen, sweeping across the eastern Pacific into the western United States, bringing with them all sorts of weather. Martin sees none of this. His arms and hands mimic the arcs, loops, and dips the fronts describe in their relentless sweep eastward against the direction of the earth's rotation, but he is pointing and gesturing at precisely nothing. In the studio, the Chroma-keyer remains as blank as the side of a newly painted barn.

It's all a trick of technology, and a weathercaster like Martin must pull it off with the adroitness of a shadow-puppet master. Even the two small remote monitors tucked away in the folds of the wall to either side of the Chroma-keyer are of little help, since Martin's eyes must look directly into the camera in order to maintain eye contact with viewers.

Bill Martin is not formally in the employ of Channel 2. In fact, he is a full-time meteorologist at Santa Rosa's Channel 50. The 33-year-old weathercaster was in Oakland participating in a unique competition, a sort of on-air audition.

When, last spring, KTVU announced it was going to hire someone to deliver the weather on its two Sunday night newscasts, it was flooded with dozens of applications, according to news director Fred Zinder. Channel 2's *Ten O'Clock News* is among the highest rated in the country; the Sunday-night job would be an excellent career move and showcase for whomever was hired.

Having narrowed the applicants down to a short list of four, KTVU decided to hold a competition, inviting each of the finalists to deliver a series of Sunday-night weathercasts. Martin was one of the four. Only Martin had serious academic credentials: a degree in meteorology from San Francisco State.

This lack of academic background among the Channel 2 candidates is not at all unusual. There is no common denominator among those who call themselves "meteorologist" on TV. The big station weathercasters in San Francisco and Oakland, as in most cities, come from a wide variety of backgrounds and possess varying credentials and abilities.

Another finalist, from Sacramento, whose name is Steve Swienckowski, told me his formal training consisted of 20 hours of science courses at the University of Kansas.

When I first met Swienckowski I immediately thought: if Plato had invented the ideal TV weathercaster, he would be this jowly but handsome man with a Styrofoam hairdo, crisp suit, and the sort of unself-conscious bonhomie that would make you spot him a block away as an obvious television personality. He stalked the hallways of KTVU like he owned the place, brimming with square-jawed confidence even though he must have been nervous. Only 31, and already a veteran of years of television weathercasting, he possessed that on-air smoothness that looks natural, but most definitely is not.

"Hi ! Steve Swienckowski, your meteorologist *du jour*," he would greet viewers, before launching into the weather.

It was an attitude I was to see again in Martin and indeed in all the weathercasters I met or studied on television, That breezy, friendly attitude, I realized, was as much (if not more) of a qualification for the job than any meteorological competence they might have possessed. Martin and Swienckowski do not look or act like talking heads. They are people you might see on the street and have a drink with -- people you might actually know. And that, I found out, is the whole idea.

On another Sunday afternoon, Martin and I sat talking in the little weather cubbyhole in KVTU's big building near Jack London Square. As a teletype machine noisily spat out National Weather Service reports and the Weather Channel played (with sound off) on a small TV, Martin told me of his earliest interest in meteorology. He'd been a geography major at Cal when, he recalled, "I was surfing at Ocean Beach and met all these characters, and they got me into it. The best meteorologists are fishermen and surfers. They have to know where the waves are, the marine layer, the wind. Because no matter what this stuff says" -- here Martin indicated a pile of Weather Service printouts stacked on the floor -- "it's happening *out there*."

To show me what he meant, Martin hauled me outside. "Do you know what that means ?" he asked, pointing to the high thin cirrus clouds that were streaking the sky. "There should be a great sunset tonight." Martin will later offer the same information to his viewers during the 5:00 p.m. broadcast. "You can't just be a scientist and recite facts. I found that out in my first year at Channel 50."

Martin's broadcast style might be labeled "the friendly neighbor." He tries to relate to his viewers as if they are sitting next to him in easy chairs. "I feel like I'm talking right to them. I'll say, 'Martha from Sebastopol called to tell me the fog is already there.' Or I can say, 'Guys, I know you have those pumpkins out there. You really ought to go out and cover them now, because a freeze is coming.' "

That kind of *gemütlichkeit* is possible in Santa Rosa, where Martin has up to 6 minutes of airtime, but not at KTVU, where the weathercast must end after exactly 2 minutes and 40 seconds, or the director will start making slashing gestures at his throat. Even so, Martin's advice on the sunset and some comments about the dense fog are typical gifts to viewers.

"What I'm learning to do is to get people to pay attention by saying a few key things and not just saying, 'It was 62 degrees today.' When the weather comes on, people are eating, not really watching the TV. You've got to say something to get them to watch."

Part of the problem, as we all know, is that the Bay Area's weather is usually quite boring. The monotonous refrain, "Low clouds and fog along the coast is extending inland nights and mornings," is as familiar to us in the summertime as a TV jingle.

And then there's the fact that all weathercasters, no matter how clever or polished, get their information from one source: the National Weather Service. As Willard Scott, the *Today Show's* weathercaster, is said to have cracked, "The hardest thing about TV weathercasting is remembering the National Weather Service's phone number."

We all know (or should) that TV news anchors are often hired more for their looks, personality, and telegenic "chemistry" than for their intellect or ability to research and interpret the news. Those activities are conducted by others, off-screen, and news anchors are little more than highly-paid readers, or "talent," in the jargon of the medium. Are TV meteorologists their equivalents in weather?

If you watch TV weathercasters, you could easily get the impression that they'd been checking their barometers and rain gauges, perhaps dressed in rain slickers, until moments before the broadcast. "And now, my forecast," the weathercaster says, as if she or he had been blearily studying charts all day. But that impression would, in most cases, be incorrect.

Most full-time TV weathercasters spend the majority of their days doing things quite unconnected with the weather. "It's fairly typical," said veteran NWS meteorologist, for weathercasters to simply "rip-and-read," the term he uses to describe what happens "when the engineer rips off [an NWS] forecast [from the teletype] and hands it to the "talent."

"They all use us as a starting point," Null told me. True, he continued, a weathercaster might occasionally "tweak around little things" in his forecast, like changing a high of 67 degrees to a high of 68. But Null claims to see his own handiwork in the majority of TV forecasts. "For the most part, I see very little deviation from what NWS puts out and what the media put out." When there is "modification," as he calls it, Null is not impressed. "There aren't any prohibitions to them doing that," he allowed. "But I have found that the times I have seen them modified, they aren't any *better*."

Null, who holds a BS in atmospheric science from UC Davis, works in NWS's Northern California headquarters, a small cinder-block building in a drab Redwood City industrial park. Inside, the building is a bewildering array of computer screens, teletypes, and video monitors. All around the room, scientists are hunched over weather charts and computer keyboards.

Null's hourly forecasts, which cover an area from the Oregon border to the Tehachapis, the Sierra Nevada to the coast, are based on an analysis of huge volumes of data, including temperature, atmospheric pressure, wind direction and velocity, relative humidity, and the state of the sea, which arrive continuously from a mind-boggling array of sources: airports, commercial and military aircraft, ships, buoys floating within 200 miles of the coast, and from fixed points on land. Also, weather balloons containing instruments are launched twice each day from Oakland airport. "I have to congeal all this data down into a cohesive forecast of about six lines," said Null dryly.

Null also looks at the output from computer models. "All this same data goes back to Washington, through the Cray supercomputers, which are located at NOAA [National Oceanic and Atmospheric Administration, NWS's parent agency], where they run these physical models of the atmosphere and timeset them out into the future using equations of thermodynamics and fluid dynamics."

And then, of course, there is the data from satellites, which have revolutionized West Coast weather forecasting. Northern California's weather comes from a vast region of the northeastern Pacific, far from most shipping lanes and air travel routes. It was once almost impossible to get information from this vast terra incognita, and thus, weather forecasting during the winter storm season was considered one of the hardest meteorological jobs in the country.

"Satellites certainly changed the way we do business," Null told me. "Probably the two biggest improvements in forecasting over the last 45 years have been weather satellites and supercomputers."

The satellites generate not only the conventional images that the NWS forwards to the TV weathercasters, but also infrared pictures. Null and other meteorologists like working with infrared, not only because infrared cameras can operate at night, but because they present a three-dimensional image of clouds, whereas visible images display only clouds' tops. Infrared intruments measure radiation emitted by cloud particles at different temperatures, and since clouds' tops are colder than their bases, these intruments can thus "dissect" clouds from top to bottom. By looking at these temperature variations over time, meteorologists can infer the wind direction and speed at various levels of the atmosphere. That gives them their best indication of the movement of troughs, huge undulating waves in the atmosphere along which weather systems ride like cars on a roller coaster. And reading troughs is the key to producing the hourly forecasts that will eventually be intoned by highly paid TV personalities.

I asked Null his opinion of the broadcast "meteorologists" to whom his forecasts are sent. "It's better for me to keep away from names," Null answered, and then he proceeded to name names. "Leo Chelino [KGO radio] does not have a degree. Pat McCormick [KTVU's longtime regular weathercaster] has no background, other than having done the weather for years. I'm pretty sure Steve Newman [KRON] does not have a degree." Null seemed to have a slightly higher regard for KGO weathercasters Joel Bartlett and Pete Giddings, both of whom received meteorological training in the Air Force and are certified consulting meteorologists, or CCMs, a title awarded by the Boston-based professional association, the American Meteorological Society (AMS), based upon a tough written examination.

KGO heavily promotes the fact that Giddings and Bartlett are CCMs, but it's not clear that the encomium means much. Dr. Keith Seitter, who is assistant to the executive director of AMS, told me that a CCM "has zero relevance to television," while KRON's Newman, who is one of Bartlett's and Giddings's chief rivals, said, "I think that Mr. Giddings has convinced KGO that [a CCM] has PR value." Even Bartlett admitted that the only reason he got his CCM was "because Pete did," and conceded that a CCM "is not something that's necessary for TV. KGO is just trying to impress people." How, then, is the competence of TV weathercasters to be judged? "I think [competence] is more dependent on how good their producers are, the people who put together the package for them," Null said, referring to full-time staff meteorologists employed by larger stations to work behind the scenes for weathercasters.

In fact, in a city like San Francisco (KTVU doesn't have a weather producer), these assistants may do what analysis and prediction there is, freeing up their bosses for non-weather-related business. At KGO, meteorologist Tim Summers "does the spade work," says Bartlett. "He'll look at the maps and charts. He's an expert at the computer and puts together the "slide show," the maps you see on the screen. He puts things together so that, when we come into the studio, we don't have to spend time ball-carrying."

At KRON, weather assistant Randy Carvalho, who has a meteorology degree from San Jose State, said he does every-thing from "ripping charts to preparing current data to setting up satellite loops to doing interpretation and forecasts" before evening weathercaster Janice Huff even arrives. "Janice will be visiting places or speaking, and it's too much trouble for her to rush in and be prepared," said Carvalho. At KPIX, evening weathercaster Brian Sussman admitted that he relies on his weather assistant to do as much as 90% of the meteorology. "You're so busy in news production meetings, promotional meetings, sales meetings, speaking engagements, and returning phone calls," said Sussman, "that there's not much time to put together a forecast."

Although having academic credentials certainly don't hurt, TV weathercasters "are hired because they're entertainers," Null declared. "That's why they make salaries that are so much higher than any operational meteorologist."

The question of salary inequity frequently arises in discussions of meteorology. While few TV weathercasters can expect to equal Giddings purported $400,000 annual salary, or even Bartlett's $225,000 (at least that's what they were rumored to be in the *Chronicle* two years ago, even a smaller media post can pay well. Last year, the American Meteorological Society conducted a survey which asked members about their salaries. The survey showed that those in government did no better than the $80,000 a handful of top NOAA administrators earn. University professors earned even less. By contrast, broadcasting, which employs about 8% of the nation's meteorologists, showed more people with salaries above $80,000 than below. It would be understandable if NWS meteorologists were to watch TV meteorologists with mixed emotions. "There's a certain amount of jealousy between the scientists and TV weathercasters," says Martin, "because guys like Jan Null are doing all the work, but the weather service doesn't pay them enough." KRON's Janice Huff, who used to work for the NWS and who now says her salary is "competitive" with that of other San Francisco weathercasters, answered simply: "I know how much [NWS meteorologists] are paid. That's why I went into TV."

But Null acknowledges some respect for TV weathercasters. "I mean, what they do is very hard. It takes a hell of a knack. I could not get up there and do that," he said, referring to the difficult on-air performance skills weathercasters must muster. Null likens the strange symbiosis between TV weathercasters and NWS meteorologists to "the brain surgeon [who] comes in and does the work, and then asks you to close up, to do the finish work." Null, of course, believes himself to be the brain surgeon. "But closing up is important. If it's not done right, the guy hemorrhages. And if it wasn't for the media, our forecasts wouldn't go anyplace. I mean, they are how we get the information out.

Many TV meteorologists, to be fair, downplay their reliance on the National Weather Service, insisting that they do their own analysis and forecasting. "It would be very easy for someone to 'buy' the NWS forecast," Bartlett told me, but we [Giddings and I] also look at all those charts and try to decide by ourselves what we think is going to happen, preferably before we look at NWS stuff so we're not swayed by it." Giddings even dropped broad hints that some NWS meteorologists produce forecasts that are less than trustworthy. "Jan Null is a very good forecaster, but there are others at NWS I don't read. We know where NWS handles things well and where they don't." Yet at KPIX, Brian Sussman said, I don't see how you could not look at NWS forecasts. They have so many people working down there. I can't downplay their involvment."

The problem is simply that there is no legal definition of a meteorologist, no licensing procedure as there is for real estate appraisers and certified accountants. "You can read a book on meteorology and call yourself a meteorologist," conceded Bartlett. "Meteorology is one of those fields where there aren't any strict requirements." AMS's Keith Seitter admitted that the definition of meteorologist is fuzzy. "AMS has a guideline," he said, "but I'm sure there are many TV stations out there who tout their 'meteorologist' when they don't come anywhere close to our requirements."

For decades, AMS has awarded a Seal of Approval to broadcast meteorologists, the goal being to "continuously upgrade radio and television programs." The first evaluation procedures for broadcast meteorologists were established by AMS as far back as 1959; since then, over 600 seals of approval have been awarded. In order to obtain a seal, meteorologists must first become AMS members, and membership criteria, according to Seitter, "have become more stringent."

Although membership used to be based only on experience, AMS officials decided ten years ago that members must have at least 20 semester hours hours of college work in meteorology or "other science and engineering" courses, a phrase which reflected the fact that meteorology is an eclectic combination of atmospheric, oceanic, and hydrologic sciences, which involve some knowledge of chemistry, mathematics, physics, and even geography and geology.

But it soon became obvious that the phrase "other science and engineering" was so broad a criterion that it could be abused. So last year, again tightening admission standards, AMS demanded that at least 12 of the required 20 credits be in so-called "core courses, defined as basic processes relevant to atmospheric or oceanic systems which must not be purely descriptive."

But AMS backed off from requiring calculus (a necessity in understanding and predicting force or motion) and it refused to require a baccalaureate. "There are many people out there who have the experience, and are doing good meteorological work, and are qualified," Seitter told me. "We shouldn't bar them from membership just because they don't happen to have a degree."

Today, all the major network weathercasters in San Francisco have the AMS seal of approval (KTVU's Pat McCormick doesn't.) Of course, since the requirements are now so much stricter than they used to be, those who have held the seal for a long time (like Pete Giddings, who's had it since 1975) earned it when it was easier to obtain. This has caused some resentment on the part of younger meteorologists, who rightfully feel they're being held to stricter standards. "You've got all these [older] guys out there who got the seal when it was easy to get," complained Martin, who doesn't yet have his and now must return to school in order to satisfy the new academic requirements. "You're gatekeeping people out of the profession."

Those weathercasters who hold the AMS seal are, predictably, proud of it. Earning the seal "gives you a certain understanding that perhaps you wouldn't [otherwise] have" said KRON's morning meteorologist, Steve Raleigh. According to Bill Martin, "Everyone's going to have the seal eventually. The pressure's building. In the 1970s and 1980s, it was enough to get someone cute who could talk, but now, we're talking about ozone holes, droughts, El Niño. You can't just have a bimbo up there pointing to highs and lows."

Despite AMS's efforts to upgrade the profession, there's little evidence that TV management--at KTVU, anyway-- attaches much importance to the seal. News director Fred Zinder says he doesn't care that Channel 2's Pat McCormick has no academic credentials in meteorology. "In weather, as in sports," he said, "there's more latitude to be less objective [than in

news reporting]. Pat's value as a well-known personality overrode the academics of it." In making hiring decisions for the Sunday weathercasting slot, Zinder said he looked primarily at applicant's videotapes, not their resumés. "How do they come across? Do they communicate well? And looks has something to do with it. Not necessarily handsome or pretty. I'm talking about poise, authority in front of the camera, those things." Besides, added Zinder, "The [weather] information all comes from NWS anyway, so really what each person has going for him is the ability to communicate and be entertaining."

Zinder's argument cuts to the quick of the issue. When McCormick first started work at KATU back in 1966, it was as host of a children's show, *Charley and Humphrey.* Following that, he went on to host *Dialing for Dollars,* quickly gaining a reputation as a trustworthy and likeable local television personality who appealed to all demographic groups. In 1973, management asked McCormick to do the weather, despite the fact that he had no interest or training in meteorology. "They wanted a weather personality," McCormick told me, "and I was well known in the market, and well-liked." To his credit, McCormick hit the ground running, reading up on meteorology and studying hard. Yet even today, McCormick readily concedes that he depends on NWS for virtually everything. "Jan Null is the Godfather, and KTVU's weathercast is the voice of the National Weather Service," he candidly told me. "I make it clear [to viewers] that we speak NWS here."

Unlike his colleagues across the bay, McCormick makes little pretense about doing his own analyses, although he says he occasionally tries (at least, in non-serious weather situations), and will even challenge NWS if he feels particularly strongly about something. What the avuncular McCormick understands, and makes no bones about, is that he was hired primarily as an entertainer, a guy whom viewers have come to know and like over the decades--the kind of Friendly neighbor, matured and seasoned, that a young Bill Martin aspires to become.

The weathercaster-as-entertainer has deep roots in television history. Quirky and even bizarre figures have traditionally been seen as ideal candidates for the weather spot. *Wheel of Fortune*'s Pat Sajak began his tubular life as a weathercaster, and so did David Letterman. (At KTVU, McCormick's predecessor was the host of the late-night horror program, *Creature Features*.) On the other side of the gender divide, weathercasting (unlike news and sports) has always welcomed women, albeit often for dubious reasons. Suzanne Somers and Raquel Welch have both done the weather. Null, with obvious distaste, even recalls "weather girls in bikinis writing backwards." I never saw that, but I remember Carol Reed and her always tight sweater in CBS in New York City. I also used to watch a rare bird named Tex Antoine do the weather for NBC. Sporting an arty little mustache and smoking through a long cigarette holder, Antoine wore a smock and a beret, and drew pictures on an easel to illustrate tomorrow's weather, making meteorology seem like a bohemian, slightly *outré* practice.

Here in the Bay Area, several years ago, KGO-TV had a weathercaster named Lloyd Lindsay Young, a frenetic and rubbery-faced man who used a different phallic object every night to point out features on his weather map: salamis, garden rakes, wheat, feathers. Operational meteorologists like Null detested Lindsay Young, who they felt disgraced the entire field. Lindsay Young, Null told me, "was one big joke. . .dictated by the media consultants."

Even if they're not as over the top as Lindsay Young, today's weathercasters are asked to do the darnedest things. Pete Giddings, lost in a yellow wind breaker, will do his broadcast from a boat filled with underprivileged kids. Janice Huff, in skimpy shorts, will do her stint from a bird-calling contest. Brian Sussman includes a weekly "adoption feature" in his spot. Granted, homeless children are a worthy cause and make for good community relations, but you never see sports announcers, much less news anchors, doing that sort of thing. Why the double standard?

There may be several reasons. "The weather's the same [in the Bay Area] every day," at least in the summer, said Raleigh, "so it frees us up. We have the availability to get out into the public." (AMS's Seitter advanced the same argument, telling me that weathercasters in the Northeast and Midwest do less community outreach because the weather in those areas is so much more complicated than Northern California's and keeps them busier.) Sussman, whose background was in theater and improvisational comedy, said the use of weathercasters for community relations may be because "TV meteorologists are used to working without a script, and have developed a talent that other on-air people don't have, which is the ability to work off the cuff."

Whatever the reason, all of the weathercasters I spoke with defended the entertainment aspects of weathercasting-- understandably so, given the fact that they need to encompass both worlds. According to KRON's Raleigh, "There will always be an entertainment aspect" in weathercasting. "It's a way of competing, in a ratings sense."

KPIX's Sussman, who actually has a degree in meteorology, called TV weather "as much of a show as an information source," but was quick to point out that that's not all bad. "You're dealing with a public that. . .I'm not sure how in-depth they want to go most of the time."

In San Francisco, a troubled Steve Newman, who conducts his segment about as straight and shtick-free as possible, told me, "I've hurt my career, because I choose *not* to inject my personality in front of the information I convey. And this is not the market to do that." Anyone who has watched Newman's dignified, unflashy, but highly intelligent approach to the weather will recognize that the last thing you could call him is an entertainer. "I've been [at KRON] for 12 years," Newman continued, "and everyone I've worked with has gone on to bigger and better things" a fact he attributes to his unwillingness to ham it up. Huff, who is KRON's senior weathercaster and thus Newman's superior, came to the station in 1990.

Back at KTUV, meanwhile, Fred Zinder is not spending much time worrying about the academic credentials of the men and women in front of the Chromakeyer. The weathercaster "is just another person on the set who adds some interest to the viewer," the KTUV news director said. "He makes the show more watchable, but he's not necessary. The anchors can do the weather."

And at KTVU on most Sundays, they will. In the early fall, Channel 2 decided to suspend its weathercasting competition; the station had decided not to hire anyone. "There was some question of whether we could use the money better

elsewhere," Zinder told me. Sunday-night anchors Griffith and Watson, he added, would read the weather as they have always done, using, of course, information supplied them by the National Weather Service.

Comment by Lynott
This essay by Heimoff displays remarkable insight and journalistic skill about this important subject. It came to my attention from a friend (since 1932 in Davenport, Iowa) living in Richmond CA.

Chapter 11, Television--Gridlock or Goldmine, in my 1987 book "The Weather Tomorrow," is a view long after my failure as a weathercaster from November 1953 to April 1968. Even in 1987 I was still brainwashed by the leadership of the AMS, hoping that academia could restore a true respect for the technology of forecasting. After attending the AMS meeting of broadcast meteorologists in June 1987 at Reno, Nevada, my recovery slowly began to return to reality.

For outstanding explanation of the deterioration of our national IQ, related to the popularity of TV entertainment, I highly recommend "Amusing Ourselves to Death, Public Discourse in the Age of Show Business" by Neil Postman, 1985, Penquin Books, 184 pages, $8.95 paper.

Paste-in Addition to Printed Book
As should be expected, and even approved after consideration of the career pressures, those involved on October 12, 1962 are presumably reluctant to add to the history of that storm. Sad stories tend to be forgotten. There are entire segments of my early life I can't recall, even when I try. Maybe one's memory doesn't want to try.

Since this book went to press, in a yellowing file of news clippings of the Columbus Day storm, I found two overlooked items. (1) Frieda's Freak Squalls Traced to Oregon Area, by Virgil Smith, Night City Editor of The Oregonian, which appeared Sunday, October 20, 1962, about a week after storm. (2) 2 Aviation Weather Forecasters at Bureau Office Write "Unofficial Autopsy" of Columbus Day Storm, printed Thursday, October 10, 1963, a year later, reviewed by an unnamed journalist. I have enlarged and pasted-up these items on three letter size sheets. Available free via SASE to me, address on copyright page.

In my opinion, there was no public prediction of high winds for Portland, "20 to 40 with gusts to 60" either in terms of knots or mph, nor any dissemination by any news medium. My guess is that such a forecast was possibly typed and reproduced on the office teletype, but never sent outside the Portland office. I welcome any contrary evidence

Contact! Science and the Public[1]

Robert M. White
President, National Academy of Engineering

This session on the public communication of weather and climate information and the resulting public understanding gives us a long overdue opportunity to examine a vital question about the interaction of science and society. In this process the public media—the press, television, and radio—are partners with the scientific and technical community. We observe, interpret, and forecast natural and man-made processes phenomena, but except for a few instances, it is the media that give us access to the public, and their representatives have a substantial role in interpreting what we tell them. The question this morning is, How are we both doing?

Understanding is intrinsically important because of the effects of science and technology on our daily lives. In a recent survey of a cross section of 1250 adults conducted by Louis Harris for the Scientists' Institute for Public Information in February 1993, it was found that people were avid in their search for science news that provides information necessary for living in the modern world. It was found, not surprisingly, that health and environmental information were of greatest interest. Over 50 percent of those questioned are viewers of television programs on science and 40 percent are reading science news. Quite simply, the survey concluded that the public wants information that can be used in coping with the modern world.

Public understanding is vital also because governmental policies are ultimately shaped by public attitudes. In today's world there is hardly a public policy that does not in some significant way depend upon the views of the public about science and technology, whether it is health care, environmental regulation, drug approval, or warnings of weather conditions. Our everyday life is guided by the same applications of technology. Information and biotechnologies are at the leading edge in transforming society, and their use is being shaped by public understanding of their utility and implications.

A quantum leap in the public fascination with the power of science and technology and the willingness to support massive government funding traces back a half-century to their role in World War II. The conduct

This space, pages 121 and 122, highlighted portions of the speech. My comment is substituted, plus bottom page 124. In requesting permission to reprint, I said it is important, and deserves wide dissemination, to potential do-it-yourself forecasters, as well as members of AMS. Photocopy is from pages 431-434, BAMS, March 1994. Dr. White is Past-President of AMS, and both a Fellow and Honorary Member.

I admire the inspirational theme of progress, need for-- (see p122)

of that conflict was dominated by the key contributions of science and technology. Allied victory could be directly traced to radar, nuclear weapons, and proximity fuses, as well as to the engineering feats such as building 100 000 aircraft in one year or construction of the invasion ports along the coast of France. At the end of that war, confidence that science and technology could be harnessed to advance economic growth and raise living standards was so great that their support became a touchstone of policies in government and the private sector.

Today, federal expenditures for support of science and technology exceed $75 billion annually. This total is matched by a similar amount expended by private industry. All fields of science and technology have been beneficiaries of this governmental and private largesse. In turn, this country and world have prospered as this investment has broken new ground with new discoveries, new inventions, and new industries.

We are daily made aware of scientific and technological wonders. New discoveries in molecular biology point the way to novel approaches to conquer disease;

---

[1]This speech was presented at the 74th Annual Meeting of the American Meteorological Society in Nashville, Tennessee, on 25 January 1994.

some forms of cancer and other genetic diseases now seem amenable to gene therapy. Developments in microelectronics and resulting advances in computer and communications technologies change the way we shop and see movies. They create new industries and jobs and render others obsolete with job losses. Other fields of science and technology, whether in materials or geophysics, present us with unprecedented new capabilities and understanding. The industrial race to convert science and technology development to new products and services has accelerated to the point that we humans, with our social and cultural structures rooted in ancient times, find it difficult to adjust to the new scientific and technological realities around us. Our systems of ethics and jurisprudence, our modes of governance, and our system of international rela-

public understanding of science, and attention to responsibilities in meterorology for improved communication, systems of ethics, exaggerated claims for achievements, haunting us later with loss of credibility), and reminder of developments in electronic transfer of information on demand. I hereby add the advent of home "production" of printing camera-ready pages, copy machines, and rediscovery of U.S. Mail to deliver legible hard copy. See notes on copyright page.

tions are being transformed. If we are to shape them wisely, public understanding of science and technology is essential.

Until recently, no scientific project was too big or complicated to be undertaken by the United States. But a watershed in public confidence was reached just a few months ago when Congress voted to kill the Superconducting Super Collider, and with it the hope of the particle physicists to advance the understanding of the fundamental particles and forces that constitute all matter. We might ask whether ultimately it was the lack of public understanding of the importance of this undertaking that brought it down? The point I make here is that public understanding of its purposes and goals is critical to the support of science and engineering. We have a real self-interest in communicating well.

How then are meteorologists doing? Ours is a unique field. No profession or field of science and technology other than perhaps that of medicine and health so directly affects the life of every business, enabling it to cope in the modern world. No field has as frequent access to the general public as does meteorology.

Few fields capture the range of environmental concerns of the nation and the world as the atmospheric sciences. Our science is central to understanding and controlling urban air pollution and formulating international agreements to arrest the depletion of stratospheric ozone. It is central to public policies governing the emission of sulphur and nitrogen oxides to reduce acid rain, and to global treaties combating a projected climate warming.

Let me share my views with you. There is good news and bad news. The good news is that we do a superb job in informing the public about the weather through television, radio, and the press in spite of the fact that we are still plagued with some sappiness in weather telecasts. The bad news is that the public is confused about what science is telling us about atmospheric environmental phenomena.

It has been 50 years since I was a line weather forecaster. In 1945 I was forecasting the B-29 bombing raids on Japan during World War II. Before that, I was a weather observer at the BLue Hill Observatory near Boston taking cloud observations under the tutelage of Charles Franklin Brooks, one of the founders of this Society. Indeed, when I watch the evening television, I wonder what Charlie Brooks, one of the world's great and original students of cloud formations, would have thought of the satellite depictions of clouds. He would have been thrilled. I also think of Harry Wexler, the former chief of research for the United States Weather Bureau, who was responsible for introducing computer weather prediction into daily practice and who, before the advent of satellites, postulated the nature of the weather patterns that would be observed from satellite altitude. What would Carl Rossby think if he could watch the progression and change of the long waves in the free atmosphere on nightly television? He would have marveled even as we do. We can be proud, and I believe satisfied, that in most television weather broadcasts we are successfully communicating with the public.

As professionals we have come to accept modern television broadcasts of weather as routine. But what the public sees is truly remarkable. The broadcasts generally commence with a broad view of the weather conditions as seen from satellite, and then move to the view from the Doppler weather radar. The changing upper air flow is depicted as the jet stream changes. Finally, there is a description of the air masses, their frontal boundaries, and the weather forecast itself. In two minutes weathercasters distill an incredible amount of weather information from a global observation and data processing system using unparalleled communication and display techniques to let the public know what the weather is going to be like. This is an incredible scientific and technological feat.

The daily telecast is only one mode available to the public to obtain weather information. It is available continuously over the NOAA weather radio and the T.V. Weather Channel. Over 50 million households turn to the Weather Channel for their weather updates. Even the print media make it easy for the public to grasp details.

No account of the success of weather communications would be complete without mentioning the remarkable job done routinely by the partnership between the weather service and the media during severe weather and flood conditions. No hurricane reaches our coast undetected with the public unprepared. With the new Doppler radars, fewer tornadoes go undetected and warning time has been extended. We've made great progress in forecasting forest fires and floods. The public media do an effective job of seeing that warnings are passed to the public quickly. In critical situations, government and private meteorologists speak directly to the public.

I wish I could report similarly good news about the public understanding of atmospheric phenomena such as acid rain, stratospheric ozone depletion, urban air pollution, and, above all, global climate change. The general public acquires its information about these phenomena through a confusing web of interpretations in the media based on views of scientists, as they communicate the results of research in meetings such as this, in congressional hearings and technical publications, and through interviews with reporters.

My purpose here is not to argue the science underlying these phenomena. I leave the discussion of scientific findings on the extent, timing, and intensity of climate change, or of the causes of stratospheric ozone depletion, or the extent to which acid rain has resulted in forest dieback, for another time. My point is that these phenomena are linked not only by meteorological conditions but also by a common confusion.

To a large extent, the public confusion is a reflection of real scientific uncertainties and debates among reputable scientists who interpret matters differently. The uncertainties and the differences of view among scientists offer the press the opportunity to emphasize what are to them the most newsworthy aspects of the interpretations. Postulated catastrophes are fair game and make exciting news. Disagreements among scientists are fair game—controversy sells well. We can't blame science and scientists for the fact that there is uncertainty and differences of view, nor can we blame the media for seeking stories that have great public interest.

In a *Washington Post* column last March, Richard Harwood phrased the dilemma of the reporters succinctly. He said, "When experts disagree among themselves, whose 'facts' and 'truths' are we (reporters) to rely on?" Let me illustrate this dilemma using the climate warming issue as an example. Two prominent national weekly magazines two years ago presented different views. A *Time* cover story was about the earth endangered by climate warming. Appearing just a few months later, the cover story in *Forbes* was about the overreaction to the climate warming threat. With two reputable magazine presenting different views, is it any wonder that the public is confused about climate change?

The confusion is abetted by television. Two programs recently presented opposite conclusions. In one, "After the Warming," the message was that the world is facing catastrophe. The other show, "The Greenhouse Conspiracy," indicated that climate warming was no problem, but rather a conspiracy of scientists to raise money.

What is the public to believe? What is our responsibility as scientists and professionals? What is the responsibility of the media?

Is there any way we can assess the depth of present public understanding of some of these issues? Recently I ran across an interesting study by the Engineering and Public Policy Department at Carnegie Melon University to learn what people understand about climate and weather. The results of that survey do not give us cause for comfort. The survey was conducted with two samples of reasonably well-educated members of the public.

I was particularly interested in whether the public distinguished between the stratospheric ozone problem and the climate warming problem. Here the confusion was almost total, with 95 percent of the respondents stating that stratospheric ozone depletion is a cause of global warming. The reply of one respondent was memorable. In discussing the stratospheric ozone hole, he thought NASA ought to send its space launches through the existing ozone hole to avoid making new ones.

Perhaps we should not be concerned and conclude that such confusion is inherent in the fact that these are extremely complicated issues about which scientists themselves disagree. As professionals and scientists, we know that the truth will eventually emerge as we test hypotheses, as we gather more data, and as we formulate new interpretations. Maybe we can dismiss the issue by reflecting that the general public does not understand the process of scientific inquiry and that neither do many of our public officials. But out of such ignorance and confusion do our public policies arise.

I believe strongly that we must not raise public expectations beyond those warranted by the state of scientific knowledge. Sooner or later, unrealizable expectations can come back to haunt us in the decreased confidence of policy makers. When our credibility goes, so goes the support for our work.

Sometimes I feel we run dangerously close to the edge. For example, I worry about some of the claims advanced for long-range seasonal and interannual forecasts on the basis of our knowledge of, and the predictability of, the El Niño phenomenon. No one doubts that there are important interactions between the oceans and the atmosphere. There is also no doubt that phenomena like El Niño must have an impact on the atmosphere over time periods commensurate with the time scale of El Niño. Nor do I find attempts at experimental forecasting of long-term weather changes on the basis of El Niño to be unwise. Indeed, it is through such experimental attempts that we test our ideas and theories.

On the other hand, it is risky to claim that our ability to predict El Niño is good enough or that the relationship between El Niño and subsequent large-scale weather conditions is predictable enough for highly accurate forecasts. El Niño has become the universal explanation in the media for all weather anomalies. The El Niño surprises of this past year that were not forecast suggest a greater measure of humility.

As another example, I worry that we have raised expectations that the investment of large sums of money in earth systems science will enable us to provide new knowledge in a short period to formulate significantly improved policies for addressing climate warming. Clearly, the investment is necessary if we are ultimately to understand the causes of and predict the consequences of global climate change. Valuable new knowledge about the global atmosphere will flow from this investment, and such knowledge will eventually be essential for the formation of wise policies, but we need to step carefully and make sure that expectations are realistic because of the complexity of the problem.

Senator Ed Muskie of Maine, expanding on a colorful phrase by Fritz Hollings, senator from South Carolina, during a hearing on pollution at which Philip Handler, president of the National Academy of Sciences, was testifying, first gave voice to the classic characterization of scientists. What was wanted was a one-handed scientist, he said, rather than one who says on the one hand this and on the other hand that. Courses of action will be chosen. What can we do as professionals, and what can reporters do to ensure an informed public?

There is an obligation on the part of scientists, as well as reporters, to make sure that the public understands that many of these issues are encrusted with uncertainties and, that reputable scientists can have differing views on many critical issues. While this is helpful, we need to do more. Unfortunately, the reporters are confronted with many institutions purporting to provide the truth. These range from government organizations to advocacy groups, industry associations, universities, and yes, professional societies like ours. It seems to me that there is a need for a more proactive role for organizations like the American Meteorological Society to present well-considered assessments and to make them readily available to the news media.

The statements of the American Meteorological Society do represent such even-handed assessments of critical atmospheric science issues. But are they getting through? Here computer and communications technology now make it possible to make information available on demand through electronic means. We need to explore new ways to get our message across that go beyond the press release. Similarly, reporters might consciously seek out such appraisals, and they would if access were easy and rapid. This is a task not only for the American Meteorological Society but also for other scientific and technological societies. Increasingly it will become an important role for all professional societies to become more active in their relationships with the policy-making arms of the government and the public media.

The need for public understanding of science and technology becomes greater with each passing year. They are the agents of change in society, and as a result, scientists, engineers, and their professional societies have an obligation to make sure that there is adequate public understanding of their work and its implications. In this way we can play an important role in shaping the directions of social change.

Thank you.

(Continued from page 122) The occasion was the annual meeting of the AMS, which had to accomodate the social aspects of membership, such as a pep talk amid the glow of group self-admiration, before gentle reminders of the unsolved problems and rugged terrain of the yet uncivilized world.

For over 11 years I've spent most of my time trying to promote the art and science of local forecasting. That activity, which ought to be the prime effort in our specific technology, is pushed aside for lack of centralized profit.

I've wasted a lot of time and money because of inexperience and natural hazards of exploring new terrain. Gadfly Press is merely a d.b.a. for self-publishing. For the encouragement of other retirees, this experience has been more satisfying than my so-called active career.

In my unalterable view, progress depends not only on discovery of new techniques, but the replacement of immature concepts with better ones. Of course that requires good judgment, which seems to be the universal item in short supply.

An apparently untapped resource is the mature skills of retirees. They are now free of retaliation from nervous misguided supervisors. In fairness, they suffered from their bosses. In attributing blame for deficiencies, always look toward the top of the administrative cylinder.

Chapter 16 Modernization and Restructuring of NWS

Everyone agrees with the need for that, except maybe for those who are accurately described as amusing themselves to death. The NWS was created 104 years ago as the Weather Bureau, administered by the Dept. of Agriculture. Now it's in the Dept. of Commerce, which seems appropriate for the connotation of an eight-letter word, Business, especially big business. I'm generally pleased how far it has come since 1940, before World War II (this country's formal entry) and before the Age of Television. I'm also very disappointed at the stagnation, even the decline of weather forecasting.

In the 1970s, and probably even earlier, there was growing awareness in the meteorological community of public needs not satisfied. In an address by Charles L. Hosler, retiring President of AMS, in January 1977, he felt that in the nongovernment sector of the profession we had failed "to be as agressive in developing new clients and markets for services that. . .society needs. Thousands of decisions are being made every day without benefit of. . .input to the detriment of the people and economy of the country.

". . .the conflict between federal and private services and between rival and competing private services will at times be severe. . . With time the delivery system will adjust itself and natural selection will operate. I feel the competition can remain a healthy one if government services keep in mind that they are there to perform those services that the people or private groups cannot perform for themselves. . . We must guard against degrading the profession through public disputes over who is the star on the team or whose forecast is best. There is no hierarchy of importance worth preserving in the face of our total dependence upon each other. . .our state of knowledge should make us all humble." [BAMS May 1977, page 402]

In BAMS for January 1983, there is a 4-page "executive summary" of *The Future of the Nation's Weather Services*, published by the National Advisory Committee on Oceans and Atmosphere, for an unspecified date in 1982. It mentioned current annual losses caused by weather amounting to "billions of dollars." Those could be reduced significantly by more timely and more accurate forecasts.

It recommended additional appropriation of $1.0 billion over next 10 years for improved equipment for the NWS. It believed the key to providing high level protection for the public and service to the economy is a strong central Federal weather service that can work closely with the private sector and other Federal agencies. That meant "don't intrude on turf of Big Brother NWS."

To shorten this summary (of the committee's summary), because data acquisition and basic analysis functions are the NWS responsibility, the NWS should also retain the basic forecasting functions.

Current policies should continue for the maintenance of a strong central weather service, and steps should be taken to prevent the establishment of multiple weather services.

In those 4 pages of fine print, the recommendations were for a simple word, *monopoly*, which means control. The NWS will do its best, but as far as the public is concerned, nobody should be allowed to do better.

The private sector should be permitted to provide forecasts "that particularize information" to meet the needs of specific clients or constituencies. (Meaning more accurate predictions for significant events before they occur, but forbidden for public use).

On Sept. 29, 1983 the AMS issued a policy statement, *The Atmospheric Environment: An Agenda for Action,"* published in BAMS January 1984. In my

1987 book, Chapter 9, The Public-Private Partnership, I wrote 6 pages criticizing that policy.

One of the rebuttals of my opponents is that "I have an axe to grind." Maybe so. How could I have been so misguided in 1949 to pursue a career as a forecaster in the Weather Bureau, where improving one's skill was cause for local harassment, rather than encouragement? And after I went on TV, the WB and AMS tried to discourage me, which succeeded, and then the WB persuaded the Forest Service never to hire another operational forecaster. As far as I know, I was the only one ever employed by the FS.

When I explained intention to retire at earliest age, 60 (having only 29 years federal service in WB, Army, and FS) which would be in mid-fire season, the FS discontinued the position, and let me go RIF, 3 months early, okay with me, at slightly lower annuity.

By December 1988 the propaganda to "modernize" the federal weather services was heating up. In that issue of BAMS appeared seven pages of 2-column 8 pt type, "The Changing Atmosphere-- Challenges and Opportunities."

These recommendations for specific actions and programs were prepared jointly by the AMS Council, and the Board of Trustees of the University Corporation for Atmospheric Research, a consortium of 57 universities.

After a one page Executive Summary, the introduction covered two pages, followed by one and one-half pages on protecting life and property through improved prediction.

As a former synoptic forecaster, I'm partly amused, and partly appalled at the volume of unreasoned assertions and the repetition of worn out propaganda, which reminds one more of a circus side show barker than a Society trying to advance a scientific technology.

This lobbying effort wrapped itself in the robes of wind shear microbursts, climate variations and disruptions, hurricanes, air quality, droughts, depleting acquifiers, land subsidence, transport of nuclear weapons, off-shore drilling rigs, space-age activities such as impact of cloud drops on the tiles of shuttles, lightning, the effects of an "El Niño," increases in atmospheric carbon dioxide and chlorofluorocarbons, tropical deforestation, global warming, decreases in ozone, rises in sea level, shifts in the paths of low pressure systems, and increases in heat waves. (Please, dear scientists, give us more scary phrases for entertainment)

Scientists and policy makers must work together. These programs will help protect life and property from weather, enhance national security, make the U. S. more competitive in the global economy, and allow for the development of effective policies. (Make that politics)

Here are two more exact quotes: "We have summarized in this document the challenges and opportunities the atmosphere presents to the administration that will take office in January 1989."

"The new administration thus has the opportunity and responsibility to make a firm commitment. . .to lead the world in thinking seriously about the future of the planet."

On March 17, 1989, hyped up by the preceding display of fireworks, the National Oceanic and Atmospheric Administration, NOAA, Department of Commerce, published its *Strategic Plan For The Modernization And Restructuring Of The National Weather Service.*

I was so moved by this outstanding effort involving 21 pages of legible 12 pt Times Roman typeface, similar to this book, that I re-pasted the entire paper on 14 letter-size pages to minimize wasted white space, and wrote a 9-page single-spaced typewriter Critique. Then I mailed the 23 pages to 92 individuals across the country.

I admit the criticisms were presented awkwardly (it takes time to learn some of the techniques of self-publishing which includes obtaining some modest equipment). The details of the critique are out of date because the recommendations have already been adopted by Congress, huge sums of borrowed money are being spent and are authorized. The public is bombarded with propaganda as never before. Here are a few comments.

During our numerous wars since 1940 meteorology has had increasing involvement, with a noticeable mililtary slant in the culture of the "atmospheric" profession. (That's a rather good word).

The word "strategic" is related to *stratagem*, a military maneuver designed to deceive an enemy. A clever, often underhanded scheme for achieving an objective. [American Heritage Dictionary, my new 3rd edition] I notice they took that word out of the original title for the grandiose modernization program under way. I had suggested a title, Impossible Dream. Now part of the dream is actually coming true, the profitable part, for the corporate elite leaders. But the dream of improved forecasts, my dream, is still fading and will continue to fade.

In my aging memory, source not remembered, are some words, "by their words ye shall know them." The best way to keep track of what goes on behind the scenes in the weather business is to read its own publications, the ones for its own members, not the material offered via the TV and print media for the general public.

For any reader interested in a career in meteorology, or do-it-yourself local forecasting (next and final chapter), I recommend membership in the American Meteorological Society. According to the latest annual report of the Secretary-Treasurer for 1993, published in BAMS for June 1994, membership categories are shown below. Dues for Associate Members are $30 per year, which includes the monthly Bulletin of AMS. I have a file back to 1937. For most of my career I was an avid supporter of the Society.

5. Membership

The membership of the Society at 31 December 1993 was:

Honorary Members and Fellows	9
Honorary Members	13
Fellows	452
Members	8363
Associate Members, Voting	126
Associate Members, Nonvoting	924
Student Members	769
Corporation Members*	159
Total	**10,815**

*Including 5 Sustaining, 6 Contributing

The August issue of BAMS is the Organization Issue. As of August 1988 the AMS had an Ethics Committee. Article VIII of the By-Laws described a Code of Ethics. Without evidence of any connection to complaints in my 1987 book about ethics, the August 1989 issue revealed the Ethics Committee had been discontinued, and the Code of Ethics in By-Laws revised to Guidelines for Professional Conduct, and moved to Article XII in the Constitution, as shown here.

ARTICLE XII. Guidelines for Professional Conduct

To enhance the benefits of the meteorological and related professions to humanity, to uphold the dignity and honor of the profession, and to provide guidance for individual members, institutional members, or for members in association with other professionals, the American Meteorological Society has adopted the following Guidelines for Professional Conduct. Only individuals and organizations who intend to abide by these Guidelines should seek admission or continuing membership in the Society; therefore, these Guidelines will appear on the membership application form and will be published at least annually in the official organ of the Society.

1. Relationship of members to the profession as a whole.

   A. Members should conduct themselves in such a manner as to reflect dignity and honor on their profession.

   B. Members who are professionally active should endeavor to keep abreast of relevant scientific and technical developments; they should continuously strive to improve their professional abilities.

C. Members engaged in the development of new knowledge should make known to the scientific world their significant results through the media of technical or scientific publications or meetings.

2. Relationship of members to colleagues.

   Members should not take credit knowingly for work done by others; in publications or meetings, members should attempt to give credit where due.

3. Relationship of members to clients and the general public.

   A. Members should base their practice on sound scientific principles applied in a scientific manner.

   B. Members should not direct their professional activities into practices generally recognized as being detrimental to, or incompatible with, the general public welfare.

   C. Members undertaking work for a client should fully advise him or her as to the likelihood of success.

   D. Members should refrain from making exaggerated or unwarranted claims and statements.

   E. Members should refer requests for service that are beyond their professional capabilities or their scope of service to those properly qualified.

   F. Members shall not use or display the official seal of the American Meteorological Society, the Radio Seal of Approval, the Television Seal of Approval, or the designation Certified Consulting Meteorologist unless duly authorized by the Society.

Guidelines 1A and 3B sound reasonable, but are deliberately designed for ambiguity. It depends on how the Executive Committee defines dignity and honor, and what practices are detrimental to, or incompatible with, the general public welfare.

My definitions of professional and scientific dignity and honor, (and we should add responsibility), and what practices are detrimental to the public welfare are substantially different from those displayed to me by the AMS. In the years 1983-1988 my conflicts with the Oregon Chapter, and the Boston headquarters became unreconcileable. In 1990 I politely resigned from each, explaining to Boston that my evaluation of its intent was that both of us would be pleased.

This story should not hinder an applicant for Associate membership. Just don't challenge any of their ideas.

Address for AMS is 45 Beacon St, Boston MA 02108.

Since January 1985 I have been a member of the National Weather Association. Annual dues are $25. Address is 6704 Wolke Court, Montgomery, Alabama 36116-2134.

The outpouring of propaganda is already a torrent, and will increase because appropriations are probably near 5 billion dollars per year for weather services in various agencies and the military establishments. More money means more advertising which brings in more money. Remember, the money is borrowed.

There is one basic theme to my "cause," my role of gadfly against the power structure in meteorology. Collectively, but with a few exceptions, those in the profession or semi-profession, don't understand forecasting, or how to do it. Even those who know, must remain silent and support the hierarchy, or lose position in the competitive world.

One need only to read and listen carefully. The hype is all about "detection" of weather events, which formerly was simply called observing the weather. Modern electronic devices will enable experts to "see" the inside of storms, etc. Then via complex communication systems warnings will be issued quickly. They usually say warnings and forecasts, to obscure the difference, which is the difference between night and day.

Warnings are always merely reports of events already occurring, or finished. To me, a true forecast is well ahead of time, several hours, such as 12 to 24 hours.

Always remember that there is a built-in time lag even for observations. The so-called "watches" are what every observer is paid to do, and now they are trying to automate most of those.

There is only one hope that I can see, do-it-yourself forecasting. That's the subject of the next chapter. I had hoped to put a lot of that in this book, but there isn't enough space. If I live long enough, I'll publish a third book on the subject.

corporation and institutional members of the AMS

Sustaining Corporation Members
Accu-Weather, Inc.
Alden Electronics, Inc.
GTE Federal Systems
Harris Corporation
Orbital Sciences Corporation
WSI Corporation

Contributing Corporation Members
Computer Sciences Corporation
Particle Measuring Systems, Inc.
Weather Services Corporation
Weathernews, Inc.
WeatherVision

Corporation and Institutional Members
AAI Systems Management, Inc.
Aanderaa Instruments, Inc.
ACT Sigmex B.V.
The Aerospace Corporation
Air Traffic Services, Civil Aeronautics
    Administration of the Republic of China
Air Transport Association of America
Air Weather Service Technical Library
Argonne National Laboratory
Atmospheric and Environmental Research, Inc.
Atmospheric Environment Service
Audichron Company, Pastel Division
Automated Weather Source, Inc.
Belfort Instrument Company
Botswana Meteorological Services
Brazilian Naval Commission
    Instituto de Estudos do Mar Almirante Paulo Moreira
Brock University Library
Caelum Research Corporation
Calspan Corporation
Campbell Scientific, Inc.
Caribbean Meteorological Institute
The Carnegie Science Center
Chanute AFB Technical Library
Climatronics Corporation
Colorado State University,
    Department of Atmospheric Science
Concurrent Computer Corporation
Control Data Corporation
Convex Computer Corporation
Creighton University, Atmospheric Science Program
Dartmouth College Library
Deutscher Wetterdienst
Dynamics Technology, Inc.
EDS Corporation
ENSR Consulting & Engineering
Edinburgh University Library
Enterprise Electronics Corporation

Environmental Instruments, Inc.
Etablissement d'Etude et des Recherche Meteo.
European Organisation for the Exploitation of
    Meteorological Satellites (EUMETSAT)
Factory Mutual Engineering Corporation
Fernbank Science Center
Finnish Meteorological Institute
Florida State University, Department of Meteorology
Foundation of River & Basin Integrated
    Communications—FRICS
Freeport International Weather Service
French Meteorological Office
Galson Mesoweather/Div. of Galson Corporation
GEOMET Technologies, Inc.
General Eastern Instruments
Gill Instruments Limited
GTE Government Systems Corporation
HANDAR, Inc.
Harvard University
Horizons Technology, Inc.
Hughes STX Corporation
ITT Aerospace/Optical Division
Illinois State Water Survey
Indiana University Library, Serials Department
Indian Institute of Tropical Meteorology
Innovative Emergency Management, Inc.
Irish Meteorological Service
Jeppesen Dataplan, Incorporated
Kaijo Corporation, Gikan
Kavouras, Inc.
Kaysam Worldwide Inc.
Kean College of New Jersey
Kipp & Zonen
Korean Meteorological Services
Laboratoire de Meteorologie Dynamique du CNRS
Lawrence Livermore National Laboratory
Lightning Location & Protection Inc.
Logicon Eagle Technology, Inc.
Loral Data Systems
Marta Systems, Inc.
Massachusetts Institute of Technology,
    Department of Meteorology
Meteoglobe Canada, Inc.
MeteoMedia, Inc.
Met One Instruments, Inc.
Millersville University of Pennsylvania,
    Department of Earth Sciences
The MITRE Corporation
Mount Isa Mines, Ltd.
Murray & Trettel, Inc., Consulting Meteorologists
NRG Systems, Inc.
National Agency of Environmental Protection,
    Roskilde, Denmark

corporation and institutional members of the AMS

National Climatic Data Center/NOAA
    Department of Commerce/Library
National Meteorological Library of the United Kingdom
National Oceanic and Atmospheric Administration
    NOAA Science Center, Washington, D.C.
National Severe Storm Laboratory
National Weather Service Training Center
New Zealand Meteorological Service
North American Weather Consultants
Northern Video Graphics, Inc.
Oceanroutes, Inc.
The Ohio State University,
    Department of Atmospheric Sciences
Oregon State University
Pacific Gas & Electric Co.
Pennsylvania State University, Department of Meteorology
Pennsylvania State University, Pattee Library
Philippine Weather Bureau—PAGASA
PRC Inc.
Purdue University
Pyrometer Instrument Company, Inc.
Qualimetrics, Inc.
RMS Technologies, Inc.
Radian Corporation
The Republic Group
Republic of Korea Air Force, 73rd Weather Group
Republic of Korea, Meteorological Research Institute
Rotronic Instrument Corporation
Royal Netherlands Meteorological Institute
Royal Observatory, Hong Kong
Rutgers University, Douglass–Cook Library
S.C.E.M. Documentation
Saint Louis University,
    Department of Earth and Atmospheric Sciences
San Jose State University
Science & Engineering Analysis Corporation (SEACOR)
Scientific Technology, Inc. (ScTI)
SciWorks
SeaSpace Corporation
Service Argos, Inc.
Service Central D'Exploitation Meteorologique
Servicios A La Navegacion En El Espacio Aereo Mexicano
    (SENEAM), Centro De Analisis Y Pronosticos (CAP)
Snow Systems, Inc.
South Dakota School of Mines & Technology
SpaceCom Systems, Inc.
Space Systems/Loral
Sterling Software
Storm WATCHER Systems, Inc.
Surface Systems, Inc.
Swedish Meteorological and Hydrological Institute, SMHI
Swiss Meteorological Institute
Systems Applications, Inc.

Technical Services Laboratory, Inc.
TECNOIDROMETEO
Texas A&M University, Meteorology Department
The Titan Corporation
Unisys Corporation, Government Systems Group
U.S. Army Atmospheric Sciences Laboratory
U.S. Army Cold Regions Research
U. S. Department of Commerce, NOAA,
    ERL/Air Resources Laboratory
U.S. Naval Academy Library
Universal Weather and Aviation
Universita di Bologna, Dipartimento di Fisica
Universitat Freiburg, Meteorologisches Institut
Universitat Innsbruck,
    Institut fur Meteorologie and Geophysik
Universiti Kebangsaan Malaysia, Library
University Corporation for Atmospheric Research,
    National Center for Atmospheric Research
University of Alabama in Huntsville
University of Arizona, Institute of Atmospheric Physics
University of Chicago,
    Department of the Geophysical Sciences
University of Copenhagen, Geophysical Institute
University of Illinois, Department of Atmospheric Sciences
University of Michigan,
    Department of Atmospheric and Oceanic Science
University of Nevada, Desert Research Institute
University of New South Wales Library
University of North Carolina
University of Northern Colorado, Library
University of Oklahoma, Department of Meteorology
University of Sheffield Library
University of Washington,
    Department of Atmospheric Sciences
University of Wisconsin—Madison,
    Space Science and Engineering Center
Uppsala University, Department of Meteorology
VCS Engineering GmbH
VIZ Manufacturing Co.
Valcom, Ltd.
Viking Instrument & Photo
Weather Bureau Pretoria, South Africa
The Weather Channel
Weather Consultants Inc.
Weather Corporation of America
Woods Hole Oceanographic Institution
WTVT Television
Yale University, Department of Geology and Physics
Yankee Environmental Systems, Inc.
R.M. Young Company
Zentralanstalt fur Meteorologie und Geodynamik
Zephyr Weather Information Service

Chapter 17 D I Y Forecasting

This is a very brief introduction to do-it-yourself forecasting. There are three essential groups of data for this purpose, facsimile maps called Difax, with at least the sea level map, and the 500 mb chart, plotted raobs for the soundings made in your nearby area, and the "hourly sequences" of surface observations, which are arranged in groups, for each state.

Samples are presented here, to show how they look, but these samples are for different dates, and have no continuity.

I have not yet learned the use of a modem, and don't have a fax yet. Soon I will explore the technique. Maybe I will be able to write a pamphlet on the topic.

Chuck Wiese gave me an assortment of discarded fax data, from which I selected these items, pruning them to fit on the pages. I plotted the Salem raob on our chart Page 43. (turn to page 136)

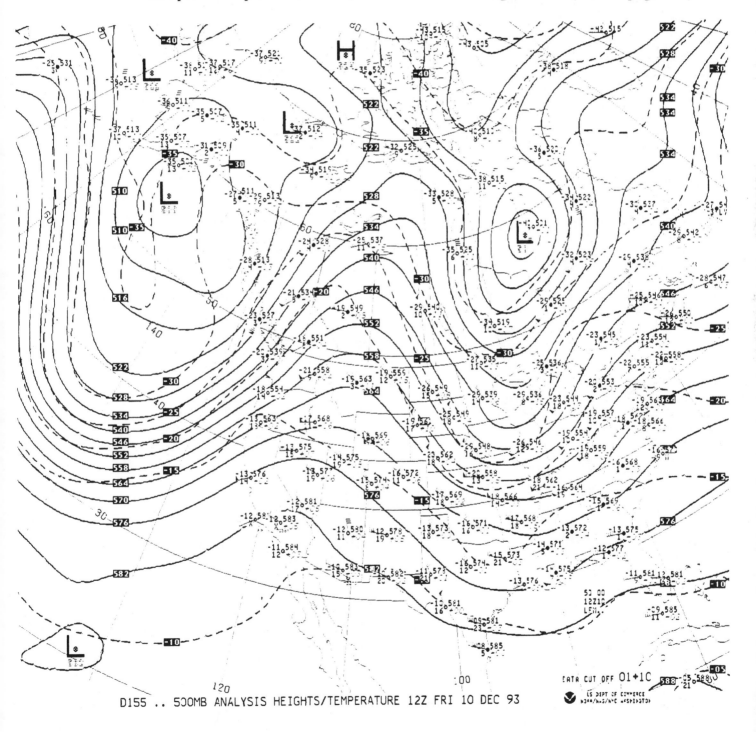

D155 .. 500MB ANALYSIS HEIGHTS/TEMPERATURE 12Z FRI 10 DEC 93

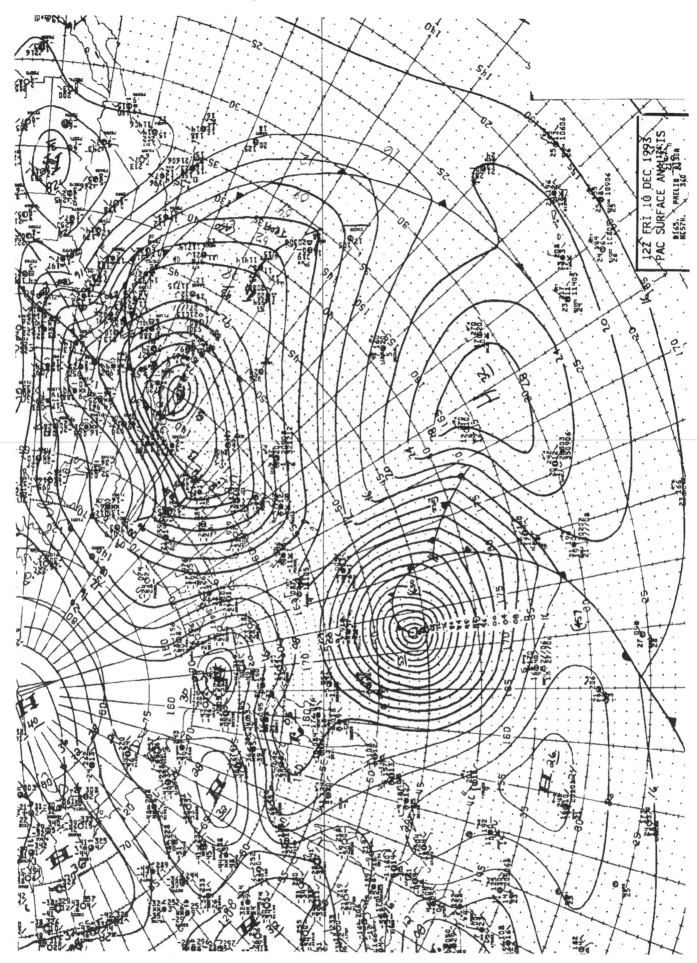

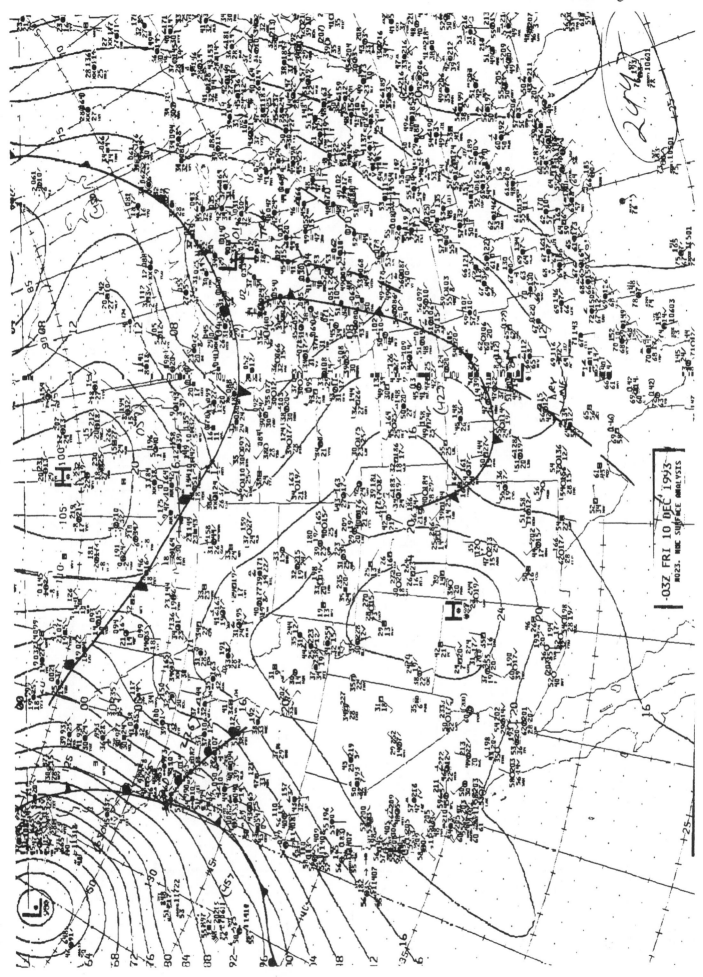

-03Z FRI 10 DEC '1993
NO23. NMC SURFACE ANALYSIS

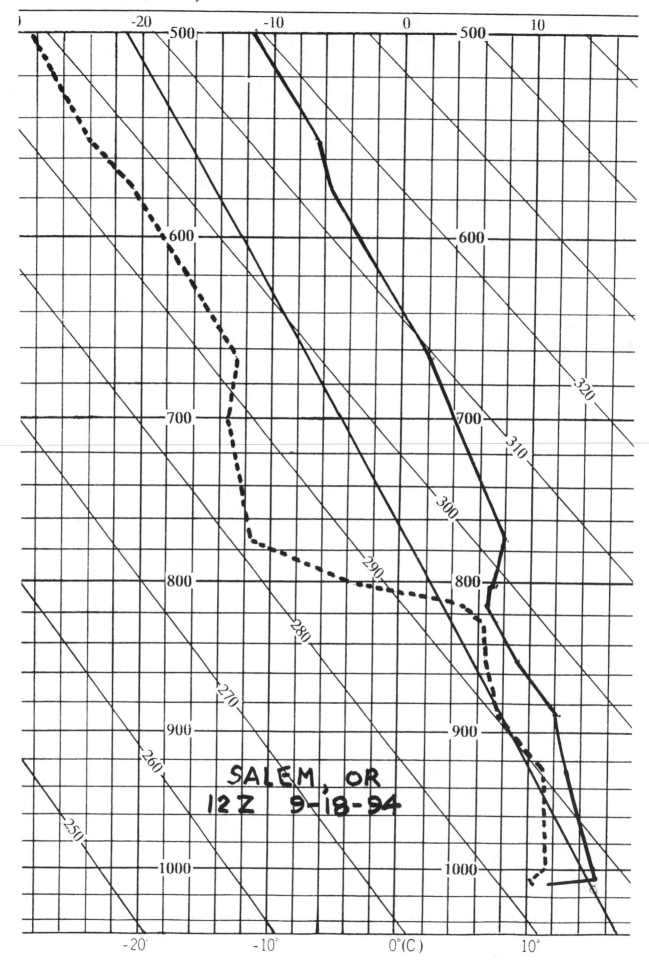

SURFACE WEATHER OBSERVATIONS   OREGON 2-16-94
                                        Time is GMT, also called Z

3S2 SA NO CURRENT DATA
4BK SA 2330 E40 BKN 60 BKN 80 OVC 15 988/55/46/1411G16/M/OCNL RW-
    PRESFR/ 82200 152/ 60 NOSPL
4LW SA 2330 E100 OVC 25 058/43/21/1816G23/M/ 720 107/ 90402 44 NOSPL
5J0 SA 2345 E90 OVC 25 54/15/0220G30/967/H54 L33 PRECP00 LAST
AST SA 2356 AO2A M38 BKN 47 OVC 7R- 987/49/45/1416/949/ 885// 56013 6010
    20048 PCPN 0003
BKE SA 2350 70 SCT E120 BKN 160 OVC 40 088/45/26/1011/977/ACSL NW-E/
    625 48
BNO SA 2348 AMOS 90 SCT E200 OVC 40 070/ 41/25/0908/971 PK WND 13 000/ 7
    44
CVO SA 2355 AWOS 70 SCT 10 50/39/0709/948
CZK SA 2330 50 SCT E90 OVC 10 48/42/1905/M/NOSPL LAST
DLS SA 2349 100 SCT E150 BKN 250 OVC 30 008/54/40/0000/955/ 734 56
EUG SA 2350 M70 OVC 10 987/49/46/3605/949/ 827 107/ 51
HIO SA 2351 3 SCT E20 BKN 41 OVC 6R-F 48/43/2507/958
LGD SA 2355 AWOS CLR BLO 120 10 50/23/1714G18/970
LKV SA 2356 AWOS M80 OVC 10 43/21/1821/967
LMT SA 2355 40 SCT 80 SCT 200 -OVC 15 020/47/22/E1730G36/960
    /BD ALQDS/ 622 1577=
MFR SA 2352 55 SCT 70 SCT E130 BKN 180 OVC 30 000/58/30/2106/953/
ONO SA NO CURRENT DATA
ONP SA 2345 E35 BKN 50 OVC 5R-F 49/48/1006/948
OTH SA 2350 30 SCT M55 OVC 12 R- 976/50/45/1304/946 / 82416 51
PDT SA 2350 E120 BKN 150 OVC 30 014/58/23/1409/957/VIRGA ALQDS/ 729
    107/ 63
PDX SA 2350 M47 OVC 15R- 021/48/44/3605/959/ 61006 102/ 51
RBG SA 2346 80 SCT E150 OVC 30 61/28/1808/946/NOSPL/ 61
RDM SA 2354 AWOS M100 BKN 10 54/19/2404/956/SLP 010/ 620 55
S47 SA 2355 10 SCT E20 BKN 40 OVC 4R-F 49/47/E1206/954
SLE SA 2353 M55 BKN 75 OVC 45R- 007/50/44/0907/955/RB05 PCPN VRY LGT
    AND INTMT/ 71702 152/ 51
SXT SA 2354 AO2A M50 OVC 10+ 985/45/25/1715G18/949/ RWU OVR CST / 8/79/
    10046 20036 TNO ZRNO PK WND 1828/2301 $
TTD SA 2356 49 SCT M75 OVC 25 48/43/0808/958

SURFACE WEATHER OBSERVATIONS   WASHINGTON 2-16-94   00 Z
                                        same as for OREGON

4OM SA NO CURRENT DATA
60S SA NO CURRENT DATA
75S SA 2345 E16 BKN 40 BKN 300 OVC 30 51/M/1514/955
76S SA 2349 10 SCT E20 BKN 50 OVC 7 50/M/1415/951
ALW SA 2349 80 SCT 120 SCT E150 OVC 20 015/64/17/1515G21/958/ 627 67
BFI SA 2345 M35 OVC 5R-F 48/47/1406/958
BLI SA 2350 20 SCT 35 SCT E80 BKN 120 OVC 20 982/51/42/1615/948/
    82005 55
CLM SA NO CURRENT DATA
CLM SA 2255 E40 BKN 80 OVC 20 52/42/2607/941
CQV SA 2331 150 -OVC 20 075/44/36/3006/972/ 727 101/ 44 NOSPL
EAT SA 2354 AWOS 110 SCT 10 44/33/0000/962/SLP 038/ 722 44
ELN SA NO CURRENT DATA
EPH SA 2350 E90 BKN 120 OVC 20 M/48/35/3109/961/ 730 50
FHR SA 2350 30 SCT E80 BKN 15 48/M/1226G33/946
GEG SA 2351 90 SCT 200 -OVC 30 049/48/34/0407/965/ 629 1077 51
GRF SA 2355 30 SCT M45 OVC 7R- 012/48/46/1403/956/ 61415 15// WR//=
HMS SA 2350 E80 BKN 110 OVC 15 016/50/32/3111/957/ 720 107/ 52 RSNK
    48/2014
HQM RS 2350 6 SCT E11 OVC 4RW-F 993/47/44/1112/951/VSBY LWR E/ 61427

KLS SA 2356 AWOS 21 SCT M32 BKN 43 OVC 4 47/41/1911G17/960/   P004
MWH SA 2346 110 SCT E200 OVC 65 48/38/3405/960
NUW SA 2355 20 SCT E40 BKN 80 OVC 7R- 986/49/37/1520G27/948/
    522 157/ 52=
OLM SA 2353 40 SCT M60 OVC 12R- 014/47/45/1809/957/FEW LWR SC W/
    51014 152/ 49
                                          WASHINGTON (CONT'D)
ORS SA NO CURRENT DATA
PAE SA 2347 11 SCT E35 OVC 7R- 49/47/1707/956
PSC SA 2345 E130 BKN 180 OVC 50 54/35/3009/958
PUW SA 2350 E200 OVC 20 49/35/0708/965
PWT SA 2355 AWOS 3 SCT 9 SCT M36 OVC 3 45/41/2504/956/   P007
RNT SA 2345 M30 OVC 4R-F 47/46/0000/958
S88 SA 2335 AWOS M37 OVC 10 52/47/1205/956/   P003
SEA SA 2350 29 SCT M42 OVC 5R-F 008/48/45/1206/955/ 61426 172/ 50
SFF SA 2345 100 SCT E200 OVC 30 51/33/1306/966
SHN SA 2359 E10 BKN 50 OVC 8L- 46/44/0804/M/ NOSPL
SKA SA 2355 90 SCT E230 BKN 25 050/45/32/0508/965/ 625 1078=
SMP SA NO CURRENT DATA
SMP SA 2256 AO2A 22 SCT M49 OVC 7 030/36/31/1008/957/ LWR CIG AND SWU NE
    TNO ZRNO
SMP SP 2304 AO2A M18 BKN 49 OVC 7 031/36/31/1007/958/ TNO ZRNO
SMP SP 2336 AO2A 24 SCT M48 OVC 7 026/36/31/0905/957/ TNO ZRNO
TCM SA 2355 10 SCT M50 OVC 7R- 013/48/46/0904/956/ 61018 15// 50
TDO SA 2345 E35 OVC 6R-F 47/47/1305/959/ 508 47 20073
TIW SA 2350 30 SCT E50 OVC 6R-F 47/45/0000/956
UIL SA 2352 E8 BKN 20 OVC 21/2RF 969/47/47/1711/944/R OCNLY R-/
    50344 172/ 50
YKM SA 2350 90 SCT E140 BKN 250 OVC 35 028/53/33/0000/960/VIRGA
    S-W-N/ 717 1078 55

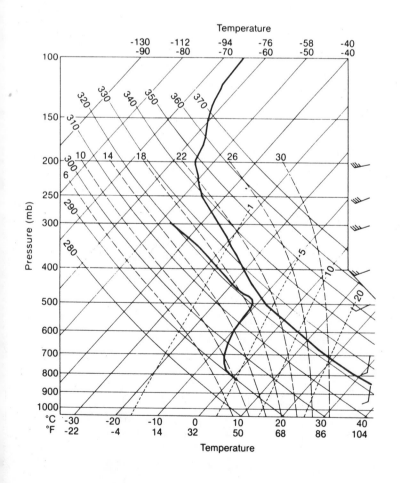

One does not need to collect synoptic data on a continuous schedule day after day. If no weather problems appear to be shaping up, skip a few days. But everyday, and at times during your waking hours, check your home barometer.

This raob plot adjacent is copied from the publication described on page 81, lower part of left column. This is called a skew-T diagram. Such diagrams are now in wide use, but I recommend the old-fashioned adiabatic chart. Also, you seldom if ever need a graph extending higher than the 500 mb chart. You don't need to waste your time studying the atmosphere up to 200 or 100 mbs.

I believe the conversion to this type of plotting is part of the hiding of data from the public, to maintain the hierarchy.

GOOD LUCK !   September 14, 1994